Entrepreneurship in Theory and Practice

Entrepreneurship in Theory and Practice

PARADOXES IN PLAY

Suna Løwe Nielsen, Kim Klyver, Majbritt Rostgaard Evald and Torben Bager
University of Southern Denmark

Case writers:
William B. Gartner, Saras Sarasvathy, Alain Fayolle, Kevin Hindle, Thomas Cooney, Anita Van Gils and Ann Højbjerg Clarke

Edward Elgar
Cheltenham, UK • Northampton, MA, USA

Published by
Edward Elgar Publishing Limited
The Lypiatts
15 Lansdown Road
Cheltenham
Glos GL50 2JA
UK

Edward Elgar Publishing, Inc.
William Pratt House
9 Dewey Court
Northampton
Massachusetts 01060
USA

A catalogue record for this book
is available from the British Library

Library of Congress Control Number: 2012939102

ISBN 978 0 85793 529 8 (cased)
ISBN 978 0 85793 531 1 (paperback)

Typeset by Servis Filmsetting Ltd, Stockport, Cheshire
Printed and bound by MPG Books Group, UK

Contents in brief

Full contents

SECTION 3: THE ENTREPRENEURIAL CONTENT

SECTION 4: THE ENTREPRENEURIAL CONTEXT

Preface

We wanted to write a different kind of entrepreneurship textbook, a textbook which embraces the messy and paradoxical world of entrepreneurs. In this world where fixed plans tend to be swept away overnight, textbooks with unambiguous guidelines and clear answers are of limited use. Certainly, there are bodies of knowledge and useful methodologies which students and entrepreneurs can and should learn from, but an entrepreneurship textbook should not pretend clear answers and a predictable journey. An entrepreneurial journey is never predefined so it is imperative to be prepared for complexity and uncertainty as well as a continuous bombardment of new challenges and opportunities along the road.

Getting close to the paradoxical world of entrepreneurs in a textbook is a challenge, in fact a paradox in itself. One way to get close to entrepreneurs and entrepreneurial processes is through cases. However, the normal use of cases in textbooks as end-of-chapter illustrations to theories and models is not very helpful. Therefore we try something else. In each chapter the point of departure is an interesting case with an immediate interpretation. Then theories and models are introduced and discussed, and at the end of each chapter we turn back to the case to look at it again at a theoretically informed level, and with a selected paradox in mind. We hope this case structure creates an element of learning-by-doing-and-reflecting throughout the book. In this book you will find cases from many countries around the world. We asked entrepreneurship colleagues for interesting case contributions and William B. Gartner, Saras Sarasvathy, Kevin Hindle, Alain Fayolle, Anita v. Gils, Thomas Cooney and Ann Højbjerg Clarke contributed with a bunch of valuable cases – many thanks!

The book is co-authored by four entrepreneurship colleagues at the University of Southern Denmark. We wanted to produce a textbook where readers, in spite of the fact that we are four authors, would not experience four different writing styles. This required close collaboration and a double writing process. Each chapter was drafted by one author, then discussed with the group, and then revised by another author – and many cases revised once more by a third author after a new round of discussion. This helped to align the writing styles, but the translation process was probably more

Figure I.1 The authors balancing and cooperating on their entrepreneurial journey

important. We decided to draft the manuscript in our mother tongue and then ask a good translator to make an English version. Here we were lucky to engage Mick Hancock who knows the entrepreneurship field well and is a good writer – thanks Mick! Also thanks to the Danish Foundation for Entrepreneurship – Young Enterprise for its contribution to cover translation costs and other expenses.

Finally a warm thank you to the IDEA Entrepreneurship Centre for co-funding and assistance, in particular to Lone Toftild and Bodil Hoeg who assisted from day one, and also thanks to Edward Elgar Publishers for smooth collaboration during the publishing process.

Introduction: the ideas behind the book

Entrepreneurship is an important and exciting field of study. The creation of new organisations along with the renewal of existing organisations is the key to job creation and growth in modern society. Entrepreneurs are exciting people who make a difference.

This textbook in entrepreneurship differs in many ways from typical textbooks on the subject.

First and foremost, we define entrepreneurship as a broad phenomenon: fundamentally about the birth of new methods and processes, their evaluation and organisation. Whilst typical textbooks are limited to understanding entrepreneurship as the creation of new and independent organisations, this book shows that entrepreneurial behaviour can also take place and be manifested within many other organisational contexts (associations, government agencies, existing businesses, etc.).

Secondly, most books focus on 'How to' develop and operate new and small businesses by referring to theory, which is already familiar from the management literature. In this book, we highlight the theory and knowledge that are unique to entrepreneurship.

Thirdly, we want to give students a global perspective; using case studies from several countries, written with the cooperation of world-renowned entrepreneurship researchers. Many textbooks use only cases from a single country, thereby failing to achieve a global view.

Of course the challenge is, in many ways, the same for an entrepreneur in Europe, the USA and other parts of the world, but the context makes a difference to particular entrepreneurial opportunities. This applies to both soft variables such as culture and hard variables such as legislation.

Last but not least, we offer an exciting, but alternative pedagogical approach to entrepreneurship education. The traditional pedagogy underpinning other textbooks typically focuses primarily on presenting the theory, which is peppered with empirical examples and cases.

The approach taken in this book is different and significant because it is based on actual entrepreneurial stories. You will meet 'real entrepreneurs' in many different contexts, and you will be challenged to make decisions on their behalf – to put yourself in their place. Only after that will you be introduced to the theories and concepts of entrepreneurship. The approach also includes carrying out exercises and investigations on your own to test the established theory and knowledge in new entrepreneurial situations.

Below we introduce the audience, ideas, content, structure and pedagogical approach. When we use the term 'entrepreneurship', we refer generally to a broad concept that captures the book's subject area as a whole. Entrepreneurship is defined as the initial emergence of new opportunities being evaluated and utilised through organising. Closely related to the concept of entrepreneurship is the concept of 'the entrepreneurial process'. We define process as the movement from discovering or creating an opportunity, evaluating it and finally exploiting it through organising. As such, the organising may lead to a new organisation, which can either be an independent organisation or a new organisation within the framework of an existing association, public institution or company. A third recurring concept is 'entrepreneur'. The concept refers to the individual who initiates, pursues and creates entrepreneurship. Many other concepts are regularly featured in the book.

The audience

Who is the audience? This book being introductory in its nature is aimed at all of you students who have no previous education in entrepreneurship. It is a book that is equally suited to all and not just 'would-be' entrepreneurs. So, it is equally suitable for a specific audience who want to start a business and a wider audience who wish to develop their entrepreneurial mind-set. If you are a member of the first group, the book will give you a great insight into how entrepreneurs act and create value. You will gain an understanding of the start-up process and among the learning points you are probably searching for, are instrumental and very specific entrepreneurial skills. On

Table I.1 Differences between audiences

	Specific Audience	Broad Audience
Career ambition	Have real ambition to start a business	Has ambition to work with entrepreneurial issues
Overall rationale	To understand start-up processes	To develop an entrepreneurial mind-set
Learning needs	Seeking practical and instrumental skills	Seeking an ability to identify, evaluate and organise opportunities

the other hand, if you are a member of the latter, broad audience, the book's value is that it introduces a set of principles to be applied in most situations that concern the creation of something new. Regardless of whether the situation is associated with design, humanities, political science or some other field, you will hopefully become more entrepreneurial in your thinking and learning and will probably seek to understand how to identify, evaluate and organise opportunities. Table I.1 shows some basic differences between the two groups.

Regardless of which audience you belong to, teaching in entrepreneurship is important to you. Students who have received this type of teaching are different from their fellow students and have a greater tendency to start new organisations compared with students in general. Furthermore, they are more efficient in accumulating financial assets, they receive higher wages and participate more in product development and other research and development activities than other students (Autio 2007).

Basic concept: theory and practice in action

There is strong evidence that entrepreneurship education should be different from normal teaching because it's about teaching you to create something that does not yet exist. Traditional teaching typically concerns how one conducts oneself within something that has already been created; for example, how to act within an existing organisation or a known market. In the teaching of entrepreneurship there needs to be room to stimulate entrepreneurial imagination, risk taking, action orientation and occupational independence. Therefore, gaining technical knowledge and skills is not enough. You also need the ability to use knowledge and link it to your own situation, activities, experiences and creativity. This book supports you in capturing the essence of entrepreneurship's complex, creative and transformative nature.

Source: Inspired by Kolb (1984).

Figure I.2 The book's use of the learning cycle

The book's concept is inspired by Kolb's (1984) learning cycle. A cycle that pushes you into entrepreneurial practice rather than simply reading about it. The cycle also means that you will be introduced to entrepreneurship from an in-depth and theoretical angle. Practice, theory, experimentation and reflection are all parts of the learning game . . . So enjoy it!

Kolb's learning cycle consists of four activities:

1. Its starting point is the practice-oriented stories of entrepreneurship, which, in this book, takes the form of text. This activates your learning process.
2. Next, it focuses on your immediate reflection and interpretation of what happens in the story and why.
3. Only at this stage are the relevant theories introduced, and we give you a taste of how the stories can be interpreted in light of the theory.
4. Based on these three learning activities you are finally ready to experiment with the knowledge you have gained by reading the chapter.

We offer some exercises that you can review to test your new knowledge. The learning cycle which is illustrated in Figure I.2, can thus start a new learning cycle.

The chapters' fourfold structure

The book's chapters are structured based on the learning cycle's logic. This means that each chapter uses a very different language that spans theoretical as well as everyday language. Finally, each chapter of the book is divided into four sections, corresponding to the learning cycle's key areas. The four sections are as follows:

- *Practical cases*. The chapters open with actual stories about entrepreneurship in the form of cases.
- *Your immediate interpretation*. This is followed by exercises that guide you to reflect on and create your initial interpretation of the entrepreneurs' stories: what happens and why does it happen?
- *Theories of entrepreneurship*. Here, relevant theories of entrepreneurship are introduced to interpret the stories further and to add theoretical angles to them. This part focuses on presenting the theory in a nuanced fashion. Therefore, the theory's presentation is built around a paradox. The paradox gives you versatile and exciting theoretical tools to interpret the entrepreneurial stories.
- *Testing the theory*. The last part of the chapter provides suggestions on how the knowledge and theory that have hitherto been discussed in the chapter may be tested in another entrepreneurial context. How can we understand the acquired knowledge and theory in light of situations other than just those outlined by the stories that were initially presented in each chapter?

Entrepreneurship: a world of paradoxes

Theories of entrepreneurship are filled with tensions and dilemmas that at first glance may seem contradictory. For example, many theories present the entrepreneurial process as a determined act that the entrepreneur can plan in advance. The entrepreneur can then predict the process, and thus what steps he must move through in order to achieve the goal: like a kind of jigsaw puzzle. These theories assume that from the beginning, a picture of the completed puzzle exists. The entrepreneurial process is then about making the right plans and taking the optimal decisions, so that the pieces can be put together in such a way that the puzzle is completed according to the picture.

Other theories take the line that that the entrepreneur does not *a priori* predict which goals are to be achieved, and how he or she can achieve them. The picture of what the entrepreneur will create does not yet exist. Entrepreneurship is simply too unpredictable to be able to plan everything in advance – it's all about creating a future in the form of a product, market or some other, as yet unknown service. Instead, an entrepreneur needs to take an improvisational approach moving step by step: like making a kind of patchwork quilt. Such a quilt is created by gradually gathering a lot of new and old materials (fabrics,

Figure I.3 The puzzle

ribbons, embroideries, buttons, etc. that exist in a variety of colours and qualities) into a meaningful pattern. From this, many different beautiful, and less beautiful, patchwork creations are produced. Seen in this light, the entrepreneur through small steps and improvisation creates an entrepreneurial process with the materials that he or she can obtain. The results of the process can be many different organisations, products or markets.

In this way the book presents theories of entrepreneurship as a collection of paradoxes. Generally, a paradox is a contradictory statement that in this book is introduced as two conflicting theoretical perspectives. The perspectives can be viewed as opposites. In this way we want to illustrate the tensions within theory, which in turn reflect the dilemmas that the entrepreneur meets in his everyday life. As an entrepreneur you will often be left in a perplexing situation where you must make up your mind on paradoxical perspectives. You must be critical and decide for yourself.

Paradoxes in the book are not only 'either-or' paradoxes, despite the fact that they are often presented in relatively extreme versions. The purpose is to distinguish the paradoxical perspectives from each other. It is easy to talk

Figure I.4 Patchwork quilt

of them as stylised interpretations, but in practice a combination of both perspectives applicable to the paradox is extremely useful in terms of understanding what's happening in the entrepreneurial process.

The book's structure

You can choose to read the book in its entirety. However, its structure also allows you to select the parts of the book that you find most relevant in light of your academic skills and interests. Thus, the book is structured around four main sections, each of which can be used independently. The sections are:

1. Welcome to entrepreneurship
2. The entrepreneurial process
3. The entrepreneurial content
4. The entrepreneurial context

Each section consists of a small group of chapters. These chapters contain a core subject area in entrepreneurship. As you can see from Table I.2, we have selected key theoretical paradoxes that are related to each discipline.

Section 1: Welcome to entrepreneurship

In the book's first section you will be confronted with two chapters. Chapter 1 introduces the entrepreneurial phenomenon. Why is it important from an individual, organisational and societal angle, and how has the phenomenon been seen in a historical perspective? Last but not least the chapter provides an insight into the key concepts that underpin the book.

Table I.2 The book's sections, chapters and paradoxes

Sections	Chapters	Paradoxes
Welcome to entrepreneurship	1 What is entrepreneurship?	Introduction – no paradox
	2 Who is entrepreneur?	Born or made?
The entrepreneurial process	3 Emergence of opportunities	Discovered or created?
	4 Evaluation of opportunities	Instrumental or legitimate?
	5 Organising of opportunities	Planning or improvising?
Entrepreneurial content	6 Resources	Exploit or explore?
	7 Networks	Rational or embedded?
	8 The business plan	Management tool or creativity curb?
The entrepreneurial context	9 Intrapreneurship	Top-down or bottom-up?
	10 Social entrepreneurship	Business or better world?

Chapter 2 looks at the decision to embark on an entrepreneurial career path. Why do some people decide to become entrepreneurs and not others? Who is the entrepreneur? Can you identify him or her in the crowd? Is an entrepreneur something you are born to be, or something we all have the potential to become? Here we expressly discuss the paradox: Born or made?

Section 2: The entrepreneurial process

Creating, evaluating and organising new opportunities are three key activities related to the formation and realisation of the entrepreneurial process. The book's second section contains three chapters. The first (Chapter 3) discusses the circumstances that lead to the emergence of a new opportunity. Specifically, there is discussion about whether opportunities exist around us at all times and are just waiting to be discovered, or whether opportunities are created by the individual? The paradox is whether opportunities are discovered or created.

The section's second chapter (Chapter 4) provides an insight into how the entrepreneur can evaluate his or her opportunity(ies). Evaluation refers to the process associated with assessing whether the opportunity makes sense in the market, or what action is needed to make it viable. We also discuss whether evaluation of opportunity(ies) is a systematic and analytical process or whether the evaluation is better understood as a legitimisation process where the entrepreneur, through interaction with the market attempts to gain legitimacy for his or her activities. Thus, the chapter presents opportunity evaluation in light of the paradox: instrumental or legitimate?

The last chapter in this section (Chapter 5) focuses on how opportunities can be organised. Opportunities are only really visible to investors, customers, etc., when they are organised. So, every entrepreneurial process develops structures and routines that can support the organising process which can lead to an independent organisation or a new organisation within an existing organisation. Can this organisational effort be planned and predicted, or is the process characterised by being improvisational? This is a question we will address in this chapter during the discussion of the paradox: planning or improvisation?

Section 3: Entrepreneurial content

The book's third section focuses on some key themes in that part of the entrepreneurial process in which opportunities are evaluated and organised. In the section's first chapter (Chapter 6) you will be confronted with the issue of resources. The chapter divides resources into three types: financial resources, human resources and social resources. It discusses how the value of a resource can be assessed. It also discusses whether the entrepreneur must use the resources he or she has control over, at any given time, to exploit an opportunity, or whether the entrepreneur must use these resources to explore new and more opportunities. This examines the following paradox: exploit or explore?

The following chapter (Chapter 7) deals with networks and networking. The entrepreneur's social and business network is important. The chapter examines the different types of networks utilised by the entrepreneur and how various challenges in the entrepreneurial process expose a need for different types of networks. Should networks be understood as rational tools that are available to the entrepreneur, or as the 'hard to manage' conditions surrounding the entrepreneur? The paradox discussed therefore is: rational or embedded?

Chapter 8 gives an insight into the business plan, which is a central element in entrepreneurship. The plan's role in the entrepreneurial process and its importance is discussed. Here we address questions such as: is the business plan a valuable management tool in the often chaotic entrepreneurial process, a tool that supports and promotes the entrepreneur in a structured and holistic understanding of the idea and its potential? Or, is the business plan an impediment to the maturing of the idea and to the consideration of new opportunities during the process? The paradox is, in other words, whether the business plan is a management tool or a curb on creativity.

Section 4: The entrepreneurial context

The final section emphasises that the entrepreneurial process does not take place in a vacuum. Different contexts help to shape the process. The section examines two interesting contexts for entrepreneurship. The first chapter (Chapter 9) introduces entrepreneurship within the context of an existing organisation. This phenomenon is often called 'intrapreneurship'. New ideas to be discovered or created, evaluated and organised, also occur within the framework of existing organisations; just as they do in the start up of new independent organisations. The question is whether this happens through management-led initiatives and supported processes, or whether it is initiative and commitment on the part of employees that creates intrapreneurship. The focus of the chapter is thus the discussion of the paradox: top-down or bottom-up?

Chapter 10 gives an understanding of the social entrepreneur who provides or creates a new organisation in an effort to achieve social objectives or to contribute to social activities; creating better conditions for people locally or globally. The title of the chapter is social entrepreneurship, but how can social entrepreneurship be created? Is social entrepreneurship a matter of creating a better world where social objectives are the social entrepreneur's only objective? This implies that profit and commercial exchanges are unheard of. Or does the creation of a better world require an economically sustainable business to be established so that the social entrepreneur can contribute to social activities? This means that social objectives are no longer the primary, but only secondary objectives because the first priority is profit and commercial exchange. The paradox of the chapter is: business or better world?

In addition to the ten central chapters, the book contains a summary (Chapter 11) of the book's discussions, emphasising the paradoxes that have been addressed. This chapter discusses whether there is a stronger correlation between the presented paradoxes, which can further support our understanding of entrepreneurship.

 LITERATURE

Autio, E. (2007) *Entrepreneurship Teaching in Öresund and Copenhagen Regions*, Copenhagen: Danmarks Tekniske Universitet.

Kolb, D.A. (1984) *Experimental Learning: Experience as the Source of Learning and Development*, Englewood Cliffs: Prentice-Hall.

Welcome to entrepreneurship

1

What is entrepreneurship?

Entrepreneurship is around us all the time and often talked about. But what exactly is it? How would you define entrepreneurship? This might seem an easy task, but it certainly is not. Reading the newspaper or watching TV, it's easy to get the impression that entrepreneurs are today's heroes. You will encounter stories of the resourceful hero, who starts his own organisation, and as a result, becomes rich and famous, e.g. Henry Ford's creation of the Ford motor company and Bill Gates's creation of Microsoft. This book's message is that entrepreneurship is much more than just starting an independent organisation. Entrepreneurship is a complex phenomenon that occurs in many different contexts, and varies in terms of its scope, process and output.

The primary purpose of this chapter is to address the question: what is entrepreneurship? There is no one answer to that question. The entrepreneurial phenomenon is broad and has many facets, '. . . there are many entrepreneurships in terms of focus, definitions, scope and paradigms' (Steyaert & Hjorth 2003: 5). One reason for the existence of many different 'entrepreneurships' is that entrepreneurship is studied within many different disciplines (economics, psychology, sociology, management, etc.). In fact, each author seems to have his own definition of entrepreneurship. With reference to Saxe's (1872) story about the blind men touching different parts of an elephant (trunk, tail, etc.) and as a result telling different stories about it, Gartner (2001) asks: 'Is There an Elephant in Entrepreneurship?'

Figure 1.1 The elephant

An elevator pitch for entrepreneurship

Before we start defining entrepreneurship, we will first provide you with a short 'elevator pitch'. This term is often used in entrepreneurship. The term usually refers to a short sales pitch or oral monologue from one person to one or more people, where a given theme is introduced in the timespan of an elevator ride. The concept is American and is frequently used in networking at various business events. Here you have just a few seconds to efficiently and quickly arouse interest in your idea, product or the like.

In the following we will stimulate your interest in the idea of studying entrepreneurship. However, there will be no question of an 'elevator pitch' in the formal sense, but it is nevertheless a relatively short sales pitch for entrepreneurship. Entrepreneurship has great value for the individual, existing organisations and society. It therefore has value for you as an individual, the organisations that you may create or work within, and the people around you.

Elevator pitch for you

Entrepreneurship has different values for different people. What value would you place on becoming an entrepreneur? Surveys among students and other populations show that it is not only the prospect of making money that motivates entrepreneurs. It is more the desire for 'independence' and the need for 'achievement' that drives the potential entrepreneur (Shane et al 2003; Naffziger et al 1994). This does not mean that making money can be ignored. In order to implement their entrepreneurial processes entrepreneurs are required to establish an organisation that is commercially viable. This means that they must, at least, earn enough money to pay necessary expenses, including remuneration for their own efforts.

You might think that entrepreneurship is of no direct value to you, but think of the changes taking place in the labour market. The trend is towards more free agents, more frequent switching between jobs, faster technological development, more choice and more ambiguous job structures. Effectively this requires each of us, to a greater extent than ever before, to act as entrepreneurs in the context of our own education and careers. We must to a greater extent create a career instead of just having a career. We can usually choose from many educational opportunities and there are often multiple career tracks to pursue after graduation, including the choice between different forms of wage earning and a career as self-employed. In the past, it was common for children to follow the same career as their parents: one was almost born to follow a particular career. Although such a career path is still to be found today, younger generations are now much more challenged to create their own future. As Down said: 'We are entrepreneurs of the self' (Down 2006: 5). Therefore it is crucial for young people generally, to know what entrepreneurship entails and to be trained in it.

Last but not least, entrepreneurship is exciting. As an entrepreneur, you are helping to create something new, typically together with others who think it is a challenging and educational experience to work in the pioneering phase, bringing new things into being.

Elevator pitch for existing organisations

Entrepreneurship is also of great value to existing organisations. Organisations may find it difficult to survive if they fail to differentiate and innovate in what is essentially a globalised world. Here there is more competition for everything from everywhere; it is also a world that seemingly has no speed restrictions (Nordström 2000). Technological advances mean that organisations' products and services constantly become obsolete. Therefore, organisations must continually renew themselves and innovate across the board (new products, materials, markets, technologies, processes, etc.).

Differentiation and renewal requires that organisations are able to create or discover new opportunities and pursue them, which is precisely the core of entrepreneurship. Therefore you see more and more organisations seeking employees who can do something beyond traditional management skills with a focus on the ability to plan, organise and coordinate; they are looking for employees who are entrepreneurial, innovative and creative. Entrepreneurship is therefore also of value for those of you that take employment in an existing organisation.

Elevator pitch for society

The value of entrepreneurship to society as a whole should not be forgotten. Especially since the 1970s, entrepreneurship has been seen as a means to generate jobs, economic growth and prosperity. In the 1970s, Bolton (1971) and Birch (1979) in particular, focused on the revolutionary idea that small businesses are more important to the economy than large businesses when it comes to creating economic growth. The idea still has currency, and the importance of entrepreneurship in a socio-economic perspective is often singled out by politicians and researchers the world over.

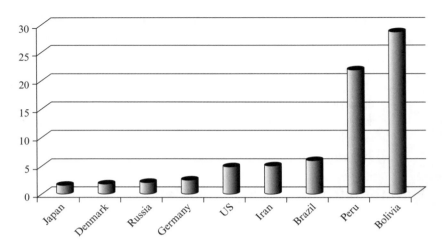

Source: Kelley et al (2011).

Table 1.1 Percentage of adult population actively engaged in start-up activity in 2010

Seen in this light it is no wonder that in many countries there is a policy objective to increase the number of growth-oriented entrepreneurs. Globally, there is great variation in the proportion of the total population that are active entrepreneurs. Generally, the prevalence of the entrepreneurially active population is higher in developing countries than in developed countries, but there is also wide variation within groups of countries. Explanations are many: culture, framework conditions, industrial structure, etc. (Kelley et al 2011). It is this proportion that politicians are trying to change in order to achieve a better level of entrepreneurial activity, both in terms of quantity and quality. Table 1.1 shows examples of the various levels of entrepreneurial activity across a number of selected countries. It shows the percentage of adults who are in the process of starting a business. As we see, variation occurs not only between developed and less developed countries, but also within each group; thus, there is also a variation among developed countries and variation among less developed countries. In Japan just 1.5 per cent of adults were in the process of starting an enterprise in 2010 but the percentage in the US was 4.8 per cent against 28.8 per cent in Bolivia.

Entrepreneurship is also acknowledged as helping to develop healthy competition in the economy, as the entrepreneur constantly pushes new ideas, products, services and processes into the market. Yes, entirely new industries and markets arise as a result of the activities of entrepreneurs. Alternative energy from wind turbines is an example of a Danish entrepreneurial adventure, which has created a new industry with great impact on our ability to solve present and future environmental and climate problems.

Therefore through the study of entrepreneurship you achieve an understanding of a phenomenon that is interesting and important both for you, existing organisations and society. Need we say more? Entrepreneurship is worth studying.

A historical flashback

Nothing comes to this world from nothing. All phenomena are part of a longer historical process of learning. Entrepreneurship also has a story. Let's go back in time and delve into this story; it will give you a better understanding of what entrepreneurship is and how this phenomenon can be defined. We've divided the field into four traditions:

1. the economic tradition;
2. the social-psychological tradition;
3. the emergence tradition; and
4. the opportunity tradition.

The economic tradition

Entrepreneurship is an old phenomenon. Going way back, warfare in particular, including the conquest of countries, was regarded as a form of entrepreneurship. Conquest and acquisition of resources was considered then as a natural part of efforts to discover and exploit new opportunities (Baumol 1990).

We have to wait until about 1755 before the entrepreneurial phenomenon is formally introduced into the literature on trade, economy and business. Cantillon (1680–1734) is often seen as an important pioneer in the field (Landström 1999). For him, the entrepreneur's function was to compensate for discrepancies between supply and demand by buying something cheaply and selling it again at as high a price as possible. The entrepreneur is a person who obtains and distributes resources at risk, thereby bringing the economy towards equilibrium (Murphy et al 2006). By the end of the 1700s, the concept of entrepreneurship had expanded to view the entrepreneur as a person who plans, supervises, organises or even owns factors of production. In the 1800s the distinction was made between those who supply funds and those who create profit (Coulter 2003).

In the 1900s, Knight saw it as the entrepreneur's function to carry the uncertainty within the economy on his shoulders. Knight distinguishes three types of uncertainty (Sarasvathy et al 2005):

- The first type of uncertainty occurs when different outcomes in the future exist and are known. Here the entrepreneur's role is to calculate probabilities and make decisions based on them. An example of this uncertainty would be to assemble a number of black and white marbles in a jar with a known distribution and ask someone, blindfolded, to pick out a ball and estimate the probability that it is black.
- The second type of uncertainty occurs when the future outcome exists but is not known in advance. An example of this uncertainty would be to assemble a number of black and white marbles in a jar without knowing the distribution and then ask someone, blindfolded, to pick out a ball and estimate the probability that it is black or white, respectively. After selecting a number of balls one forms a picture of the likelihood that the next ball is black.
- Knight calls the last type of uncertainty the true uncertainty. This occurs when the future outcome does not exist and it is therefore not possible to know anything about it. The entrepreneur receives profits as compensation for handling the real uncertainty. An example here might be where a jar is filled with an unknown and ever changing bundle of things such as balls, cakes, sweets, insects and more, and then a person is asked to estimate the probability of picking out a black ball. No picture of probability can be formed.

However, it is the function that Schumpeter (1934) attaches to the entrepreneur that really provides the root of today's understanding of entrepreneurship. According to Schumpeter the entrepreneur bears no uncertainty about the economy – that is carried by the capitalist who allocates funds to the entrepreneur. Instead, the entrepreneur is an innovator who, by combining existing things, generates new opportunities and organisations in the economy: he or she is the main source of development in the economy. Schumpeter assumes that the starting point is an economy in equilibrium until an entrepreneur generates new opportunities by combining existing things, thereby creating a market imbalance. However, at the same time, the imbalance contributes to developing the economy. The new option can take the form of:

- the introduction of new products or quality thereof;
- the introduction of new production methods;
- the opening of new markets;
- the utilisation of new supply sources;
- the reorganisation of an industry.

Schumpeter assumes that new organisations will outperform existing organisations and create waves of change in the economy. He talks about this process as creative destruction: new projects and organisations are constantly being formed and others are shutting down. If an entrepreneur is successful, copycats imitate the entrepreneur and enter the market. As the market becomes saturated, a new equilibrium emerges in the economy. Of course one can raise objections against Schumpeterian theory, such as: is the new always better than the old? Why is uncertainty not related to the entrepreneur's actions? Nevertheless, there is no doubt that Schumpeter's views are relevant in view of the link between entrepreneurship, innovation and economic growth.

The social-psychological tradition

From the 1960s until the 1980s entrepreneurship was often defined from the perspective of a psychological mentality. McClelland's (1961) work The Achieving Society kick-started these thoughts. This work presents the story of why some people concentrate on economic activity and are remarkably successful when others are not. In addition, it is a story about why some societies do better economically than others, despite the fact that they have a similar starting point. The need to achieve among the actors in a given society is identified as the key to the mystery. This need is linked to the entrepreneurial personality, which means that psychological explanations are gaining ground in entrepreneurship research. Specifically, psychological differences between entrepreneurs and non-entrepreneurs are of scientific interest (Carland 1984). One of the first studies to map the personal traits of successful entrepreneurs was by Hornaday and Bunker (1970). They pointed to many different entrepreneurial qualities, such as 'energetic participation in endeavour', 'confidence', 'desire to be your own boss' and 'need to accomplish' (Hornaday & Bunker 1970: 51).

After the 1980s, this literature fades away having been subject to criticism on three main fronts:

- Studying individual personality traits, such as the need to achieve, tends to ignore the influence that personal traits have on each other, and how environmental factors play a role in entrepreneurial behaviour.
- The psychological perspective has also led to such a wide range of traits and factors that the entrepreneur has been presented as an 'Everyman'.
- Finally, the studies did not make it possible to empirically identify the entrepreneur's personality in the crowd. In particular, Gartner's article: 'Who is the Entrepreneur? Is the Wrong Question' (1988), has

contributed to a showdown with the psychological way of thinking, at least in the sense of universal personality traits of entrepreneurs.

The psychological research route has, over the years, been supplemented by a sociological tradition where the emphasis is placed on relationships between people rather than on the individual. One can therefore talk about a social-psychological tradition concerned with man as an entrepreneurial player both individually and in groups (Aldrich 1999). The social-psychological tradition will be further elaborated in Chapter 2.

The emergence tradition

Newer theories have focused on understanding entrepreneurship as an organising process that leads to a particular output, namely the formation of a new organisation. What distinguishes entrepreneurs from non-entrepreneurs is not personality traits but the fact that entrepreneurs form new organisations (Gartner 1988). This idea was introduced in the theoretical field in the 1980s. Here, entrepreneurship is seen as an organisational phenomenon; entrepreneurship being 'synonymous with the behavioral act of new venture creation' (Pittaway 2003: 22).

By defining entrepreneurship as a process of organisational formation, entrepreneurship becomes synonymous with the building of new structures, because organisations are characterised by having a certain degree of formal policy, administrative structures and goals. There is however an important distinction between conventional organisation theory and the theory of entrepreneurship because the starting point for conventional organisational theory 'begins at the place where the emerging organisation ends' (Katz & Gartner 1988: 429). This means that entrepreneurship research focuses mainly on the process that leads to the creation of a new organisation, whilst organisation theory is mainly interested in what happens once the organisation has been created and developed.

From the beginning, this literature was largely behavioural in nature. This means that it has focused on the activities of the entrepreneur during the process of creating a new organisation. Carter et al (1996) reveal, for example, what activities 71 entrepreneurs are involved in during the start-up process.

The opportunity tradition

The emergence tradition has a competitor. We call the competitor 'The Opportunity Tradition'. Rather than defining entrepreneurship in terms of organisational formation, the opportunity tradition defines entrepreneurship as: 'discovery, evaluation and exploitation of opportunities to introduce new goods and services, ways of organising, markets, processes and raw materials' (Shane 2003: 4). Here, renewal or opportunity emergence is seen as the core of the entrepreneurial process and opening up to entrepreneurial activities may result in multiple outputs, including a new and independent organisation. Other possible outputs include entrepreneurship within the framework of existing businesses, voluntary organisations and public institutions.

Within the opportunity tradition the decisive factor is that entrepreneurship should be seen as something innovative. Entrepreneurial activities involve creativity and have the potential to change the existing economic market conditions. Eckhardt and Shane (2003) say that entrepreneurship involves the creation of new goals, new products or new means-end chains. It is not enough to optimise the existing targets, means or means-end chains – speaking about entrepreneurship, the creation or identification of new targets, means or means-end chains, is crucial. The focus is thus on the minority of organisations, either new or existing, which bring new products, processes, markets and reorganisations with them. This is based on opportunities that add something new to the world we already know. Opportunities are thus a key concept in the opportunity tradition. Eckhardt and Shane define opportunities as 'situations in which new goods, services, raw materials, markets and organising methods can be introduced through the formation of new means, ends, or means-ends relationship' (Eckhardt & Shane 2003: 336).

The book's starting point

Historically, the concept of entrepreneurship has been understood in a variety of ways. Many of these perceptions co-exist today and are still developing. This highlights the importance of positioning yourself within the range of perceptions, when writing a project or saying anything about entrepreneurship. The following section identifies and positions this book's perception of entrepreneurship.

A complementary approach

In the literature you will find many different ideas of how to understand the entrepreneurial process. Some believe that this process can be depicted as a phase or lifecycle sequence. This view holds that all entrepreneurial processes pass through the same stages and that these stages can be identified in advance. Some stage models deal with the organisation's overall lifecycle from the earliest staring point through to the end, for example, Kroeger (1974: 42) distinguishes between: 1) initiation, 2) development, 3) growth 4) maturity and 5) decline. Others zoom in on the earlier stages, when the idea is developed, the first concrete start-up steps are taken and the new organisation begins to take shape (Davidsson 2006; Carter et al 1996). The period before start-up is often called the 'gestation' or 'discovery' phase and the period just after launching, the 'early stage' phase. In some studies the entrepreneur is referred to as being 'nascent' in the period before the start and as the 'owner-manager' after starting up (Kelley et al 2011). The period before start-up can be further divided into the time when the idea arises and is being explored ('potential entrepreneurs') and the later phase, taking concrete steps to start the business without it actually being launched ('nascent entrepreneurs'). In the literature on organisation start-up and development phases you will often find analogies to biological processes, where the distinction is between the organisation's inception, birth, childhood and adulthood. Despite similarities in many stage models and the common reference to biological processes, there is no universal agreement about the number of phases and their descriptions.

Today, the emergence and opportunity traditions represent two dominating perspectives in entrepreneurship research aiming to improve our understanding of the entrepreneurial process. They are often presented as competing perspectives. This book is based, however, on the idea that the two traditions can be viewed as complementary. The argument is that the entrepreneurial process in practice involves the emergence (discovery or creation) of opportunities, evaluation of opportunities and the organisation of opportunities. Opportunity emergence is concerned with the entrepreneur discovering or creating a business opportunity; for example by combining something that already exists to a completely new or improved product. Opportunity evaluation focuses on the entrepreneur's assessment of the opportunity in terms of whether it is attractive to the market or not. Opportunity organising occurs when the entrepreneur tries to exploit the opportunity by implementing it, so that those in the market can see, understand and act upon it.

That the emergence and opportunity traditions can be seen as complementary approaches is also underlined by Bygrave's and Hofer's definition of the entrepreneur: he or she is a person 'who perceives an opportunity and creates an organisation to pursue it' (Bygrave & Hofer 1991: 14). Or Shane's understanding of the core of entrepreneurship: 'Entrepreneurship is an activity that involves the discovery, evaluation and exploitation of opportunities to introduce new goods and services, ways of organising markets, processes and raw materials through organising efforts that previously had not existed'

Figure 1.2 How
entrepreneurship is
construed in the context
of this book

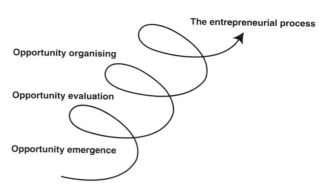

(Shane 2003: 4). The opportunity concept is central here, but note that there is also talk of 'organising efforts'.

Let's illustrate the complementarity of the two traditions with an example: the formation of a new student association. Student associations usually reflect a political position or a particular interest among a group of students, such as environmental issues or the relationship between developed and developing countries. A group of politically concerned students might believe they will have better opportunities to influence key decision makers through their new association. A key issue for consideration here is whether there is 'room' for another association established in the traditional way or whether there is a need to organise themselves in an alternative way, such as through a virtual network. According to the 'emergence tradition' one can understand this case as a traditional process of collective organisation, whilst someone viewing this from the viewpoint of the 'opportunity tradition' would emphasise that this case constitutes a different and new opportunity to perceive a student association. Both traditions thus add something to our understanding of a specific case.

Figure 1.2 illustrates this book's perception of entrepreneurship as a tripartite process involving the emergence, evaluation and organisation of opportunities. Both the emergence and opportunity traditions are involved. The figure is drawn as a spiral in order to emphasise that this book rejects the idea that the process is linear. The process is not one of clear and definable phases that naturally build on each other. Instead, it is often iterative, parallel and overlapping.

Chapters 3, 4 and 5 will elaborate on the above figure. Chapter 3 focuses on opportunity emergence and thus its discovery or creation. Chapter 4 looks at opportunity evaluation and Chapter 5 on the exploitation of opportunities through organising.

Figure 1.3 Core themes for entrepreneurship

Central themes

The processes associated with emergence, evaluation and organisation of new opportunities are extremely complex. A multitude of different factors come into play, such as environment, demography, the entrepreneur's previous experience and career, personality, self-understanding, strategic choices, etc. In particular, this book highlights four themes that influence the process. The themes are: 1) the individual, 2) resources, 3) network, and 4) the business plan. They are illustrated in Figure 1.3.

Why are these issues important? The entrepreneurial individual plays a major role in the development of entrepreneurship. After all, it is an individual or a small group of individuals who initiate and implement the process. Furthermore, it is in the minds of individuals that imaginative and creative processes occur.

Resources are a necessary input in discovering or creating an opportunity and organising it. They are the materials that form the foundation for entrepreneurship. Resources can be broadly defined as human, social and financial resources.

Networking is also crucial. Despite the fact that entrepreneurship is, in many ways, a lonely journey, it must be emphasised that this process is also very much a network journey. The entrepreneur interacts constantly with others (bankers, potential customers, consultants, other entrepreneurs, etc.) and creates networks. These networks are absolutely crucial for him or her to gain access to the knowledge, resources, etc., which are essential for the development of entrepreneurship.

The business plan, understood as a written document, is not necessarily a part of all entrepreneurial processes, but some degree of planning is present in all of these processes. The business plan can also have different meanings. Sometimes it's important to create a basis for resource acquisition and evaluation of the entrepreneurial process. Other times the purpose is to support the entrepreneur in the planning process.

Chapters 2, 6, 7 and 8 deal with each of the four themes in greater depth, which is why they are only touched upon in a superficial manner here. So, as you read the book, you will not only gain a greater understanding of key activities in the entrepreneurial process, namely the emergence, evaluation and organisation of opportunities. You will also understand the key issues that affect these activities.

The significance of context

So far we have talked about entrepreneurship as a phenomenon that takes place in a vacuum. We have not touched on how the entrepreneurial process is influenced by the unique context that surrounds it. A tendency to ignore the context is also found in entrepreneurship research. The focus tends to be on the flower (the new organisation) and the gardener (entrepreneur), whilst the garden (context) and its influence remains a mystery: it is a serious shortcoming (Hindle 2011).

The context within which entrepreneurship develops makes a difference because the context affects the type of network and resources that the entrepreneur has access to during the opportunity emergence, evaluation and organising processes. Similarly, different contexts play a part in affecting the entrepreneur's options. For example, there is agreement that contexts where norms and values encourage entrepreneurship, and also give rise to a higher level of entrepreneurial activity among its members (Gnyawali & Fogel 1994). Finally, disparate contexts confront the entrepreneur with different barriers and opportunities.

An entrepreneur within the context of a university may feel constrained by academic norms with their focus on contemplation and knowledge generation, rather than action and commercialisation. This can give rise to tensions in the entrepreneurial process. But the university context also gives the entrepreneur a lot of opportunities, for example in the form of unique knowledge that can be used to develop his or her opportunity. Last, but not least, entrepreneurs, when they break with their familiar contexts, may experience a feeling of loneliness if the context does not legitimise their entrepreneurial actions.

The importance of context has led us to design two special chapters in the book, which are often omitted from textbooks on entrepreneurship: namely a section on intrapreneurship (Chapter 9) and a chapter on social entrepreneurship (Chapter 10).

The international variation

Finally, this book has an international angle. Even though this book emphasises the universal concepts and ideas about entrepreneurship, international specifics are presented when regarded as relevant. After all, entrepreneurship develops within national, regional and local contexts and is influenced by the rules, norms and values that exist therein. Therefore there is great variation in entrepreneurial activity between countries.

Of course, legislation plays a role. In some countries and sectors, entrepreneurial activity is impeded or prohibited as a formal activity and often develops informally. This applies especially in communist and socialist countries where the State has a full or partial monopoly to organise economic activity. In all countries there are also rules for the creation of new firms and often there are also special rules for subsidies or preferential treatment for start-ups. Typically, entrepreneurs in the initial phase have access to concessional loans and cheap or free advice, fully or partially supported by national, regional and local authorities. The authorities can thus both inhibit and promote entrepreneurial activity, which obviously affects the entrepreneur's opportunities and incentives.

However, it's not just the formal laws and rules that play a role. Also important are the unwritten rules, i.e. culture-related norms and values in society. One example is the large variation from country to country in the perception of what activities women and men should undertake in public and economic life. Can women, for example, be presidents, ministers, police officers and generals? The answer varies enormously from country to country – and in many countries there has been a significant shift in these perceptions throughout history. Something similar applies to the role of the entrepreneur. In some countries it is considered acceptable for a woman to start and conduct business while in others it is controversial and is considered to be contrary to the accepted female role. This of course affects the proportion of female entrepreneurs in those countries. In most countries, the majority of entrepreneurs are men, but in some countries there are more women. In 2010, an extensive study of entrepreneurial conditions showed that in Ghana there were more female than male entrepreneurs, while in Korea there are five times more male than female entrepreneurs (Kelley et al 2011).

Ready for departure

We hope that you now have a better understanding of why it is valuable to study entrepreneurship, what entrepreneurship is and how this book perceives the phenomenon. That was certainly the aim of this chapter. Now you are going on an exciting journey where you have the opportunity to immerse yourself, from both a practical and a theoretical angle, in the central issues of entrepreneurship. You know the itinerary, but before the final departure, we want to be absolutely sure that you pack your bag with the right concepts. Therefore we'll end this introduction with an overview of key concepts that are crucial for understanding the book.

- *Entrepreneurship*: a broad concept that generally speaking can be defined as: emergence of new opportunities which are evaluated and exploited through organising
- *The Emergence Tradition*: a tradition within entrepreneurship research that emphasises the creation of new organisational structures which function as a frame for an opportunity related to a specific market demand
- *The Opportunity Tradition*: another tradition within entrepreneurship research that focuses on the break with existing structures via emergence of new opportunities
- *The Entrepreneurial Process*: the movement from discovering or creating an opportunity, to evaluation of the opportunity, to finally exploiting it through organising
- *Entrepreneur/Intrapreneur*: the individual who initiates, strives for and organises entrepreneurship
- *Paradox*: a conflicting statement which will be introduced in the book as two conflicting theoretical perspectives
- *Perspective*: a theoretical approach which represents one of the two statements that pertain to the paradox
- *Opportunity*: an idea which is evaluated as capable of creating value for others

- *Opportunity Emergence*: the process in which the opportunity emerges led by individuals who discover or create the opportunity
- *Opportunity Evaluation*: the process in which the entrepreneur evaluates to what extent the idea represents an attractive opportunity
- *Opportunity Organising*: the creation of some meaningful structures that support the realisation of the opportunity, for instance to collect resources, to coordinate activities and to involve others so that the wanted output can be obtained.

 LITERATURE

Aldrich, H.E. (1999) *Organisations Evolving*, London: Sage.

Baumol, W.J. (1990) 'Entrepreneurship: Productive, Unproductive and Destructive', *Journal of Political Economy*, 98(5), 893–921.

Birch, D.L. (1979) *The Job Generation Process*, Cambridge: MIT Program on Neighbourhood and Regional Change.

Bolton, J.E. (1971) *Small firms: Report of the Committee of Inquiry on Small Firms*, London: Her Majesty's Stationery Office.

Bygrave, W.D. & Hofer, C.W. (1991) 'Theorising About Entrepreneurship', *Entrepreneurship Theory & Practice*, 16(2), 13–22.

Carland, J.W. (1984) 'Differentiating Entrepreneurs from Small Business Owners: A Conceptualisation', *Academy of Management Review*, 9(2), 354–359.

Carter, N.M., Gartner, W.B. & Reynolds, P.D. (1996) 'Exploring Start-up Event Sequences', *Journal of Business Venturing*, 11(3), 151–166.

Casson, M. (1982) *The Entrepreneur*, Totowa, NJ: Barnes and Noble Books.

Coulter, M. (2003) *Entrepreneurship in Action*, Upper Saddle River, NJ: Prentice Hall.

Davidsson, P. (2006) 'Nascent entrepreneurs, empirical studies and development', *Foundations and Trends in Entrepreneurship*, 2(1), 1–76.

Down, S. (2006) *Narratives of Enterprise: Crafting Entrepreneurial Self-identity in a Small Firm*, Cheltenham, UK and Northampton, MA, USA: Edward Elgar Publishing.

Eckhardt, J.T. & Shane, S. (2003) 'Opportunities and Entrepreneurship', *Journal of Management*, 29(3), 333–349.

Gartner, W.B. (1988) 'Who is the Entrepreneur? Is the wrong Question', *American Journal of Small Business*, 12(4), 11–32.

Gartner, W. B. (2001) 'Is There an Elephant in Entrepreneurship? Blind Assumptions in Theory Development', *Entrepreneurship Theory & Practice*, 25(4), 27–39.

Gnyawali, D.R. & Fogel, D.S. (1994) 'Environments for Entrepreneurship Development: Key Dimensions and Research Implications', *Entrepreneurship Theory & Practice*, 18(4), 43–62.

Hindle, K. (2010) 'How community context affects entrepreneurial processes: a diagnostic framework', *Entrepreneurship & Regional Development*, 22(7), 599–647.

Hornaday, J.A. & Bunker, C.S. (1970) 'The nature of the entrepreneur', *Personnel Psychology*, 23(1), 47–54.

Katz, J. & Gartner, W.B. (1988) 'Properties of Emerging Organisations', *Academy of Management Journal*, 13(3), 429–441.

Kelley, D., Bosma, N. & Amoros, J.E. (2011) 'Global Entrepreneurship Monitor, 2010 Global Report', GERA/Babson.

Kroeger, C.V. (1974) 'Managerial Development in a Small Firm', *California Management Review*, 17(1), 41–47.

CASE STUDY (continued)

your life, but there are moments when conditions are more favourable. And I felt that, in my case, all the conditions were met. I therefore made the decision to stop looking for a job, and to stop responding to the people I had met during interviews. From then on, I devoted myself totally to my start-up project.

This start-up project had no *a priori* reason for being. It was a project in wine, born out of my own interest and passion for it. At least, if it did not work out, I would have learned something about wine, which, for somebody like me, who loves cooking, can always be useful in everyday life. I am aware today that this is not the way you go about developing a business plan, but there was this thought, in the back of my mind, that if it did not work out straight away, it was so interesting that I would find the energy to turn it into something viable. It is true that the wine sector is a tough one, where there is little money to make, which creates little value. The wine trade has existed in France for over 20 centuries, and people involved in the sector consider it in very traditional terms, be they involved in production, wine-making, or buying and selling. The wine sector also has regional particularities; you do not pull the same levers when you are in Burgundy, the Bordeaux region, Côtes du Rhône or Alsace. I immediately knew that understanding its specificities would be a very complex task. In order to better know the sector and understand its workings, I spent a year visiting the vineyards, tasting the wines, meeting people and giving the project time to mature. The initial idea, which I never put into practice, was to apply the Tupperware concept to wine selling: individuals organise sales parties at home where people can taste the wine, hosts get rewards, etc. The idea was to work with wine lovers and set up a network of knowledgeable customers who would organise home sales parties to sell carefully selected quality wines. But what works with plastic containers does not necessarily work with wine: the profit margin on plastic containers is high, whereas margins are low in the wine sector, so I quickly arrived at the conclusion that the initial idea was not viable. I rethought the original concept and opted for wine brokerage instead, which was in the end a rather conventional idea, especially when it came to implementation and distribution. By that time, I had come to realise that there were specific markets that could be commercially attractive, like hotel chains and restaurants. I had identified these targets because without a large sales force, it was out of the question to go and visit private people to sell them a couple of cases of wine at a time. It seemed more logical and efficient to target hotel and restaurant chains in order to negotiate with head office and then sell throughout their hotel and restaurant network. I also realised that this type of clientele used wholesalers dealing in all kinds of beverages: water, soft drinks, coffee, tea, wine, etc. But wine is not a product like any other, it is not water – even if it does contain some – it is not coffee, it is something that requires a specific kind of expertise! So I met with several hotel chain managers, who at least agreed to lend me their name so I could go and visit the local hotel managers. And this is how it all began! My first customers were chain-owned hotels, my very first customer was the Holiday Inn hotel chain.

At the beginning, I was on my own, I was working from a very old flat in Lyon. It was funny in a way: the staircase was a very narrow stone vaulted staircase, and I had to take the cases up

---

CASE STUDY (continued)

the stairs. The first few months, there were many of them, and after a while, there were more wine cases than there were personal things in the flat, I was no longer accommodating the business, it was the business which accommodated me, because there were even cases in the bath: they were everywhere! . . .'

Your immediate interpretation

What does the story tell you about the entrepreneurial individual? What is your initial impression? The following exercises can help you interpret the story.

- Make a list and discuss the personality traits revealed in the narrative. Who is Rémi?
- Rémi presents his stories for you and your fellow students. Your tutor asks you to give a brief statement of whether or not he can be defined as an entrepreneur. What are the arguments for and against? How do you define an entrepreneur?
- One of your fellow students emphasises that Rémi does not start up alone, but together with others. Does this tell you something about the entrepreneurial individual? Why do you think that entrepreneurs often start up in teams rather than alone?
- You have decided to start your own organisation, but you want to start it with others. What key issues would you consider in your efforts to put together the perfect start-up team? What characteristics, skills, networks, etc. should the other members of your start-up team possess?
- You meet one of your friends. She has already started two organisations. In discussing what makes an entrepreneurial person she claims that she was born to become an entrepreneur. What do you think about this argument?

Theories of entrepreneurship

As mentioned earlier, the number of entrepreneurs varies across countries, depending on, among other things, countries' unique economic, cultural and social situations. However, the individual level is also crucial for understanding the kind of people that generate, evaluate and organise new opportunities and thereby adopt the role of entrepreneurs. Theories, which have primarily been of a psychological nature, can give us some answers as to the characteristics of entrepreneurial individuals, but they point in different directions.

According to Korunka et al (2003) the development of theory about the entrepreneur as an individual can generally be considered in three phases. The first, 'optimistic' phase, particularly dominant in the 1960s and 1970s, essentially believes that entrepreneurs are born with a variety of traits that produce a universal and specific entrepreneurial personality that we can identify. By revealing this personality, it is possible to differentiate the entrepreneur from other individuals.

In the 1980s however, another, more critical phase of theoretical development arose. Here, the entrepreneur is seen as a much more complex phenomenon and it is not enough merely to look for personality traits. This allows the introduction of more dynamic and diverse theories, which among other things, focuses on the process and the interaction between individual and environment to explain the entrepreneur and entrepreneurship. It also opens up the possibility that individuals are not born as entrepreneurs, but are made into entrepreneurs. Anyone can evolve to become an entrepreneur over time. Whether individuals are motivated to try their hand at entrepreneurship will be the result of specific situations and experiences encountered during their lives.

A third and more recent phase, around 2000, focuses, once again on the individual's personality. However, rather than concentrating on identifying individual traits this research develops a more dynamic understanding of the entrepreneurial personality through the analysis of cognitive processes, intent, identity, etc.

In short, this chapter will introduce you to the paradox of whether entrepreneurs are:

Born or Made?

Types of entrepreneurs

Before we plunge into the paradox it is important for you to remember that an entrepreneur is not simply an entrepreneur. We can distinguish between different types of entrepreneurs according to the various entrepreneurial opportunities and challenges they face. Here is a breakdown of entrepreneurs in six different groups, inspired by Ucbasaran et al (2001):

- 'Novice' entrepreneur (a person with no entrepreneurial experience)
- 'Habitual' entrepreneur (a person with previous entrepreneurial experience)

- 'Serial' entrepreneur (a person who is constantly establishing and selling organisations)
- 'Portfolio' entrepreneur (a person who owns several organisations simultaneously)
- 'Nascent' entrepreneur (a person who is in the process of considering the establishment of a new organisation – he or she can be either a 'novice', 'habitual', 'serial' or 'portfolio' entrepreneur)
- 'Intrapreneur' (a person acting entrepreneurially within an existing organisation). This type of entrepreneurship is discussed, thoroughly, in Chapter 9.

Within the literature you will find many other interesting classifications of the entrepreneur, see Wickham (2006) for an overview. Now, let's get back to the paradox.

The entrepreneur is born

The 'entrepreneurs are born' perspective represents what we, earlier in this chapter, referred to as the optimistic phase. Despite the fact that psychology has played a crucial role in this phase, we begin with the economic tradition, which was reviewed in Chapter 1. This tradition considers the function performed by the entrepreneur, within the economy, to be crucial (Casson 2003), but doesn't delve into who the entrepreneur is as an individual and thus the important individual personality traits that are relevant to entrepreneurship. As Herbert and Link state: 'the entrepreneur has been a shadowy and elusive figure in the history of economic theory. Referred to often, but rarely ever studied or even carefully defined, the entrepreneur winds his way through economic history, producing results often attributed to faceless institutions or impersonal market structures' (Hérbert & Link 1988: 11). Some economists, including Schumpeter (1934), stress the importance of the entrepreneur's character traits and personality. Overall, he sees the entrepreneur as a particularly innovative individual – 'A Great Man' who through creative destruction creates new waves of change in the economy. This distinguishes the entrepreneur from the 'ordinary' people who are more 'routine' in their activities. Entrepreneurial activity comes from special individuals who have the:

- desire to establish a private kingdom: 'First of all, there is the dream and the will to found a private kingdom, usually, though not necessarily, also a dynasty';
- will to conquer: 'Then there is the will to conquer: The impulse to fight, to prove oneself superior to others, to succeed for the sake, not

of the fruits of success, but of success itself. From this aspect, economic action becomes akin to sport – there are financial races, or rather boxing-matches';

- joy of creating: 'Finally, there is the joy of creating, of getting things done, or simply of exercising one's energy and ingenuity' (Schumpeter 1934: 93–94).

The idea of the entrepreneur as a special individual has been continued in research focused on identifying the traits that make up the unique entrepreneurial personality. But can it really be true that one must be a special person to be an entrepreneur? Well, to discover or create opportunities, evaluate and pursue them through organising involves risk taking, the ability to find creative solutions, the need to perform, personal ambition and much more. They all sound like traits that are related to one's personality. One may wonder if there are certain people who are more likely to have these traits whilst certain other people prefer a more secure and conventional career path?

Character traits in the limelight

As mentioned in Chapter 1, entrepreneurship research from around 1960 up to 1980 focused on describing the entrepreneur as a person in possession of a particular set of traits (e.g. Hornaday & Aboud 1971; Hull et al 1980, Begley and Boyd 1987). In short, the entrepreneur is assumed to be a kind of 'describable species that one might find a picture of in a field guide, and the point of much entrepreneurship research has been to enumerate a set of characteristic describing this entity known as the entrepreneur' (Gartner 1988: 12). One of the aims of character trait research is to find out what differentiates the population of entrepreneurs from other groups in society. It would be quite rewarding if you could point out entrepreneurs in the crowd and support these unique entrepreneurs, so as to accelerate economic growth in society. The thinking behind trait research is that some people have certain attributes that make it more likely that they will find or create an opportunity and pursue it through organising. Personality traits are: 'constructs to explain regularities in people's behaviour, and help to explain why different people react differently to the same situation' (Llewellyn & Wilson 2003: 342), and research has focused on identifying individual or sets of traits, predicting entrepreneurial behaviour.

Over time, the range of character traits that have been identified as important to entrepreneurship is long. For example: apt to take risks, need to perform, independent, aggressive leader, self-efficacy, is action-and goal-oriented, innovative, intelligent, creative, tolerant of uncertainty and a desire to make money. These are enough to make you think that the entrepreneur is an extraordinary super-human – a hero or heroine. See Gartner (1988) for a more detailed overview of the key contributions to trait research.

However, some traits seem to have attracted more attention and spent more time in the limelight than others, such as risk-taking propensity, need for achievement, need for autonomy, self-efficacy, and internal locus of control; these are also known as Entrepreneurship's Big Five (Vecchio 2003). Thus, there are results showing that entrepreneurs exhibit a higher need to accomplish than others, they are more willing to assume risk; possess a greater need to be his/her own boss; believe they are able to control their surroundings rather than being led by them, and have a more developed faith in their own work-related powers and thus believe in their own abilities in relation to performing a given activity.

Since classic trait research assumes that the identified personality features are stable over time and that the entrepreneur has acquired these more or less at birth, we see this research as an example of a 'born entrepreneur' mind-set. Like in Hans Christian Andersen's story of the Ugly Duckling, it is origin and not growing up that decides who you are and what you become. 'Being born in a duck yard does not matter, if only you are hatched from a swan's egg.' The consequence is '. . . once an entrepreneur, always an entrepreneur, since an entrepreneur is a personality type, a state of being that doesn't go away' (Gartner 1988: 12).

Is it in the genes?

As a further development, of the discussion about entrepreneurs as 'born', there is even a search for the specific genetic set-up, which increases the likelihood that an individual will perform entrepreneurial activity (Nicolaou et al 2008). Entrepreneurship research has often suggested that people with entrepreneurial parents exhibit a greater tendency to become involved in entrepreneurial activity in comparison with individuals whose parents are not entrepreneurial. But can this be explained at a genetic level? According to Shane (2010), research shows that genes indirectly increase an individual's odds of ending up as an entrepreneur. Through the influence of genes on the individual's personality traits, cognitive skills and activity level, the chances of entrepreneurship are increased. For instance individuals with a high level of activity, high intelligence and dyslexia have a greater tendency to become entrepreneurs. Personal characteristics 'self-esteem, novelty seeking, risk-taking propensity, disagreeableness, extraversion, emotional stability, openness to experience and conscientiousness' (Shane, 2010: 165) also seem to increase the likelihood of the genetically determined entrepreneur.

If certain individuals demonstrate a genetic tendency to engage in entrepreneurial activity this makes it much easier for us to point out the entrepreneur in the crowd. Identification of entrepreneurial genetic components also raises ethical questions about how you will manage the new knowledge. A consequence of genetics may be that only a limited supply of entrepreneurs exists in a given society, and only a certain amount of people will be born with the 'right' genes. If one follows this logic, entrepreneurship education makes less sense in general, because an entrepreneur is something you are: it's not something you can learn or develop into.

The entrepreneur is made

As we discussed in Chapter 1 the classic psychological literature – especially traits literature – has been subject to criticism. The subject area has been controversial since the late 1980s, which has given rise to what we referred to earlier as the critical phase in relation to answering the question: Who is the entrepreneur? As Gartner emphasises 'I believe the attempt to answer the question "Who is an entrepreneur?" which focuses on the traits and personality characteristics of entrepreneurs, will neither lead us to a definition of the entrepreneur nor help us to understand the phenomenon of entrepreneurship.' (1988:12)

Focusing on upbringing and demography

One criticism of trait research that has been raised is how little it takes account of environmental factors. This has led to the idea that the entrepreneurial personality is shaped not only by birth but also that early childhood and demographic factors are important. Factors such as birth order, entrepreneurial parents, encouraging parents, work experience, education, gender, age, etc. are assumed to influence whether you become an entrepreneur (Hisrish & Peters 2001); it is from such factors that the idea of becoming an entrepreneur has begun to sprout.

In terms of age, The Global Entrepreneurship Monitor Survey 2010 (www.gemconsortium.org, last accessed 21 May 2012) shows that worldwide the 25–34 year age group contains the highest percentage of people involved in the earlier phases of entrepreneurship, followed by the age groups 35–44 years and 45–54 years. Early stage entrepreneurial activity is less prevalent among 18–24 year olds and least prevalent among 55–64 year olds. When it comes to gender, the same study illustrates that in overall terms, women are less likely to be involved in entrepreneurship. There is however considerable variation in the proportion of female entrepreneurs across countries depending on the opportunities and normative, formal and cultural conditions, which confront women in different countries. In The Republic of Korea there is one female entrepreneur for every 20 male entrepreneurs, whilst there are six female entrepreneurs in Ghana for every five male entrepreneurs. In Western Europe, women are primarily entrepreneurs in Belgium and Switzerland where there are four female entrepreneurs for every five male entrepreneurs. This corresponds roughly to the proportion in the USA too.

A wider picture of the entrepreneur

Born out of another critical response to trait research is the idea that one can explain the entrepreneur's person in a broader and more process-oriented context. Here, a series of components are seen as interacting with the entrepreneur to discover or create opportunities, evaluate and organise them. It views the entrepreneur as being formed by the interaction between the individual and a number of more environmental components. The interaction between the entrepreneurs' market and life situation, network characteristics, type of organisation, access to resources, demography, etc. has a bearing on who will become entrepreneurs and who will not. You simply weave a broader and more dynamic theoretical framework than hitherto to capture what makes an entrepreneur and entrepreneurship.

In creating this framework we use contingency theories which have developed out of the idea that systems consist of various interacting components. Contingency theory implies that something is 'determined by/is contingent upon the situation'. Whether an individual becomes an entrepreneur or not, depends therefore on the situations and experiences that the individual encounters. Furthermore, the interaction between the various components makes the formation of very different entrepreneurial processes and entrepreneurs possible. Consequently, 'The process of starting a business is not a single well-worn route marched along again and again by identical entrepreneurs. New venture creation is a complex phenomenon: Entrepreneurs and their firms vary widely' (Gartner 1985: 697). So there is no single way in which an entrepreneur is created. One of the better-known contingency theories of entrepreneurship is Gartner's (1985) model depicted in a simplified version in Figure 2.2. The model shows how the entrepreneurial process is seen as a result of an interaction between four components (individual, organisation, environment and process).

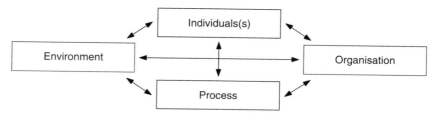

Source: Gartner (1985: 698).

Figure 2.2 Gartner's contingency model

Contingency theories provide us with a good overview of the mechanisms at play in entrepreneurship, but they tell us much less about the entrepreneur as a person. Instead, they focus on the interaction between certain structural or system components; factors external to the entrepreneur as subject (Jones & Spicer 2005).

The entrepreneur's cognitive processes

The critical phase has led to the point where entrepreneurs are no longer seen as an homogeneous group of individuals, and it has largely moved beyond the unilateral studies of traits and the idea that entrepreneurs are born (Baum et al 2007). At the same time, one cannot ignore the entrepreneur as a person in a field such as entrepreneurship, and scholars have, over time, gained a renewed interest in studying the entrepreneurial individual. So, in recent years we have seen the germination of an interesting research approach (the third phase of literature on the entrepreneur), which once again is more directly concerned with studying the entrepreneurial individual, focusing on, among other things, cognitive processes (Mitchell et al 2002). Cognition represents the study of how the mind and our thoughts are organised. It's about the entrepreneur's intellect rather than traits; how he or she understands and what he or she thinks about what is taking place in their environment and within themselves. It is the study of how the brain processes the impulses and the information that the entrepreneur receives from the environment. Therefore, although the entrepreneurial personality is the primary unit of analysis, there may also be an interactionist approach where both the individual and the environment play a role in creating entrepreneurs (Chell 2008). The cognitive approach can be used to understand why some individuals find or create opportunities and pursue them, while others do not; why some even choose to become entrepreneurs and others do not; whether entrepreneurs think differently from others, etc. (Mitchell et al 2004). Shaver and Scott (1991) take this approach in seeking knowledge about how the business world is represented in the cognitive processes of individuals, in both those who create new businesses and those who do not.

According to Shane (2003), the literature has specifically identified three cognitive characteristics that make entrepreneurs exploit opportunities:

- Entrepreneurs are more optimistic in their impulse processing than others. They therefore have a tendency to seize opportunities despite uncertainty about the outcome.
- Entrepreneurs have more willingness to generalise based on small samples than others. They therefore have a tendency to take big decisions, despite the fact that they don't have much information available.
- Entrepreneurs use their intuition more than others. Entrepreneurs thus tend to refrain from collecting information as they possess an inner feeling or belief that exploiting a given opportunity is the right thing to do.

Identity and the entrepreneur

Another emerging branch of research is focused on understanding the entrepreneur as an individual through identity research (Down and Reveley 2004; Downing 2005; Stepherd and Haynie 2009; Hoang and Gimeno 2010). There are many different definitions of what an identity is. Some understand identity as a relatively stable core that individuals carry with them into the entrepreneurial process, and which guides the individual in the unknown situation (Sarasvathy and Dew 2005), while others increasingly see identity as a constantly changing socially constructed phenomenon. One definition focuses on how entrepreneurs make sense of themselves within their environment. Identity is defined as 'a person's sense of who he or she is in a setting' (Weick 1995: 461). According to this definition, a person's understanding of him/herself is constantly changing depending on who the person interacts with and in what contexts he or she participates. Identity thus takes the form of a continuous social process in which the entrepreneur is trying to create meaning and understanding of: who I am, what I do and what I experience. All this affects how the entrepreneurial process functions and entrepreneurs are created.

Similarly, an individual is assumed to have multiple identities. The entrepreneurial individual is not just an entrepreneur. He or she are perhaps also a parent, soccer player, student, half-day employee or pensioner. These other identities play a part in how individuals understand and perform the entrepreneurial identity. We cannot therefore always expect the individual to be fully dedicated to the entrepreneurial identity. It is also easy to find someone who is involved in the entrepreneurial process, but does not see himself as an entrepreneur. For example, he sees himself primarily as an engineer, and the entrepreneurial process is only a tool for facilitating his identity as an engineer.

According to this research, all people can potentially develop an entrepreneurial self-understanding. Who it is that actually creates such an understanding depends on the social relationships the individual is involved in along with their existing self-image or desire for certain future identities. Because identity creation is taking place constantly and is a part of everyday life, this way of thinking breaks with the perception of entrepreneurship as an extraordinary hero-phenomenon.

The individual's process towards entrepreneurship

Before we finally resolve the paradox 'born or made', we will spend some time studying the process through which the individual goes in his journey toward entrepreneurship. As we will discuss, the process can be influenced by whether the entrepreneur sees himself as a born or made entrepreneur. Figure 2.3, developed by Fayolle (2003), shows the individual's journey toward entrepreneurship as being divided into phases. If we are all potential entrepreneurs, the individual's process towards entrepreneurship is understood as being based on an indifference situation where individuals are not yet aware of entrepreneurship (Phase 1). However, an entrepreneurial awakening may occur, which stimulates the individual's interest and desire for entrepreneurship (Phase 2), which in turn can help individuals become motivated to engage in entrepreneurship and develop entrepreneurial intentions (Phase 3). This in turn can trigger the decision to act as an entrepreneur (Phase 4) from which, over time, arises one or another result of the operation (phase 5).

In some cases, the individual passes the entrepreneurial awakening stage very early in life. From childhood he or she dreams of becoming an entrepreneur and has therefore intended to pursue this career for a long time. At times, these types of people may say that they have always seen themselves as entrepreneurs, and they may even perceive themselves to have been born entrepreneurs.

Ajzen's 'Theory of Planned Behaviour' also reflects the process of intention prior to action. The theory suggests that action presupposes a conscious intention to carry out the action. Intention is an indicator of how hard an

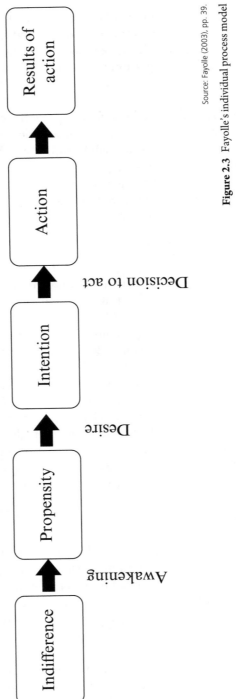

Figure 2.3 Fayolle's individual process model

Source: Fayolle (2003). pp. 39.

individual will work to achieve something – for example entrepreneur-ship, and 'as a general rule, the stronger the intention to engagement in a behaviour, the more likely should be its performance' (Ajzen 1991: 181). It follows that entrepreneurial actions are not random or simply a result of social stimuli. They are also the result of an internal rational individual inten-tion to perform an entrepreneurial act. Ajzen's theory gives us some tools to explain and predict entrepreneurial intention, as intention is referred to as the crystallization of three variables:

- Perceived behavioural control: how difficult or simple the individual perceives the entrepreneurial project.
- Subjective norms: the extent to which individuals perceive a social pres-sure to perform or not perform the entrepreneurial action.
- Attitude towards the behaviour: the degree to which individuals will choose the entrepreneurial action, rather than another action – view of the action's favourability (Ajzen 1991: 183).

As a rule of thumb, the more the individual experiences behavioural control, the greater the respect awarded to the action by society, and the more the individual considers the act to be favourable, the stronger the individual's intentions to become a entrepreneur; which increases the individual's need to discover or create an opportunity.

Nevertheless, action sometimes precedes the individual's intention to journey toward entrepreneurship, for example, when an individual more or less randomly creates an opportunity he finds interesting and begins to develop it further, without really having a clear intention of becoming an entrepreneur. Shane concludes: 'People can and will discover entrepre-neurial opportunities without actively searching for them' (Shane 2000: 451). New opportunities are discovered or created often as a result of our daily interaction with others in different contexts – that is, through exter-nally oriented activities. The entrepreneurial opportunity can, over time, lead to the intention to become an entrepreneur, for example when the individual is curious to explore the possibilities of its potential, has no other career opportunities or is pushed into entrepreneurship by others who find the option attractive. Basically this is a more unconscious initiation of the entrepreneurial process, where the entrepreneurial awakening and intent forms over time in parallel with the individual beginning to act as an entrepreneur.

This type of entrepreneurship strongly underlines how we all have the potential to end up as entrepreneurs, although we may have no intention of

Table 2.1 The paradox: Born or made

	Born	Made
Who is the entrepreneur?	Special super-individuals	All are potential entrepreneurs
Perception of the entrepreneur	Stable over time – once an entrepreneur, always an entrepreneur	The entrepreneur is created through a process
Stimulation	Internal character features	External factors
Research focus	Character features attached to the entrepreneurial personality	The interacting individual and contextual factors that create individuals, cognitive processes and identity
Objectives	To be able to predict and point out the entrepreneur in the crowd	To understand the entrepreneur and how an entrepreneur is created

doing so. Who will become entrepreneurs is difficult to predict. It depends on the circumstances, whom we meet, opportunity, chance, our needs, self-perception, and much more.

Entrepreneurs: born or made?

The entrepreneurial individual has lived a somewhat turbulent life, from a theoretical viewpoint. From being a shadowy figure to being regarded as the 'bees knees' and subsequently being considered as a non-trendy area of research, the individual has again become interesting. Attempts to describe and identify universal and invariable facts concerning the entrepreneur's personality and character traits have not met with much success. Nevertheless this research still, in many ways, seems to maintain many of the ideas of entrepreneurs as heroes who are more or less born for this profession. A contrary view is that entrepreneurship is not something you are; it is something one becomes. Life experiences, people you meet, one's self-perception, situations you get into, knowledge and experience you gain, etc. all combine to create entrepreneurs. Who will become an entrepreneur is not pre-determined and there are no general laws related to the personality that limits the number of us that can become entrepreneurs. We are all potential entrepreneurs. The 'born or made' paradox can be summarized as shown in Table 2.1.

The table shows how two perspectives have dominated research into the entrepreneurial individual. One perspective suggests that entrepreneurs are born. This means that entrepreneurs are special super-individuals who are born as entrepreneurs and remain entrepreneurs all their lives. It is primarily internal character traits that are assumed to determine entrepreneurial behaviour. Therefore, research has – at least in its classic form – primarily focused on the study of stable character traits associated with the entrepreneurial personality. The objective of this research is to be able to point out the special entrepreneurial person in the crowd.

Conversely, the other perspective that views entrepreneurs as made, emphasises that we are all potential entrepreneurs. The creation of entrepreneurs is a process in which primarily external factors play a role, which is underscored by the focus of this research. The research also includes reflections on cognitive and identity-related processes that are linked to the entrepreneurial individual, with the aim of understanding the individual, and how that individual, in interaction with external processes, is created.

A theoretical interpretation

Let us now return to the story about the French entrepreneur Rémi, attempting to understand the story from the 'born' and 'made' perspectives.

The born perspective

Through the lens of the born perspective, Rémi's story is about a man with certain inherited personal characteristics that do not fit into the role of corporate employment. He is born to be an entrepreneur, and therefore he skips a successful and promising career in a major world leading firm. The formal structures of the large organization simply do not give him room to express who he is.

At first, the entrepreneurial personality trait influences Rémi unconsciously. Rémi has never considered the possibility of being an entrepreneur, yet, from unconscious processes his personality traits make him perform an entrepreneurial pattern of behaviour. This behaviour is especially triggered by meeting an entrepreneurship teacher when he joins an MBA programme. After this, the entrepreneurial traits have an all-consuming effect on Rémi as he becomes more and more aware of the fit between the entrepreneurial career option and his personality. Entrepreneurship can satisfy his distinctive personal needs.

Yet, when confronted with difficulties Rémi, during the start-up process, turns his attention towards the employment career option. He goes to job interviews. In the end, the entrepreneurial career option is however the winner. It underscores the born perspective's suggestion that once an entrepreneur, always an entrepreneur. Rémi does what he was born to do although he has some doubts.

Moving into the traits constituting Rémi's entrepreneurial personality, many of the traits from the born perspective can be associated with Rémi. Foremost, his story indicates that he holds a high need for autonomy. He leaves the corporate context to be free to accomplish personal goals of self-fulfillment rather than corporate goals. He is passionate about building a private kingdom to realise his personal lifestyle preferences. Also, Rémi's story shows a high level of risk-taking propensity. He enters the risky and hard-hitting French wine sector with an almost empty backpack in terms of sector relevant knowledge, networks, experiences, etc. To comprehend the game of this wine sector, he travels around in the sector for a year. It indicates that Rémi holds a high internal locus of control. By actively gathering information on the wine sector, he perceives himself able to control the events of his entrepreneurial process as it unfolds within the boundaries of the sector. Moreover he seems to believe that he is competent to create a new venture within this sector. It makes Rémi's story one about a high level of self-efficacy.

In this way, through the lens of the born perspective, we can conclude that Rémi is born with distinguishing entrepreneurial traits. They explain why Rémi enters entrepreneurship and the events of the new venture creation process.

The made perspective

The made perspective provides us with a very different understanding of what is going on in Rémi's story. Initially, Rémi does not hold any entrepreneurial intentions. He has not considered entrepreneurship as a potential career. After all, entrepreneurship has not been a part of his upbringing and he is working for a large company. It is from interactions with others and his contextual external circumstances that Rémi experiences an unanticipated entrepreneurial triggering. An entrepreneurship teacher evokes his interest in entrepreneurship with the question: 'Why not start a business?'

Thinking about new venture creation as a career option, Rémi seems to engage in a process of redefining himself and his career. Increasingly, entrepreneurship appeals to him, and eventually he seems to surrender to the entrepreneurial identity although he still finds his old career identity

Section 2

The entrepreneurial process

3

Emergence of opportunities

The entrepreneurial individual is crucial to understanding entrepreneurship, but many see the discovery or creation of opportunities as the core of entrepreneurial theory. An opportunity is an idea that is believed will create value for others. Without opportunities entrepreneurship cannot occur. Furthermore, many believe that a focus on opportunities is what makes the theory of entrepreneurship unique. But, what is an opportunity and where do opportunities come from? This is the theme of this chapter.

In order to discuss opportunities, we introduce another concept: the idea-concept. Ideas come before opportunities, but not all ideas grow and turn into opportunities. Some ideas remain at the idea level, because evaluation does not suggest that the idea can flourish and be realised. When we think of ideas and opportunities, it is therefore important to distinguish whether a market can be realised or not. If it is judged that a market cannot be realised the idea remains an idea. However, if it appears realistic that a market can be realised, the entrepreneur may take the initiative to develop the idea into an opportunity.

Entrepreneurship in practice

Now it is time to introduce a new real-life entrepreneurial story. This story is about one of the most successful and admired entrepreneurs in the world. It is the Starbucks case which has been developed for this textbook by Saras Sarasvathy.

CASE STUDY

Serving the Starbucks Coffee Story

(Devised by Saras Sarasvathy)

In 2011, Starbucks Corporation owns and operates over 17,000 coffee shops and stores in 55 countries.

The first Starbucks store opened in Pike Place Market in Seattle in 1971. Inspired by another

CASE STUDY *(continued)*

gourmet coffee entrepreneur, Alfred Peet, three friends – English teacher Jerry Baldwin, history teacher Zev Siegl, and writer Gordon Bowker – opened the shop to sell fine fresh-roasted coffee beans from around the world. Each founding partner invested a little over $1,000 and each also took out a bank loan of $5,000. The founders were fans of the American novel Moby Dick and named the store after the first mate on Captain Ahab's ship. In the early days, the founders purchased green coffee from Peet's and eventually began sourcing directly from coffee growers.

For about two decades bracketing the time the original Starbucks store was founded, coffee consumption in the US had been on a downward trend – declining from about three cups per capita per day in 1963 to two in the mid 1980s. Most people bought their undifferentiated mass-marketed coffee from grocery stores and had not even heard of specialty coffees from other countries. Also, in 1971, Seattle was facing a tough economic downturn called the Boeing Bust. Its largest employer, Boeing, had recently cut over 60,000 jobs and other industries were also in a slump. It is reported that a sign near the Seatac airport read: 'Will the last person leaving Seattle turn out the lights?'

In this dismal economic climate and in the face of falling demand for coffee, Starbucks opened in the form of a narrow storefront in Pike Place Market. The founders of the little shop were not watching the trends, but wanting to fulfil their own desire for fine fresh-roasted coffee. Through frequent visits and conversations with Alfred Peet they had learned that imparting to their customers their own appreciation for good coffee involved educating them about its origins, aromas, flavours, preparation and different ways to enjoy it in their daily lives.

The current chairman, president and CEO of the company, Howard Schultz, was working for Hammarplast, a company that made everyday plastic products. In 1981, Schultz noticed that a little store in Seattle was buying increasingly large quantities of a rather simple plastic drip coffeemaker. He decided to investigate. Almost as soon as he got to know the founders and their passion for coffee, Schultz was drawn into becoming part of the enterprise. Here is how he describes what he felt on the plane flying back home from Seattle to New York after his first visit to Starbucks:

'I could feel the tug of Starbucks. There was something magic about it, a passion and authenticity I had never experienced in business. Maybe, just maybe, I could be part of that magic. Maybe I could help it grow. How would it feel like to build a business, as Jerry and Gordon were doing? How would it feel to own equity, not just collect a pay check? What could I bring to Starbucks that could make it even better than it was? The opportunities seemed as wide open as the land I was flying over.'

He joined the company a year later, and a year after that visited Italy where he fell in love with the idea of a coffee-bar, the ambience, the romance and the notion of a place for conversation and community. But the original founders of Starbucks were not particularly enthralled about moving into the coffee-bar business. So Schultz started his own Il Giornale coffee-shops with investment from Ron Margolis, whom he calls 'the unlikeliest investor you could imagine'.

CASE STUDY *(continued)*

Margolis and Schultz were total strangers. But Schultz's wife knew Margolis' and when she mentioned Schultz was in the process of starting a coffee-bar, Margolis expressed an interest in funding it. When Schultz met with Margolis, fully prepared with his business plan and eager to talk about financial projections, Margolis waved away the documents and only wanted to know about the details of Schultz's vision for the business. As Schultz describes it, 'The more I talked, the more enthusiastic I grew, until suddenly, Ron interrupted me, "How much do you need?" – and then proceeded to write a check for $100,000.'

He learned a lot in the process. He tried out several different features and offerings, many of which now form the core elements of the Starbucks experience, such as: the décor, the music, the Barista, the names for cup sizes on the menu, the ordering process and so on and so forth. Schultz made several changes in response to feedback, but also ignored feedback when he felt it might compromise the distinct identity he was trying to create. As he worked out the details in conjunction with customers, employees, investors and people in the community, he became increasingly convinced he wanted to purchase the original Starbucks company and wanted to name his growing chain the same.

When he sought to obtain financing to accomplish this, Schultz encountered every argument possible about why coffee could never be a growth industry. Here is the gist of his pitch to counter the arguments:

'What we proposed to do . . . was to reinvent a commodity. We would take something old and tired and common – coffee – and weave a sense of romance and community around it.

Figure 3.1 A Starbuck's cup ready for the coffee drinker

CASE STUDY *(continued)*

We would rediscover the mystique and charm that had swirled around coffee throughout the centuries. We would enchant customers with an atmosphere of sophistication and style and knowledge.

Nike is the only other company I know of that did something comparable. Sneakers were certainly a commodity – cheap and standard and practical and generally not very good. Nike's strategy was first to design world-class running shoes and then to create an atmosphere of top-flight athletic performance and witty irreverence around them. That spirit caught on so widely that it inspired myriads of non-athletes to lace up Nike shoes as well. Back in the 1970s, good sneakers cost $20 a pair. Who would have thought anyone would pay $140 for a pair of basketball shoes?'

In 1987, Schultz managed to raise enough funding from about 25 of over 240 people he talked to. Their investment enabled him to purchase the Starbucks brand. The rest is history, as they say.

Your immediate interpretation

The Starbucks story gives you an idea of the emergence of opportunities. How will you spontaneously interpret it? Here are some suggestions for what you might consider.

- You are going to write a letter to the editor of the local newspaper about the importance of opportunities. Why do you find them important? In light of the Starbucks story, how will you define an opportunity? Are both ideas and opportunities at play in the story and how?
- A reader asks: where do opportunities come from? With respect to the Starbucks story, how do you answer the reader's question? Another question posed by the reader is: who were the entrepreneurs who built Starbucks? What are they capable of doing which other people are not?
- Ask yourself: if Howard Schultz had not noticed the increase in sales of coffeemakers and gone to investigate, would he still have started Il Giornale or built some other highly successful company such as Starbucks? If yes, what would he have had to do differently?
- Think carefully: have you ever had an idea which you think has the potential of getting transformed into an opportunity? If your answer is yes – describe how you got the idea. And list three things you would do to transform it into an opportunity.

Theories of entrepreneurship

Theories of opportunities are generally about what the opportunities are, why, when and how they exist, what form they might take, and what role the entrepreneur plays in the process of their formation. Now we are going to take the bull by the horns and provide you with one or more perspectives on the nature of opportunities: it is not an easy task.

As in discussions about who the entrepreneur is, so there is also disagreement about what the opportunity is. Generally there are two perspectives on this issue. One emphasises that opportunities are around us all the time. They are just waiting for us to 'fall over' them – to discover them. On the other hand, the second perspective sees opportunities are something belonging to the future, which is *created* through the manner in which the individual acts and interacts with other people as well as his or her ability to reflect on these. Thus, opportunities do not exist independently of human activity and interference. This chapter introduces you to the two perspectives that form the paradox:

Created or discovered?

Opportunity versus idea

We began this chapter by noting that an opportunity is an idea that is evaluated as being able to create value for others and a market can be realized. The criteria for the evaluation are whether the idea is:

- Anchored: bound to a product, a service or an experience that creates value for others
- Attractive: others are willing to pay for the value that represents the idea
- At the right time and place: the environment is mature enough to receive the entrepreneur and his or her idea
- It can be done: the opportunity is practically feasible (Barringer & Ireland 2008).

The last point refers to the entrepreneur's possession of, or ability to acquire access to, the resources, expertise, legitimacy and knowledge required in order to make the idea of value to others. If the idea is evaluated as creating value for others (and not only for the entrepreneur himself) to such an extent that others are willing to pay for the value, and it comes into existence at the right time and place, and it can be realised, the idea is considered to be a real opportunity. With that in mind, do you think that the following diagram in Figure 3.2 is an image of an opportunity?

The figure illustrates how an opportunity is often differentiated from an ordinary idea – a thought. Ideas have the potential to become opportunities, but they do not meet the above criteria for an opportunity. You might have a really good idea, but all your competitors also have the same idea, and besides, the market may not be ready for your idea. As a result, the idea remains an idea, and it never turns into an opportunity. However, it is important to mention that it is often difficult to draw a clear dividing line between an idea and an opportunity. This is a fluid transition, which will also leave its mark on the discussions in this book.

The extent of intentions and capabilities

If one talks about opportunities, one should also discuss intentions. It doesn't really matter whether individuals have discovered or created opportunities if they do not intend to exploit them through organising. At the same time, one can argue that it is immaterial whether the individual has intentions to exploit an opportunity, if they have not discovered or created one, i.e. if they are not in possession of an opportunity.

This discussion was formally introduced by Bhave (1994), who identified two different paths to entrepreneurship. In the first path, the entrepreneurial process starts with the individual intending to start an organisation and then looking for an opportunity. In the second path, the entrepreneurial process begins with the individual, more or less randomly, discovering or creating an opportunity, after which the intention to exploit it develops. This way of thinking has already been touched upon in Chapter 2.

Bhave's (1994) deliberations identify that a society at any given time consists of a population where some have an intention to initiate entrepreneurship, some are in possession of an opportunity, some are in possession of both an opportunity and an intention, and some are in possession of either an opportunity or an intention. In 2004 the Danish team within the Global Entrepreneurship Monitor (GEM) (www.gemconsortium.org, last accessed 22 May 2012) collected data that points to the extent of opportunities and intentions within the Danish population. GEM is an international research project that aims to identify:

● correlations between a country's entrepreneurship activity and socioeconomic growth;

Figure 3.2 Is this an opportunity?

Table 3.1 The extent to which opportunities and intentions are carried by Danes (per cent of the population)

		Opportunity	Opportunity
Intention	Yes	Yes	No
		Potential entrepreneurship	Waste of intention
		7 per cent	3 per cent
Intention	No		
		Waste of opportunity	No entrepreneurship
		16 per cent	74 per cent

Source: GEM Denmark (2004).

- how entrepreneurial activity varies across countries; and
- which national framework conditions encourage a country's entrepreneurial activities.

Over 60 countries have participated in GEM since the project began in the late 1990s. Data on entrepreneurship are collected annually in each of the participating countries. The most essential data collection is a population survey of a random sample of at least 2,000 adults. It is this data collected in 2004, to which we refer in Table 3.1 when determining the extent of opportunities and intentions in Denmark.

The table shows that approximately 74 per cent of the Danish population is completely uninvolved with entrepreneurship, while 7 per cent are in possession of an opportunity, which they intend to exploit; they are potential entrepreneurs. However, the two interesting categories are intention waste and opportunity waste: 3 per cent of the Danish population is located in the former category. These are people with the intention of starting an organisation, but who lack an opportunity to exploit. From a society's point of view this is a waste of intentions. In fact, about 30 per cent of Danes $(3 / (3 +7))$, that intend to start an organisation are in need of a concrete opportunity.

The second interesting category is opportunity waste, where we find 16 per cent of the Danish population. People in this group are in possession of an opportunity, but they have no ambitions to exploit it through organising. A full 70 per cent of them $(16 / (7 + 16))$, have an opportunity that they do not intend to exploit. Again we can see a major waste from society's point of view. Thus, Table 3.1 clearly shows that the main loss in relation to Danish entrepreneurship is the lack of intention to exploit the opportunities that the Danes actually possess.

However, there is considerable international variation in both the extent of intentions and the extent of opportunities across countries. In the international GEM report of 2010 Kelley, Bosma and Amoros (2011) show that the proportion of people who think there are good opportunities for starting a business in the area where they live varies greatly. They sketch out a pattern relative to the stage of economic development in countries. The less economically developed a country is, the greater the proportion of the population that believe there are good opportunities for starting a business. This immediately seems counter-intuitive – you would of course expect that there are more business opportunities in countries that are economically developed. However, according to Kelley et al (2011) this arises because the population in countries with different stages of development have different types of businesses in mind. In the less developed countries, such as Uganda, many of the business opportunities envisaged are necessity driven rather than opportunity driven. People start businesses because they have no other sources of income. It also means these necessity-based businesses are often less innovative and without growth potential.

One can therefore conclude that the waste of intention and waste of opportunity will vary across countries according to their economic development stage. But it is likely to be an important issue around the world.

Types of opportunities

In discussions about what an opportunity is and how it arises, two theorists are frequently referred to: Schumpeter (1934) and Kirzner (1973). As mentioned in Chapter 1, the core of Schumpeterian theory is that opportunities will emerge through new combinations of existing resources. They are also characterised by the fact that they break with the existing perceptions and ways of doing things. A fun example of how existing knowledge can be combined in producing something new is the story of an industrial designer who in 2000 took out a patent for a new type of bulletproof vest. The vest is based on the knowledge and study of insects. Some insects are soft on the inside, but have a robust and animated skeleton on the outside. The vest was designed according to those principles and thus broke with the existing construction of bulletproof vests. The industrial designer got the idea for the vest when he saw a programme on insects on the Discovery Channel. Therefore, by combining the existing knowledge of bulletproof vests with the knowledge of insects, the designer created a whole new, more flexible and comfortable vest.

On the other hand, Kirznerian opportunities are characterised by the entrepreneur's use of existing market information to see whether there are 'holes' in the market in terms of resources that can be used more efficiently than they are currently. In other words: is there potential value in the market that has not yet been optimally used by others? Here, the entrepreneur focuses on optimising and making the existing market effective. For example, the establishment of yet another hair salon on yet another street corner can be an example of a Kirznerian opportunity if the salon fills a potential market that has not yet been exploited. Figure 3.3 provides a simplified illustration of the differences between Schumpeterian and Kirznerian opportunities.

Figure 3.3 further elaborates the difference between the two types of opportunities from a market perspective. Schumpeterian opportunities can be understood as a violation of the existing balance that exists in markets, because they break with existing ways of doing things. It follows that an opportunity in the Schumpeterian sense need not occur because the existing market has a need for the new opportunity. The opportunity arises because existing knowledge is recombined; creating development in the light of the known market. In some cases, the new opportunity, as mentioned in Chapter 1, even reorganises entire industries.

Kirznerian opportunities, however, can be illustrated as a compensation for disequilibrium and are instrumental in creating a balance in the markets. Often, the equilibrium in markets occurs when unmet needs are suddenly covered by new opportunities. For example, an entrepreneur may discover how a hitherto very costly product can be made cheaper or faster. Therefore, the Kirznerian opportunity will not be innovative in the same manner as a Schumpeterian opportunity. It is instead helping to provide equilibrium in the markets.

We can conclude that Kirznerian and Schumpeterian opportunities play different roles in the market. However, they can also be seen as complementary approaches to opportunities. While Schumpeterian opportunities create imbalance in the market, Kirznerian opportunities bring the market back into equilibrium. Therefore, Figure 3.4 is drawn as a ring.

A Schumpeterian opportunity

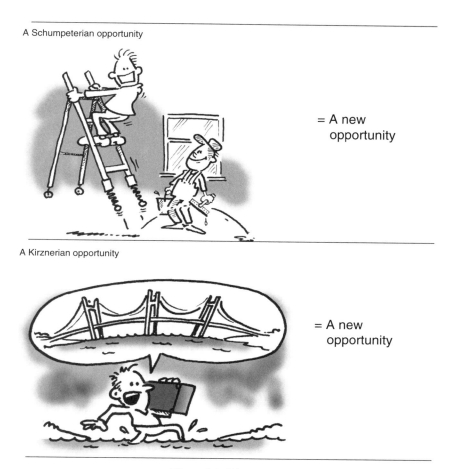

= A new
opportunity

A Kirznerian opportunity

= A new
opportunity

Figure 3.3 Schumpeterian versus Kirznerian opportunity

Discovering opportunities

Now we're going to look at the process that leads to a new opportunity. The Kirznerian opportunity can be said to be objective in nature. It is simply a part of our environment (profit gaps in the market) just waiting to be discovered. The concept of objectivity refers to the fact that the opportunity exists independently of human intervention, time and place. It follows that we can take it for granted that opportunities exist as part of our world despite the fact that we are not always aware of them. Shane and Venkataraman put it that: '. . . the opportunities themselves are objective phenomenon that are not known to all parties at all times. For example, the discovery of the telephone created new opportunities for communication, whether or not people discovered those opportunities.' (Shane & Venkataraman 2000: 220)

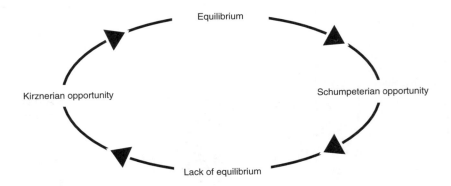

Figure 3.4 Two perceptions of opportunities

However, if opportunities are objective, why don't we all 'fall over' them? Why do only some individuals in our society spot the opportunities? The answer to this question is multi-faceted. Some entrepreneurs proactively seek opportunities. However, many opportunities emerge as a result of the entrepreneur discovering an opportunity without consciously seeking it. Kirzner introduces the concept of 'alertness' to capture this type of discovery. The term refers to: '. . . the ability to notice, without search, opportunities that have hitherto been overlooked' (Kirzner 1979: 48). We might say that 'alertness' refers to a kind of built-in alarm system within the entrepreneur that responds to unforeseen opportunities that he or she then turns her attention to more or less unconsciously and involuntarily. This entrepreneur discovers new opportunities without actively searching for them.

However, if we continue with the discussion about 'alertness' the question remains as to whether all people have a constant preparedness for opportunities, or whether some people are more likely to discover opportunities than others. In this context Shane and Venkataraman state that: 'recognition of entrepreneurial opportunities is a subjective process' (Shane & Venkataraman 2000: 220). This means that although the opportunity is objective, the discovery of the opportunity is linked to the individual. For example, the individual's information and experience in a particular field will, in most cases, lead to a greater degree of awareness of solutions and new ways of tackling challenges. Shane (2000) examines this by allowing a group of entrepreneurs with diverse backgrounds to see the same technology. They arrived at very different ways of looking at the technology as a potential opportunity, depending on the information and experience they possessed.

Access to information
(including life experiences,
social networks and search processes)

Ability to discover opportunities
(including capacity to absorb,
intelligence and cognitive processes)

Source: Inspired by Shane (2003).

Figure 3.5 The individual and opportunity discovery

Figure 3.5 illustrates the opportunity discovery process of the individual.

The figure emphasises that access to information is important to opportunity discovery, and explains that such access will depend on our life experience, social networks and our efforts to seek opportunities. Research shows that the more people seek out opportunities, the more likely it is that they discover an opportunity. Additionally, the figure indicates that our ability to discover opportunities depends on our absorptive capacity (i.e., our ability to interpret information in a useful manner, for example, to see solutions to the problems we face), intelligence and cognitive processes. The latter refers to the fact that we all have a different cognitive set-up, which according to Chapter 2 refers to how the entrepreneur understands and thinks about what is taking place in his / her environment and within him / herself. The perception of opportunities will then be different between entrepreneurs, depending on how his or her brain works. Entrepreneurs typically see an opportunity more optimistically than others and act faster on the opportunity than others despite the lack of information because they possess an inner belief that the opportunity has potential.

Creating opportunities

If you believe that opportunities are not objective phenomena in our surroundings, there's nothing to discover: many share this belief. Opportunities are not '... concrete realities waiting to be noticed, discovered, or observed by entrepreneurs' (Gartner et al 2003: 104). Instead, opportunities are something created by humans: 'opportunities and markets have to be invented, fabricated, constructed, made' (Sarasvathy 2008: 181). Without human intervention, there would be no opportunities. They talk about opportunities as subjective realities. As we see it, Schumpeterian opportunities are examples of the fact that human action is pivotal to the creation of opportunities. They are not based on existing information on markets, prices, consumer preferences, etc. Instead, what is central is the human ability to act creatively, by creating new combinations; where creativity refers to the ability to think innovative thoughts. In addition, this perspective suggests that the interaction between people plays a role in the creation of opportunities.

We can therefore conclude that if opportunities are not objective phenomena, they can instead be seen as social constructs, which are created in everyday life through entrepreneurs' interaction with others, their contexts and themselves. On this subject, Fletcher says: '... entrepreneurial activities, features, and characteristics are not "objects" given a fixed or static ontological status as they come into being. Instead, they are dynamic and constantly emerging, being realized, shaped and constructed through social processes' (Fletcher 2003: 127). Instead of seeing opportunities as objective truths that are present at all times and potentially visible to all, they are an everyday phenomenon. 'We need to recognize that the entrepreneurial activities of everyday life have a great capacity to move us in new and unexpected directions' (Boutaiba 2004: 24). Figure 3.6 is an illustration of how opportunities are created in the interaction between the entrepreneur, other people and their contexts in daily life.

Often our daily interaction leads to the reproduction of things that already exist. Humans can to a great extent be controlled by routine. But sometimes something new occurs, such as a new opportunity. Figure 3.6 shows, indirectly, how opportunity creation is not merely a matter of discovering an optimal opportunity. Because opportunity creation is based on daily interactions, the key point instead is: What occurs here and now? What can be done? What makes sense in light of the current situation? Is it possible? In other words opportunity creation is very much a pragmatic part of everyday life.

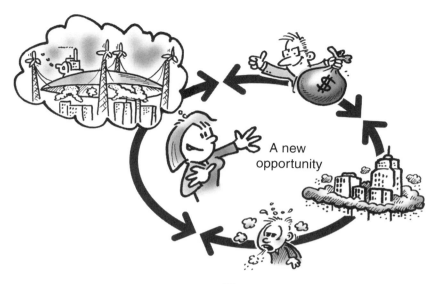

Figure 3.6 A model of opportunity creation

Listen for example to the story of how the opportunity linked to eBay was born. The entrepreneur behind eBay says:

> So people often say to me – 'when you built the system, you must have known that making it self-sustainable was the only way eBay could grow to serve 40 million users a day.' Well . . . nope. I made the system self-sustaining for one reason: Back when I launched eBay on Labor Day 1995, eBay was not my business – it was my hobby. I had to build a system that was self-sustaining . . . Because I had a real job to go to every morning, I was working as a software engineer from 10 to 7, and I wanted to have a life on the weekends. So I built a system that could keep working – catching complaints and capturing feedback – even when Pam and I were out mountain-biking, and the only one home was our cat. (Sarasvathy 2008: 189)

The story is a good example of how opportunity can arise as a result of everyday interactions. The entrepreneur is trying to create an opportunity that can be achieved in light of the other people he interacts with (Pam) and his context (his work). At the beginning he did not know that the opportunity would end up with eBay, as we know it today. He started only in a small way, to create an opportunity, and he took his starting point in everyday challenges.

Last but not least, it follows from the above that opportunities are constantly evolving. Opportunities change constantly as a result of the interaction.

Table 3.2 The paradox: Discovered or created

	Discovered	Created
Opportunity character	Objectively given unit in the environment	Dependent on the interactions of the individual
Opportunity emergence	Involves discovery	Involves creation
Opportunity source	The individual who is attentive towards existing market information	The individual who creates by means of his or her creativity
Opportunity status	The opportunity is stable	The opportunity is dynamic
Opportunity type	Kirznerian hole in the market	Schumpeterian market ruption

Opportunity creation is a process where the entrepreneur does not necessarily determine the development. The entrepreneur is just one of many actors who have influence on the process.

Opportunities: discovered or created?

The focus of this chapter has been a review of two perspectives on opportunities. One perspective argues that opportunities are discovered, while the second perspective sees opportunities as being created. Table 3.2 summarises the two perspectives that make up the paradox: discovered or created.

As shown in Table 3.2, the discovery perspective views opportunities as given objects in the environment. Their formation involves the individual's discovery of 'holes' in the market in the form of untapped resources. This makes clear that the source of opportunity is the individual's awareness of current market information. It is assumed that the opportunity discovered remains the same over time – it is stable. In terms of type, this form of opportunity is Kirznerian.

On the other hand, the creation perspective views opportunities as being closely linked to the individual's actions. The individual is again rooted in a social context, which is why he or she interacts with others and the environment in general. All of this contributes to the creation of opportunities and emphasises that the process of emergence requires the intervention of a creative individual. Since the process that creates opportunities is a result of interacting elements (such as the entrepreneur himself, other individuals and their contexts), the opportunity is constantly changing – it is dynamic. This perspective refers partly to Schumpeter's thoughts on the opportunities as new creative combinations of the existing order.

If you think it makes no sense to see opportunities as being either created or discovered, you can choose to take the same stance as Sarasvathy et al (2002). They stress that some opportunities '. . . lie buried in the soil waiting to be dug out by the alert individual. Yet, others require several stakeholders, including founding entrepreneurs to act effectually to "create" them (or nurture them into being) in a dynamic and interactive process of contingency, design and negotiation' (Sarasvathy et al 2002: 2). Opportunities are thus not necessarily a question of 'either / or'. There are perhaps both opportunities requiring discovery and opportunities requiring creation.

A theoretical interpretation

There are many interpretations of one story. What follows, is two different interpretations of the Starbucks story that began this chapter, in light of the discovery and creation perspectives.

The discovery perspective

Viewed through the discovery perspective the Starbucks story is basically about an existing and available market opportunity which, yet, has not been discovered – it is untouched. Selling fresh-roasted quality coffee represents some unexploited value, a 'hole' in the market. The three original founders of Starbucks seem to have spotted this 'hole' more by luck than judgement. They just follow their dream. Yet, it can be argued that the CEO of a company selling plastic products, Howard Schultz, represents the alert Kirznerian entrepreneur of the Starbucks story. His alert capabilities make him constantly scan the market for opportunities. Being attuned to changes in the market, he discovers that a small store in Seattle is buying an increasingly number of plastic drip coffeemakers.

The alertness of Schulz seems to unfold rather unconsciously. After all, he is not actively searching for opportunities, and it is only after meeting the original Starbucks trio that he begins to dream of building a new organization. He wonders: 'How would it feel to own equity, not just collect a pay check?' It is especially Schulz's professional experiences, knowledge and access to information on the plastic product market combined with competences to interpret this information and turn it into a valuable opportunity that makes him discover the Starbucks opportunity. In this manner, he spots what others did not spot.

Although the three founders have done some of the work in terms of formulating the opportunity, Schulz does not just imitate what they are doing.

Based on further market analysis of the special roasted coffee business and the idea that coffee is not just a hot and dark beverage – it is an entire ritual – Schulz digs deeper into the opportunity 'hole'. Especially, inspired by Italian coffee bars he finds inspiration to a large scale development of the opportunity. In this way, Schulz extends the original Starbucks opportunity and opens up for the opportunity to grow to a massive international success despite many critics argue that coffee cannot be a growth industry.

The creation perspective

It is also possible to perceive the Starbucks case through the creation perspective. Then it is a story about the Starbucks opportunity as emerging from a process of creation, imagination and social interaction. After all, there are no trends in the market – at the point in time of the establishment of the first Starbucks shop – which suggest that opening such a shop will be a success. On the contrary, the market shows no need for fine coffee, thus, there is no opportunity to discover.

Rather than taking departure in the existent market, the three founders invent the Starbucks opportunity using their creativity, imagination, own vision and taste. It shows that the opportunity is indeed a result of subjective processes. Since there are no market trends to watch and they hold little professional knowledge of fine-roasted coffee, the trio very much interact with an experienced gourmet coffee entrepreneur, Alfred Peet, to form the opportunity. In this way, the opportunity is from the beginning emerging from social interaction.

Yet, the creation perspective is particularly apparent from Howard Schulz's activities. His is innovating the original Starbucks opportunity through additional creative thinking and social interaction. Combining the original concept with a wealth of experiences, ideas, etc. emerging from his visits to Italy, and everyday interactions with investors, customers, employees, own imagination of future needs, etc., Schulz reinvents coffee as a commodity. The process reflects that opportunity creation is a dynamic and continuously evolving process of social interaction. Opportunities are not fixed or permanent.

Schulz's innovative efforts turn a coffee industry, focused on mass-marketed coffee from grocery stores, upside down. He builds a completely new and unique culture around coffee appealing to millions of people around the globe. Transforming an industry as we knew it, Schulz is a Schumpeterian entrepreneur who carries out creative destruction.

Above, you find two interpretations of the Starbucks start-up process based on the perspectives: discovered or created. Yet, the author behind the Starbucks case, Saras Sarasvathy, suggests a third interpretation derived from the effectuation perspective. In this book, you learn about effectuation theory in Chapter 5. This perspective puts forward that idea that the emergence of opportunities is not a matter of either discovery or creation. Saras explains in a private communication:

> Both discovery and creation processes go into transforming ideas into opportunities. If the original founders had not acted on their personal passion for better coffee and the inspiration they found from Alfred Peet, Howard Schultz may have had nothing to 'discover', at least not in the specialty coffee business. Yet, if Schultz had not been 'alert' to the increased sale of coffee machines and followed up with an investigation, his desire for becoming an entrepreneur and his ambition to achieve great success may not have been given an outlet for action. Also, even after he 'discovered' Starbucks, he had to do a lot of 'creation' to get it to be the opportunity it is today. Everything he did in building and growing Il Giornale involved discovery (about the tastes and preferences and pains and prejudices of all his stakeholders including customers, suppliers, employees and investors) as well as large amounts of co-creation – these stakeholders actively participated in forming the identity of the company that is embodied in its brand and consists in its main asset.

Sarasvathy furthermore outlines that whereas new opportunities emerge from unique mixtures of discovery and creation, the action of the entrepreneur is always effectuated action. Sarasvathy explains it this way: effectuated action involves entrepreneurs' interactions 'with other people and with the objective environment around them in ways that end up transforming the people they interact with into stakeholders who in turn reshape and co-create the environments around them' (Sarasvathy at al 2008).

Testing the theory

It's time for you to get back on track. Make sure you keep the above theories and discussions in mind when you are out in the field carrying out your own tests on opportunities and their emergence.

? EXERCISES

1 **Study of technological progress and opportunities,** Search the Internet. Make a list of three major technological advances that have occurred since you began your education. Describe two opportunities that have emerged in the wake of these advances. Can you come up with additional opportunities that have arisen as a result of these advances, but have not, as yet, been exploited?

2 **New case study.** Find an article – any newspaper article or a magazine article – about an entrepreneur. If this is not possible then interview an entrepreneur you know. Analyse how the entrepreneur's opportunity emerged, making reference to the above theories and discussions

3 **Draw your opportunity library.** It appears from this chapter that your identification of new opportunities depends, among other things, on the information that you already possess. Information may be a result of your life experience, education, your spare time, your hobbies or socializing with friends, classmates, family, etc. Take a piece of paper. Draw your brain. Imagine your brain as a library with a lot of books that contain the information that you possess. Now type the names of the books: are they about gardening, football or arithmetic? Now assess the combination of the library's books and determine what opportunities you have the potential to discover or create.

 LITERATURE

Barringer, B.R. & Ireland, R.D. (2008) *Entrepreneurship: Successfully Launching New Ventures*, Upper Saddle River: Prentice Hall.

Bhave, M.P. (1994) 'A Process Model of New Venture Creation', *Journal of Business Venturing*, 9, 223–242.

Boutaiba, S. (2004) 'A Moment in Time', in Hjorth, D. & Steyaert, C. (eds) *New Movements in Entrepreneurship*, Cheltenham, UK and Northampton, MA, USA: Edward Elgar Publishing, 22–57.

Fletcher, D.E. (2003) 'Framing Organisational Emergence: Discourse, Identity, and Relationship', Hjorth, D. & Steyaert, C. (eds) *New Movements in Entrepreneurship*, Cheltenham, UK and Northampton, MA, USA: Edward Elgar Publishing, 9–46.

Gartner, W.B., Carter, N.M. & Hills, G.E. (2003) 'The Language of Opportunity' in Hjorth, D. & Steyaert, C. (eds) *New Movements in Entrepreneurship*, Cheltenham, UK and Northampton, MA, USA: Edward Elgar Publishing, 103–125.

Kelley, D., Bosma, N. & Amoros, J.E. (2011) 'Global Entrepreneurship Monitor – 2010 global report', GERA/Babson College.

Kirzner, Israel (1973) *Competition and Entrepreneurship*, Chicago: University of Chicago Press.

Kirzner, Israel (1979) *Perception, Opportunity, and Profit*, Chicago: University of Chicago Press.

Sarasvathy, S.D. (2008) *Effectuation: Elements of Entrepreneurial Expertise*, Cheltenham, UK and Northampton, MA, USA: Edward Elgar Publishing.

Sarasvathy, S.D., Dew, N., Velamuri, S.R. & Venkataraman, S. (2002) *A Testable Typology of Entrepreneurial Opportunity: Extension of Shane & Venkataraman (2000)*, University of Maryland and University of Virginia.

Sarasvathy, S.D., Dew, N., Read, S., & Wiltbank, R. (2008) 'Designing organisations that design environments: Lessons from entrepreneurial expertise', *Organisation Studies*, 29(3), 331–350.

Schumpeter, J.A. (1934) *The Theory of Economic Development*, Cambridge, MA: Harvard University Press.

Shane, S. (2000) 'Prior Knowledge and the Discovery of Entrepreneurial Opportunities', *Organisation Science*, 11(4), 448–469.

Shane, S. (2003) *A General Theory of Entrepreneurship: The Individual-opportunity Nexus*, Cheltenham, UK and Northampton, MA, USA: Edward Elgar Publishing.

Shane, S. & Venkataraman, S. (2000) 'The Promise of Entrepreneurship as a Field of Research', *Academy of Management Review*, 25(1), 217–226.

4

Evaluation of opportunities

Opportunity evaluation is a key theme in entrepreneurship. An entrepreneur cannot simply expect that the opportunity and the organisational effort he plans to make in order to exploit it will be viewed by the market as attractive and in the right place at the right time. It is not certain that the market can and will fulfil the value that the opportunity and its organisational implementation represents. The opportunity may simply prove to be unprofitable. Therefore, the entrepreneurial process involves the evaluation of each opportunity, whereby the entrepreneur seeks to determine whether the idea that he or she intends to pursue, creates value in the eyes of the market and can thus be considered as a real, strong and feasible option. You could say, 'evaluation is the key to differentiate an idea from an opportunity' (Keh et al 2002: 126). Entrepreneurs normally have no difficulty in generating new ideas, but far from all ideas are actually opportunities, and it is often particularly interesting for the entrepreneur to assess whether the idea represents an economically viable option, at least in the long term.

As mentioned in Chapter 3, it can often be difficult, conceptually, to determine whether you are dealing with an idea or an opportunity. The transition from an idea to an opportunity is a broad and grey area. Therefore, there may be many situations where you think that the wrong term is being used. For example, some may argue that this chapter should be called 'evaluation of ideas' and not 'evaluation of opportunities'. It is therefore important to read the chapter flexibly with regard to the concepts of 'opportunity' and 'idea' and just remember that evaluation is the very process where the entrepreneur seeks to assess whether the idea represents an opportunity or not.

Entrepreneurship in practice

Now, let's move into the Danish fashion scene and meet an entrepreneur who has greatly helped to define that scene. The entrepreneur's name is Naja Munthe and the organisation called Munthe plus Simonsen (www.muntheplussimonsen.dk, last accessed 21 May 2012). Here is the story of the organisation's start-up. In particular, note how Naja and her partner Karen evaluate the potential of their idea, both initially and during the process. How do they find out whether it is viable and represents a real entrepreneurial opportunity that creates attractive value to others?

CASE STUDY

'The sky is the limit'

(Devised by the authors)

Naja and Karen had a very successful start to their entrepreneurial journey. Their clothing line was a tremendous success, more or less from the beginning. Customers wanted the luxury bohemian style Naja and Karen delivered. Naja said: 'We rode on a wave of success, where, basically, we couldn't do anything wrong . . . Karen was always saying: "The sky is the limit" and I thought that was kind of cool, because then there were no limits. It became our motto.' However, the outward tempestuous journey filled with success turned and moved in a more sombre and negative direction in 2006. Munthe plus Simonsen was threatened with bankruptcy and went into administration. Had Naja and Karen's idea not, after all, had what it takes to survive in the market?

Figure 4.1 Naja Munthe and Karen Simonsen

CASE STUDY *(continued)*

Next stop the big city

Naja and Karen met each other in the 1990s as students at the Design School in Kolding (Denmark's seventh largest town), where they quickly became friends and worked closely together. After graduation, neither of them had any specific career plans. One cold winter day in 1994 Karen, who had found herself a boyfriend in Copenhagen (the capital of Denmark) asked: 'Shall we go to Copenhagen and start a company?' Naja nodded yes, although she also points out: 'it was not very prudent. We did not have definite and finely-honed plans for what we should do.' They formally established a business but it was not based on a clear idea. Instead, they filled their time with whatever jobs they got offered: 'We started basically from one end and offered our services for all kinds of things.' The two girls worked as TV presenters, stylists, writers, lecturers and much more.

Themselves as customer

In parallel with undertaking these jobs, Naja and Karen put together their first clothing collection in 1995 without any careful thought as to the potential customer group: 'When we designed our very first collection, we didn't think about who our end customer was. For very many years, we used ourselves as a target group. We only thought about what we liked.'

Therefore, it is not surprising that Naja and Karen tried to sell their first collection by calling their favourite, nationally renowned shop, Norgaard, in central Copenhagen. However, it was necessary to call several times since the store's staff did not seem particularly interested in what the two young designers had to offer. Eventually the staff became tired of their many calls, and gave them a minute to present their clothes, but they were not to expect anything to come from it. The proprietor of the store ended up buying their entire collection. That experience taught Naja: 'Never take no for an answer. You have to go on and on. One thing you can be confident of, out there in the real world is that there are a lot of doors that are closed.'

A couple of dressmakers?

The two young girls experienced many difficulties in opening the doors. The Danish fashion industry was at this point in its own fledgling start-up phase, and Naja and Karen met the challenge of helping to create and shape the industry as a whole. They had no one to lean on. There were no role models or precedents to guide them. With no guide, they were left to find their first supplier through the yellow pages, which ended up with them accidentally hiring a cushion factory to sew their first collection. 'When we opened the door to the factory we were greeted by a sight we had not imagined. They made plastic cushions for homes, and the last thing they knew about was making clothes.' It was not easy to attract media attention in an attempt to market the collection either. Naja says: 'Also in relation to the media, which is how you make a living these days, it was extremely difficult to get any attention, particularly as a designer. We were just seen as a couple of blond dressmakers who sat around stitching together dresses for ourselves.'

As a result of their enormous drive and fighting spirit Naja and Karen did, after all, manage to push through the barriers. They knew how to draw attention to themselves and their products

CASE STUDY (continued)

through a lifestyle where only the best is good enough, and through promotion of their own expression rather than a commercial expression. 'We made it a point of honour not to be commercial . . . We were not focused on an end-user, or whether things were economically viable.' So when Magasin (a major Danish department store) approached them with a desire to promote their products, they said no. Magasin is too commercial.

In the early years, their lifestyle and 'only the sky is the limit' philosophy led to Naja and Karen buying a lot of expensive furniture, renting 1,600 m2 of office space, opening stores and setting up showrooms in the heart of the most dominant fashion cities and hiring expensive models. For example, they hired Cindy Crawford for one of their campaigns. These activities were successful in marketing terms. They received a lot of positive feedback in the form of high earnings and various Danish prizes such as the branding award of the year, and Naja was awarded the prize for being the year's Danish businesswoman. However, the success would unfortunately end.

Suspension of payments

'If you are employed as a checkout assistant at a supermarket and drink champagne every night, at some point in time your income will not be quite in proportion with your consumption. The same thing happened to us.' In 2006, Naja and Karen were staring bankruptcy in the face and subjected to a suspension of payments. According to Naja, there are several explanations for things going wrong, such as poor business insight, lack of counselling, evaluation of the market, and a number of stupid errors. An example of the latter is that they forget to cater for an expense of 1 million Danish kroner (approximately US$200,000) in postage for sending out a Cindy Crawford catalogue.

Naja and Karen used the suspension of payments crisis as a timeout to think about how to create a more robust business structure with a balance between revenues and expenditures. After receiving a capital injection they rolled up their sleeves and cut back in every imaginable area of the organisation. 'We shut that one down, we have to dismiss them, we make savings here, we cancel this showroom. Can we afford this? Yes, but only 50 per cent.' Naja and Karen began to think more economically, commercially and strategically about how they could optimise the organisation through 'lean business'. 'There was clearly a greater focus now on earnings and managing an economically viable business . . . There was also greater emphasis on not being so egocentric in our expression. We were still faithful to what we are, but we also thought about others . . . thinking commercially and about the end-user.' Nevertheless, they still didn't undertake any formal market research to understand who the customers were. Information about core clients was picked up for example, through distributors, employees and vendors. These same stakeholders were also involved in redefining Munthe plus Simonsen's design line.

Last but not least, Naja and Karen began using the franchise organisational model, rather than owning shops. In this way they spread the risk and involved people with local business knowledge about who buys their products, where and why.

CASE STUDY *(continued)*

Postscript of a divorce

In 2009, Naja and Karen chose to end the long marriage between them within the fashion industry. Karen was bought out by Naja (still using the company name Munthe plus Simonsen) and started up for herself. Naja faced the challenge of continuing one of the most influential design brands in the Danish fashion industry and she now sets – especially in light of the financial crisis – business acumen and market rules high on the agenda rather than the champagne approach guided primarily by personal preferences. Naja and Karen both seem to have found a way forward after the divorce, but they've also learned a lot from Munthe plus Simonsen's very turbulent and challenging journey.

Your immediate interpretation

Now it's your turn to get involved. Think about the Munthe plus Simonsen story and give your interpretation of how Naja and Karen evaluated whether their idea was valuable in light of the market and hence whether the idea represented a real opportunity. Below are some prompts for reflection, which can help you interpret the story.

- A well-known newspaper gives you the task of writing an article on how Naja and Karen evaluated whether their idea represented a profitable opportunity. What would you focus on? Did they evaluate the idea at all? If yes, what characterises the evaluation process?
- Your description is so convincing that Naja and Karen immediately appoint you as their personal adviser. What recommendations do you give them as to how they can streamline their evaluation of an idea in the future? Undertake the task as follows. First list two or three positive aspects of the way they have so far evaluated opportunities. Then list two or three negative features associated with their evaluation process. Finally, give your opinions on how they can turn the negative aspects into something positive and improve their evaluation processes in the future.
- One day Naja comes past your office. She is considering conducting a market analysis of core customers and competitors. The analysis must support an assessment of the feasibility of a particular idea, including how that idea can be adapted, modified, etc., so it better reflects market conditions. Provide suggestions as to what evaluation-related advantages and disadvantages may be associated with performing such an analysis.

Theories on entrepreneurship

As you read the literature on entrepreneurship, you will quickly discover that opportunity emergence and organising are two key issues. Discussions about opportunity evaluation are less noticeable. 'Little is known about how entrepreneurs actually evaluate opportunities' (Keh et al 2002: 125). That we know no more about this subject is a mystery when you consider how central it is to the entrepreneurial process. After all, the evaluation tells the entrepreneur whether he or she can expect the idea to become an economically viable opportunity, or what the entrepreneur must do to achieve it. Finally, the evaluation is in many ways a bridge between the emergence and organising of opportunities since it tells the entrepreneur whether it makes sense to use resources to pursue this opportunity by organising activities.

Based on the existing literature about how opportunities are evaluated in the entrepreneurial process, we will highlight two perspectives on opportunity evaluation, which make up this chapter's paradox: *instrumental* or *legitimate*.

The first and most familiar perspective emphasises how opportunity evaluation is a means to achieve a particular result or goal. Different formal business administration techniques and methods are needed to assess the extent to which it is possible to achieve the goal. As mentioned, the goal is often to create a profitable organisation that can survive in the market. Thus, evaluation is perceived to be an instrumental and decisive action. The evaluation process is characterised by the entrepreneur systematically pursuing specific and predefined rules of analysis.

Conversely, we find the 'legitimacy perspective', which emphasises that the creation of legitimacy is essential for the evaluation of options. According to this perspective, the entrepreneur's success depends on whether he or she can get others (including the entrepreneur's organisation) to accept the opportunity as being valuable and attractive. If successful, the entrepreneur may rightly judge that the idea represents an opportunity. The entrepreneur will evaluate this opportunity positively.

When a new idea occurs, its legitimacy is typically low because it is unknown. This is known in the scientific literature on the topic as 'liability of newness'. Therefore, the entrepreneur's challenge is to find market players that will support the idea with, among other things, resources. This requires legitimacy – that others accept it as a valid opportunity in a market context. Without legitimacy, the idea could not be considered a real opportunity, because it cannot be realised. The legitimisation process is fundamentally a social process in which the entrepreneur, through interaction with the market, achieves an impression of whether the idea represents an opportunity or not. Systematic analysis is not employed and social interaction determines how the evaluation process unfolds and its outcome. Rather than a formal evaluation process with a specific start and end point, it is more one of continuous evaluation, which takes place as a natural part of everyday entrepreneurial processes, and which the entrepreneur makes more or less unconsciously or strategically.

The paradox that will be explored in this chapter on opportunity evaluation, is therefore whether the evaluation is:

Instrumental or legitimate

What is evaluation?

Traditionally, evaluation is defined as 'the systematic determination of merit, worth, and significance of something or someone using criteria against a set of standards' (Hindle 2010: 108). Generally, evaluation can take many forms (classical evaluation, impact evaluation, user evaluation, etc.). An example of a well-known evaluation tool is Cost-Benefit analysis, where the effects are evaluated in light of the costs. We often associate evaluation with a retrospective and systematic assessment of performance and processes that have been associated with a given activity; for example, evaluation of a government initiative that has run over a period of years. Has the initiative been accomplished in accordance with the set targets in terms of the direct and indirect resource consumption? So, evaluations are often carried out in connection with something that has already been undertaken. Moreover, the activity being evaluated needs clearly established goals. However, the reasons for undertaking an evaluation vary greatly and may be for the purpose of control, documentation, legitimation, strategic manoeuvre or learning.

The process of evaluating entrepreneurial opportunities differs in significant ways from the typical evaluation process. The evaluation aims to determine whether the concept represents a future attractive option in a market that may not even exist yet and this makes the idea's evaluation and development difficult to predict. Within entrepreneurship we are therefore faced with a challenging, forward-looking evaluation (ex-ante), not a retrospective evaluation (ex-post). It's about visualising and predicting the future to determine whether the idea can form the basis for a profitable and sustainable organisation. 'The entrepreneur must forecast future prices and goods and resources and use intuitive judgement to gauge market potential' (Keh et al 2002: 130), and he or she has limited access to information on past performance, such as the development in sales figures.

In entrepreneurship, the purpose of evaluation is not to verify or substantiate something that has already happened, but to assess the future potential of an idea. This makes the evaluation process more uncertain, complex and risky. The decision to implement an opportunity is made in a situation where the entrepreneur does not know the future conditions (uncertainty) and he or she must take into account many factors (complexity). Uncertainty is closely associated with risk. The entrepreneur's perception of risk associated with an entrepreneurial project is therefore an important element in the evaluation process. If he or she determines that the risk is low, the probability of the project's realisation will be high and vice-versa.

This shows that the assessment of whether an idea is valuable for others and feasible is, in essence, a cognitive and emotional process, meaning that it takes place in the minds of the entrepreneur (Grichnik et al 2010). The entrepreneur may seek other people's advice to support the process or utilise various tools, but ultimately it is his or her decision. Since cognition varies from person to person, two people with the same idea and in the same situation may very well end up taking different decisions. One may be more optimistic and willing to take a risk than the other and therefore seek to pursue an opportunity from which the other refrains.

Finally, the entrepreneurial evaluation characterised by the need for, and extent of, the necessary evaluation activities vary according to the idea's complexity and unique circumstances. Consequently there are more questions to answer when evaluating an idea for 'new high-tech equipment for offshore structures' than the idea of 'a home delivery service for breakfast rolls and bread'.

The instrumental evaluation

The instrumental perspective is the most widespread in the literature (textbooks, research articles, reports, etc.) on the evaluation of opportunities. Perhaps this is because the perspective, in a situation filled with uncertainty and risk, provides the entrepreneur with some clear and simple guidance on how he or she can evaluate and even predict whether an idea is or may become profitable. Basically, the instrumental perspective consists of a series of tools and guidelines to gather information that can support the evaluation process. The tools and guidelines are rational and analytical in nature. By applying these, the entrepreneur, expects to gain insight into whether the idea represents a real present/future opportunity or not, including whether the opportunity is attractive to the entrepreneur him/herself given his/her unique expertise, resources and circumstances (Haynie et al 2009). In other words, the instrumental perspective seeks to give the entrepreneur control over the evaluation process with the entrepreneur's own situation as a starting point. Such an evaluation is believed to enable the entrepreneur to assess in advance whether he or she can achieve his/her goals before the actual organising of the opportunity is begun. It reflects how evaluation according to the instrumental perspective is something that happens before the actual entrepreneurial activity and the decision to exploit the opportunity: well before the entrepreneur seriously commits to involving other actors (such as investors), arranges access to resources (such as capital) and establishes technology (such as machinery). Haynie et al write: 'Evaluations of opportunity attractiveness – that is, the potential of the opportunity to generate competitive advantages and entrepreneurial returns to the firm – likely proceed and are separate from the decision to exploit.' (Haynie et al 2009: 338)

The instrumental collection of evidence to underpin the evaluation takes place as an analytical process where the entrepreneur is recommended to divide the evaluation into areas. There is no consensus on which areas are key, but a good proposal comes from Barringer and Ireland (2010). They suggest that the entrepreneur should specifically focus on four areas:

- Product / service
- The market / industry
- Organisation
- Financing.

The evaluation's main interests are therefore: are customers interested in the entrepreneur's product / service? Is there room in the market for such a product / service in light of competitors, market trends, etc.? How must the entrepreneur organise him/herself to reach customers? What financial resources are necessary to realise the idea? Of these areas, some researchers consider evaluation of the market / industry as particularly important: 'Unquestionably, the analysis of the industry and market in which the business will operate is the most important analysis of the entire feasibility study. Without customers – without an industry and market that are receptive to the business concept – there is no business.' (Allen 2006: 90)

Source: Inspired by Barringer & Ireland (2010).

Figure 4.2 A procedural model of opportunity evaluation

Typically, the evaluation will follow certain pre-defined phases. Based on Barringer and Ireland's key areas above, a procedural model might look as depicted in Figure 4.2.

The model shows how the entrepreneur can assess whether s/he ought to pursue the idea further, through analysis of the four areas of 'product / service', 'market / industry', 'organisation' and 'funding'. In support of the analysis of each area the literature often refers to traditional management theories. For example, in connection with analysis of the market / industry, tools such as 'SWOT analysis' (Pahl & Richter 2007) and Porter's 'Five Forces Model' (Porter 2008) are often referred to.

As mentioned, there is no universal agreement on these areas. Some research-ers, such as Hindle et al (2007) and Allen (2006), specifically emphasise the importance of evaluating the human factor, i.e. the attributes and skills of the entrepreneur or entrepreneurial team. This is also included in Barringer and Ireland's (2010) organisational dimension. For example, an engineer may be an excellent engineer and inventor, but incompetent as a salesman and manager. Many investors, especially venture capitalists and Business Angels who invest in risky projects with high news value, place great emphasis on evaluation of the human factor when contemplating whether to invest in the new opportunity or not.

Evaluation is thus undertaken by considering both external factors, such as the market and internal factors such as the human factor. Together, the struc-tures and processes of these external and internal factors create a picture of whether the entrepreneur's idea can result in a product, process or service that creates value for others and is thus feasible.

One way of getting an overall picture of the idea's chances of being realised is the business plan, which will be discussed in detail in Chapter 8. It is considered by many researchers within the instrumental perspective as the key to entrepreneurial success: 'Some entrepreneurs are impatient and do not want to spend the time it takes to write a business plan. This approach is usually a mistake. Writing a business plan forces an entrepreneur to think carefully about all the aspects of a business venture. It also helps a new venture to establish a set of milestones that can be used to guide the early phases of the business rollout.' (Barringer & Ireland 2010: 49)

Evaluation of opportunities with great potential

Opportunities differ in scope and potential. Some are small and local, others large and global. Some result from a new organisation being created, others unfold within an existing organisation. But how does one evaluate the potential of a specific opportunity in advance? What criteria can be used to identify opportunities with great potential, and find the tools that enable systematic evaluation ex-ante?

Wickham (2004) emphasises three key criteria for evaluating opportunities. He refers to the importance of assessing the possibilities of its potential in light of the 'scale', 'scope' and 'span'. The first refers to the opportunity's size, and 'scope' to the value that it provides in the short and long term. 'Span' refers to the opportunity's durability over time – is it a one-hit wonder or does it have lasting potential? A successful opportunity may well be a flash in the pan, as long as its 'scale' is great. As an example, Lance Armstrong launched a yellow rubber wristband with the inscription 'Live Strong' during the Tour de France in 2004. The goal of the bracelet was to raise money for cancer research, and in general to make the world more aware of the disease and the importance of living life fully while you have it. The bracelet was a huge sales success and created a fashion the world over. But as the Tour de France 'yellow fever' died down, so did the bracelet's popularity.

Hindle et al (2007) base their model on slightly different criteria. A particular feature of this evaluation model is that it takes place on three levels. First the idea is assessed as to its viability, then its development potential and finally, whether it can be implemented. For each of these levels five dimensions, similar to Barringer and Ireland's four dimensions, namely product, market, industry, people and money, are evaluated. The model is developed based on two PhD dissertations on opportunity evaluation. Accuracy in evaluations of a large number of innovative ideas based on the model has, through testing, proved to be high and it is believed therefore to provide a clear identification of the idea's potential. The model should not be regarded as a kind of oracle as it rests on evaluation of different areas that are highly subjective. What

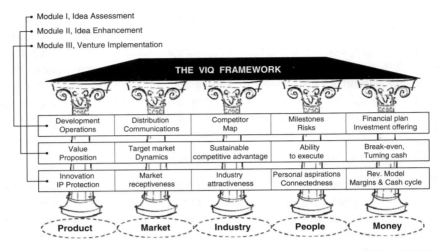

Source: Hindle et al (2007).

Figure 4.3 The VIQ model

it does provide is primarily a systematic evaluation process. In addition, it constitutes the starting point for dialogue, for example between investor and entrepreneur, between consultant and entrepreneur, and between students themselves if they are asked to assess whether a particular idea is a possible opportunity.

Figure 4.3 shows the model's components with five pillars and three levels. The model is called the Venture Intelligence Quotient (VIQ).

Module 1 (Idea Assessment), indicated on the left-hand side of the model, covers the evaluation of whether the idea, which constitutes the foundation for the entrepreneurial process, is worth pursuing. The second module (Idea Enhancement) focuses on strengthening the idea. Can the elements that constitute a successful opportunity be developed based on the idea? In other words, the idea's potential is identified and understood. The third module (Venture Implementation) deals with the effective implementation of the idea. This section provides suggestions as to how the entrepreneur can actually build a new organisation based on the idea. This covers the last part of the VIQ tool; issues that this textbook focuses on in Chapter 5.

As previously mentioned, the five columns refer to five dimensions:

- Product = the essence of the idea, which may be a product, service, experience or process

- Market = the group of clients and organisations who are interested in the idea and have the resources to acquire the product or service that the idea represents
- Industry = organisations offering the same or substitute products, services, experiences or processes
- People = the entrepreneur / the entrepreneurial team
- Money = the financial dimension.

Evaluation through the creation of legitimacy

Evaluation is not, however, always an instrumental process of evaluation with the areas defined in advance of actual entrepreneurial activity. Furthermore, it is not always the case that evaluation is a systematic, time-limited and analytic process geared to a particular objective and based on certain specific tools to downplay the complexity of the situation. Some entrepreneurs simply don't use such logic to evaluate their ideas; or they combine this logic with other evaluation methods. Some reasons may be that few ideas are so 'ready' that it is possible to test them here and now, through an instrumental evaluation process. In addition, the entrepreneur may not have 'time' to sit down and carry out a detailed instrumental evaluation, because the idea must be exploited here and now or else its potential opportunities dwindle, e.g. other competing actors may seize the opportunity before the entrepreneur. Finally, one can also, in light of the complexity and risk surrounding entrepreneurial evaluations, easily put a big question mark over whether it is possible to predict which ideas represent successful opportunities in the future. This is especially true when the entrepreneur has a very innovative business idea, such as Skype, which gives rise to considerable evaluation challenges in all directions. Maybe entrepreneurs instead of evaluating instrumentally simply have to act and create legitimacy for themselves and their processes.

As an alternative to the instrumental perspective, evaluation can also be seen as an integral part of everyday entrepreneurial processes. Only by acting on the idea, confronting others with the idea and testing its attractive aspects, negative aspects, capacity development, etc. in a social context, is it possible to get an understanding of whether the idea represents an opportunity. Here, the evaluation focuses on whether the idea is attractive to others rather than just the entrepreneur, or how the idea could be modified so that it is attractive to others. The latter says that there may be a need to continually reassess the idea depending on the feedback that the entrepreneur receives from the environment. All this underlines the legitimacy of the perspective. Instrumentation models may incorporate an assessment of legitimacy, but the basic mindset is totally different from the legitimacy perspective.

What is legitimacy? In short, something is legitimate if it complies with the norms, values, beliefs, practices and procedures that are accepted by a particular social group (Johnson et al 2006). According to a famous definition, legitimacy is 'a generalized perception or assumption that the action of an entity is desirable, proper, appropriate, within some socially constructed system of norms, values, beliefs and definitions' (Suchman 1995: 574).

It follows that the entrepreneur's idea can be considered a legitimate option when the economic, social and political surroundings accept its existence as a valid part of the market. According to this approach, the environment plays an important role in determining when there is 'room' for a given entrepreneurial process, and when not. This is especially evident when a new type of organisation or a new industry is evolving. 'Organization populations emerge when the goods and services they provide are seen as legitimate and desirable by the host society' (Reynolds 1991: 57). Therefore we can say 'certain kinds of organizations simply cannot be founded before their time' (Aldrich 1999: 75). As previously indicated, the more innovative and 'new' the entrepreneur's idea, the more problems he can expect in convincing others of the idea's relevance and legitimacy, as the environment may have difficulty understanding the idea, and what to do with it. Aldrich and Fiol put it thus: 'The first organization of its kind faces a different set of challenges than the one which simply carries on the tradition pioneered by many predecessors' (Aldrich & Fiol 1994: 663). As a consequence the 'new' entrepreneur simply lacks the acquaintance and confidence of others, which is critical for them to become engaged in the emerging opportunity. Another consequence of being an innovative entrepreneur in an emerging market is that he or she lacks role models to lean on. Role models are seen as critical to entrepreneurial success.

Without the necessary legitimacy, the entrepreneur will have difficulty in raising the necessary capital, recruiting employees, getting customers etc. 'Among the many problems facing innovative entrepreneurs, their relative lack of legitimacy is especially critical' (Aldrich & Fiol 1994: 645). An empirical study of a large number of organisations in their early years confirms that the ability to survive depends on the ability to achieve legitimacy (Delmar & Shane 2004).

Legitimacy cannot be obtained and evaluated from behind a desk and through symbolic actions and planning. It is primarily through action and interaction with other actors, not least the other market players that the entrepreneur can determine whether others perceive the opportunity to be legitimate. To emphasise the point Quinn (2004) recounts a story about how he and a group of colleagues invited a consultant to assist them in finding their core competency as a foundation for an entrepreneurial project. The consultant asked them to write a list of their views on their core competencies. They were then told to throw away the final list, as it was not usable. Instead, they were advised to email friends and business partners to get them to identify their core competencies. The moral is that our 'best' self is when we create value in the eyes of others and not our own eyes. Our best self is the self that is legitimate in the eyes of others, and this we can only find by interacting with others. As Quinn writes, 'Reading what these people have written, I felt approved and received.' (Quinn 2004: 128)

Legitimacy as a process

Johnson et al (2006) indicate the process by which new objects – such as a new idea – gain legitimacy and are thus evaluated as a real possibility. The process consists of four phases: 1) innovation, 2) local validation, 3) diffusion and 4) general validation. The first phase covers the creation of the idea. The next phase is characterised by local stakeholders who must be convinced that the new opportunity is possible to relate to and makes sense in the context of existing norms, values, procedures, etc. Once accepted in the local environment – or other close relationship-based contexts – the new opportunity can start to spread into other contexts. 'As the new object spreads, its adoption in new situations often needs less explicit justification than it may have needed in the first local context.' (Johnson et al 2006: 60) As a result of the spread, the new object will, over time, become more widely accepted as a natural part of the environment. The legitimacy process can thus be seen as ripples that spread across the water and eventually disappear completely and become an integral part of a larger sea. The spread is dependent on social interaction and acceptance, which controls the progress of the process.

Strategies for building legitimacy

As previously mentioned, evaluation according to the legitimacy perspective take place more or less consciously from the entrepreneur's side. Here we indicate various deliberate actions that the entrepreneur may make to convince the environment of legitimacy in terms of the idea's relevance. For example, the entrepreneur may imitate other organisations that have already been accepted into the environment, or may seek to obtain official certificates to emphasise that the idea actually makes sense in light of the existing (Shane 2003). Furthermore, it may be appropriate for entrepreneurs to cooperate with others to gain legitimacy in society, for example through a new trade organisation or a new network, rather than seeking legitimacy separately. Another strategy for building legitimacy is to focus on creating trust among key stakeholders that will provide the entrepreneur with access to knowledge, resources, etc. Trust is important because it is fundamental to all types of interaction between people. The entrepreneur has various opportunities to build trust. For example, he or she can convince others that the option makes sense, by acting 'as if' the opportunity was already a successful reality. 'Founders can behave "as if" the activity were a reality – producing and directing great theatre, as it were – may convince others of the tangible reality of the new activity.' (Aldrich & Fiol 1994: 651)

Many other approaches can be used to promote legitimacy, including practical/symbolic actions such as producing a business card, letterhead and a website. Legitimacy can also be obtained by the entrepreneur drawing on people who have high legitimacy within a particular business area, for example by using a mentor or by putting together a management or advisory board. Finally, contact with an existing organisation that has legitimacy can provide a route to greater legitimacy. If an entrepreneur can write 'trusted by' a well-known organisation on the business card, it helps to overcome his 'liability of newness'.

According to the legitimacy perspective the entrepreneur rarely pursues a practical strategy in relation to creating legitimacy. Instead, the process of legitimacy tends to be experimental and exploratory, with the entrepreneur, through his daily actions in the market, looking out for signals that tell him or her if the idea is perceived as legitimate. Metaphorically, the entrepreneur carries his idea under his arm and goes into the field to test it by trying to convince others of its merits, so as to evaluate the idea's degree of legitimacy – is it worth pursuing further? Through his attempts to convince others of the idea's virtues the entrepreneur receives various forms of feedback that tell him or her if the idea is the basis for a realistic opportunity. Feedback can take the form of resources, knowledge, new opportunities, barriers, etc., which of course can actually serve as physical inputs for shaping the idea into an opportunity, and later an organisation. However, feedback also has symbolic value as it tells the entrepreneur whether others perceive his or her opportunity as legitimate. This leads to a clarification of whether the entrepreneur's idea makes sense, and thus whether it is appropriate to pursue it further as an option.

So the idea is evaluated according to the legitimacy perspective through exploration and experimental activities and social interactions rather than through the utilisation of systematic and analytical tools prior to the actual entrepreneurial process. Evaluation takes place in the process and it

Table 4.1 The paradox: Instrumental or legitimate

	Instrumental	Legitimate
Evaluation perception	Tool to achieve a certain objective	Legitimacy creation
Evaluation objective	To state the direction for action	To convince the actors of the market of the idea
Evaluation criteria	They should be formulated before the process	They emerge during the entrepreneurial process
Evaluation process	Rational, systematic and analytic	Social, interactive, experimental and exploring
Evaluation character	Evaluation and entrepreneurial action are two separate activities	Evaluation and entrepreneurial action are two inseparable activities

is also here that the criteria for what should be evaluated are created. As a result, evaluation becomes a progressive and procedural journey where the entrepreneur, over time, creates an assessment of the idea as a potential opportunity.

Different types of entrepreneurs experience different challenges in relation to the creation of legitimacy. For the engineer, who has created a physical prototype of his idea, it is often relatively easy to create legitimacy around it, as market participants have something concrete to relate to. Conversely, someone who intends to sell a consulting service or a cultural performance is faced with the challenge of creating legitimacy on a more intangible product, which essentially is the person himself.

Evaluation: instrumental or legitimate?

You have now been presented with two different perspectives on the evaluation of opportunities; namely the instrumental perspective, and the legitimacy perspective. These are summarised in Table 4.1.

As the table shows, the instrumental perspective views evaluation as a means for achieving a particular goal. The goal indicates directions for action so that it can be determined how and whether the idea can become a viable opportunity. Evaluation criteria are defined prior to the actual evaluation process and the evaluation itself is limited in time by a specific start and end point. The criteria often emerge from different analytical frameworks such as the VIQ tool or the business plan. These frameworks often indicate a linear, rational and systematic chain of analytical evaluation activities that the entrepreneur must undertake to achieve the goal. Finally, the instrumental perspective often looks upon evaluation and actual entrepreneurial action as two separate activities. First evaluation and then action based on the evaluation's recommendations.

In contrast, the legitimacy perspective emphasises that legitimacy building is the focal point of the evaluation process, which takes place on a continuous basis and aims to convince market participants of the idea's excellence and potential. Here, the criteria for evaluation are not determined in advance, but in the legitimation process, where interaction with the market will gradually signal what criteria are relevant: the evaluation process is social, interactive, experimental and exploratory. By presenting the social environment with the idea, the entrepreneur has the opportunity to build trust, acceptance and understanding which will often end up in a continuous reassessment, adjustment, alteration, etc. of the idea, depending on the feedback that the entrepreneur receives from others. The entrepreneur takes the idea into the market and tests it. This highlights how, according to the legitimacy perspective, the evaluation process and the entrepreneurial act are two inseparable processes.

A theoretical interpretation

In light of the above theory, we now offer our interpretation of the Munthe plus Simonsen story with which we started the chapter; firstly through the lens of the instrumental perspective, and then according to the legitimacy perspective.

The instrumental perspective

At first glance, it may be difficult to understand the story of Munthe plus Simonsen from the instrumental perspective. At the start of the entrepreneurial process Naja and Karen had no definite idea or specific target that they aimed to achieve through rational and analytical processes – quite the contrary. However, looking at the story over time, it seems that Naja and Karen became increasingly focused, goal-oriented and concerned with planning in terms of their activities. In particular, the suspension of payments caused them to stop, analyse and systematically evaluate what they could do to create a clothing line and business model that the market would find attractive. Evaluation was an exploratory and experimental process for them, which resulted in Naja and Karen clarifying their goal and, through analysis of the budget, identifying the financial cuts that were necessary to achieve that goal. In other words, they really cut the business down to the bone through a systematic financial evaluation. The goal then was to create a mature and economically viable organisation, and they knew that they must continually look at how they could optimise the business and what economic consequences were associated with which activities. It was no longer enough for them that they were making great clothes – it also had to be a profitable business.

After starting out refusing to be a commercial organisation Naja and Karen began to think commercially and analytically. In part, the focus moved away from what they liked and their own lifestyle by, for example, thinking about who the end-user was and why they should buy their clothes. As part of the more commercial orientation, Naja and Karen effectively made a rational analysis of the client group and therefore an analysis of the product's potential in light of the market: enabling them to integrate the market's needs and desires in their designs. This was achieved by including distributors, employees, vendors, etc. in the evaluation of the Munthe plus Simonsen target group, and in the redefinition of the organisation's design line. Last but not least, Naja and Karen sought to create a more stable and profitable situation through franchising. This may indicate that a form of organisational assessment took place.

In other words it is clear that the suspension of payments gave rise to a more instrumental approach to evaluation, with goals being set prior to the evaluation process, and systematic analysis tools being put into service.

The legitimacy perspective

Taking the opposite view the early part of the Munthe plus Simonsen story provides plenty of evidence of the legitimacy perspective. It is a tale of two young girls who encounter great difficulty in convincing the world that they have an attractive product and in generally achieving legitimacy as entrepreneurs. In particular, the fact that Naja and Karen started up within an industry that was not yet in itself an accepted part of the market, created legitimacy challenges for the young entrepreneurs. They were not just trying to convince the outside world about their own collection, but also about the value of a whole new industry. As a result, the media, sales channels, etc. initially rejected them, and they had no role models to lean on.

However, their organisation spread like ripples on the water and became increasingly viewed as legitimate; primarily because Naja and Karen appeared to have a good insight into how to create positive awareness and credibility in the fashion world. This is evident in that they first and foremost pushed their way through to Norgaard, a respected retailer in central Copenhagen. Since this particular sales channel itself enjoys widespread social acceptance in the fashion world, others easily accepted their collection as attractive. Naja and Karen opened the door to the sales channel by daring to explore, being persistent, not taking 'no for an answer' and by showing off their products. Drive, persistence and interaction with the 'right' people are hallmarks of Naja and Karen's creation of legitimacy.

Another interesting way that Naja and Karen entered the market through the creation of legitimacy was by acting 'as if' they had a very precious product, which was already widely accepted in the fashion industry. They acted 'as if' and made symbolic gestures that gave them a successful and prestigious image and status in the fashion industry, such as hiring famous supermodels, setting up in expensive office buildings with exclusive furniture and establishing shops and showrooms in key fashion cities from an early stage of the entrepreneurial process. Through these actions Naja and Karen also stand out from the crowd, which is very advantageous in an industry like the fashion industry. It is obvious that the evaluation process at the beginning is very much an integral part of the entrepreneurial process. This is expressed by virtue of the fact that Naja and Karen did not seem to use legitimacy as a deliberate strategy. In fact, from an early stage they made it a point of honour not to relate their designs to the market or to bother about what others thought of them and their collection.

Naja and Karen's exploratory and experimental approach to opportunity evaluation led, at the beginning of the story, to positive feedback from the market, which was carried through in the way that they apparently hit an upward market trend with their clothes. Important feedback also came in the form of growing earnings, and prices, both of which can be construed as official certificates creating additional legitimacy around Munthe plus Simonsen. Naja and Karen certainly got that right. They created an attractive option, which emerged at a time when the bohemian style was popular. In fact there is strong evidence that Naja and Karen's actions and the example they set not only created legitimacy for their own organisation, but also contributed to the growing legitimacy of the Danish fashion scene as a whole.

Unfortunately, however, legitimacy is not something you have in perpetuity once it is acquired. You can also lose legitimacy, as the late stages of the Munthe plus Simonsen story reveals. The fact that the organisation was subject to a suspension of payments makes it clear that Naja and Karen did not have legitimacy in everyone's eyes. They understood the rules of legitimacy in the fashion industry at an image and collection level, but they had not understood in detail how business legitimacy is created, despite having won awards such as businesswomen of the year. In view of that, the restructuring of their business can be seen as an exercise in repairing some of the legitimacy that they have lost in the business world as a consequence of the suspension of payments.

Testing the theory

The interpretations, thoughts and discussions throughout this chapter have prepared you to develop your own tests for understanding opportunity evaluation. Here are some exercises that you can start with.

 EXERCISES

1 **Conceptualising Evaluation.** First, undertake a brainstorming exercise that results in you writing down all the words that you associate with evaluation. Then organise the words into some broad definitions of what evaluation is. Finally determine whether your definitions of evaluation reflect the instrumental perspective, legitimacy perspective, or a combination of the two.

2 **Consultant.** As you know, Munthe plus Simonsen has had a stormy voyage. Imagine that Naja and Karen contact you wanting to hire you as a consultant. They ask specifically for an analysis of the following:

   1. What are the two most beneficial things that they have done in terms of evaluation?
   2. What are the two most negative things they have done?
   3. What could they have done to turn the negative things into something advantageous?

3 **Write your own review narrative.** Start with a business idea (either an idea you already have or a new thought). Turn on your computer and write a narrative about how you would evaluate the idea. You have 10 minutes to write your narrative. Working in pairs, read your narratives to each other. Analyse together, whether the narratives provide evidence that you would make an evaluation from the instrumental perspective, legitimacy perspective, or a combination of the two.

 LITERATURE

Aldrich, H.E. (1999) *Organisations evolving*, London: Sage.

Aldrich, H. & Fiol, M.C. (1994) 'Fools Rush in? The Institutional Context of Industry Creation', *The Academy of Management Review*, 19(4), 645–670.

Allen, K.R. (2006) *Launching New Ventures: An Entrepreneurial Approach*, Boston: Houghton Mifflin Company.

Barringer, B.R. & Ireland, R.D. (2010) *Entrepreneurship: Successfully Launching New Ventures*, Upper Saddle River: Prentice Hall.

Delmar, F. & Shane, S. (2004) 'Legitimating First: Organising Activities and the Survival of New Ventures', *Journal of Business Venturing*, 19, 385–410.

Grichnik, D., Smeja, A. & Welpe, I. (2010) 'The importance of being emotional: How do emotions affect entrepreneurial opportunity evaluation and exploitation?', *Journal of Economic Behaviour & Organisation*, 76, 15–29.

Haynie, M.J., Stepherd, D.A. & McMullen, J.S. (2009) 'An Opportunity for Me? The Role of Resources in Opportunity Evaluation Decisions', *Journal of Management Studies*, 46(3), 337–361.

Hindle, K. (2010) 'Skillful Dreaming: Testing a General Model of Entrepreneurial Process with a Specific Narrative of Venture Creation', *Entrepreneurial Narrative Theory Ethnomethodology & Reflexivity*, 1, 97–137.

Hindle, K., Mainprize, B. & Dorofeeva, N. (2007) *Venture Intelligence: How Smart Investors and Entrepreneurs Evaluate New Ventures*, Melbourne: Learnfast Press.

Johnson, C., Dow, T.J. & Ridgeway, C.L. (2006) 'Legitimacy as a Social Process', *Annual Review Sociology*, 32, 53–78.

Keh, H.T., Foo, M.D. & Lim, B.C. (2002) 'Opportunity Evaluation Under Risky Conditions: The Cognitive Processes of Entrepreneurs', *Entrepreneurship Theory and Practice*, 27(2), 125–148.

Quinn, R.E. (2004) *Building the Bridge as You Walk on It: A Guide for Leading Change*, San Francisco: Jossey-Bass.

Pahl, N. and Richter, A. (2007) *SWOT Analysis – Idea, Methodology And A Practical Approach*, Santa Cruz: GRIN Publishing.

Porter, Michael E. (2008) 'The Five Competitive Forces that Shape Strategy', *Harvard Business Review*, January, 86–104.

Reynolds, P.D. (1991) 'Sociology and Entrepreneurship: Concepts and Contributions', *Entrepreneurship Theory and Practice*, 16(2), 47–70.

Shane, S. (2003) *A General Theory of Entrepreneurship: The Individual-opportunity Nexus*, Cheltenham, UK and Northampton, MA, USA: Edward Elgar Publishing.

Suchman, M. (1995) 'Managing Legitimacy: Strategic and Institutional Approaches', *Academy of Management Review*, 20(3), 571–610.

Wickham, P.A. (2004) *Strategic Entrepreneurship*, Harlow: Pearson Education Limited.

5

Organisation of opportunities

It is now time to exploit the opportunity; this requires organising ability. Organising is essentially about developing some meaningful practice, structures and systems that we call organisations. The process itself involves the coordination of elements such as people, resources, strategies, competition, technologies, etc., and it evolves in a complex milieu of interacting individuals. The process of getting organised is seen as a tool to realise the opportunity and take it to the market through the formation of new independent organisations or organisational units within existing organisations (Allen 2006). One can also envisage the entrepreneur taking his opportunity to market through the purchase of a franchise unit or by selling the opportunity to an existing organisation. In this chapter we will however concentrate on what the organising of opportunities through new organisational formation involves.

Entrepreneurship in practice

Before we go into a lengthy theoretical explanation of how opportunities can be exploited through the organisation, it is time, once again, to meet an entrepreneur. His name is Claus Meyer and is a well-known chef from Denmark. Just listen to his story about how he organised his entrepreneurial activities, including an established restaurant Noma, which in 2010 and again in 2011 was named the world's best restaurant by Restaurant Magazine. In parallel with organising the process he went from being a university student to a successful serial entrepreneur.

CASE STUDY

A famous chef, 'It just happened'

(Devised by the authors)

'I've never wanted a big company. I wanted great successes, but not many employees, high turnover or seven or eight companies, which it probably is right now. It's something that just happened. I've never worked with plans. Until a few years ago I didn't work with budgets, and the idea of having a board is only four years old. We never took bank loans. I've only done that once and it was not a success . . . So we started in the easiest way.' This is how Claus describes his approach to entrepreneurship. In 2010, the Meyer Group (including subsidiaries) consisted of a number of food companies that together employed more than 300 people.

Claus grew up in the Danish 'food culture' of the 1960s and 70s: a time characterised by many women leaving the kitchen in favour of paid labour. Danish households were filled to the brim with frozen vegetables, minced meat, frying margarine and other foods that made life easier and kept costs down – often at the expense of food quality and the consumer's experience. At the beginning, Claus had no special interest in food, but as a young man he found himself in the house of a famous chef in southern France. The experience founded a mission for life within him. He would transform and improve the Danish / Nordic food culture: put the experience, the soul, the quality and sincerity back into the food, but how? Claus had no plan as to how he might realise his mission.

Others might have undertaken training as a chef, but not Claus. Instead, he enrolled on a course as a student at Copenhagen Business School, and consequently Denmark's most famous chef never trained as a chef. At the business school he took a business administration degree, specialising in starting and developing businesses. Claus chose this approach because, to a great extent, he already saw entrepreneurship as a future career path: both his father and grandfather having been self-employed.

As a 20-year old young man Claus started his first entrepreneurial project: 'take away food' from his two room studio apartment in Copenhagen. He delivered the food on his Raleigh bicycle. Later he talked the business school's rector into letting him take over the school canteen. It was the beginning of a long entrepreneurial journey: many organisational projects have been set up in the years since (The Chocolate Company, Meyer and Tingstroem staff restaurants, corporate 'pampering' outings / team building, fruit breeding, Noma, Meyer's Deli, etc.). Figure 5.1 provides an overview of the Meyer Group organisations in 2008.

The mission comes into focus

'I had the best idea of my life about four years ago: it synchronised the last fifteen years of my life. I didn't want to go into the restaurant business, but I got an offer . . . a nice place . . . an old warehouse in Christianshavn. My idea was to build a Nordic gourmet restaurant.' Colleagues laughed. Nordic food is not 'fine' – not worthy of a gourmet restaurant. The restaurant would be ridiculed as the 'whale-restaurant'. Nevertheless, Claus established the restaurant, Noma,

CASE STUDY *(continued)*

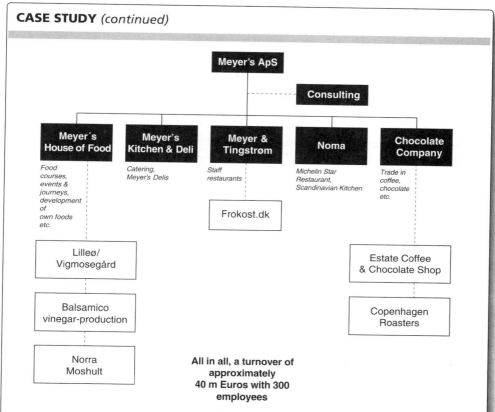

Figure 5.1 Organisation diagram: The Meyer group

with his partner Rene Redzepi, who has experience in the gourmet business. They cultivated the unique history, taste and origin of Nordic cuisine. Nobody had thought of it before. Thai, French and Indian cuisine, we all know, but what is Nordic cuisine? Neither of the two entrepreneurs had dreams of creating great economic success: it was about something bigger. As with Claus' mission in life their real success criterion was to define the Nordic kitchen and create a common mission among Nordic farmers, small and large businesses, citizens, politicians, etc. to promote Nordic food of high quality. It all led to a huge success. In 2008, Noma was awarded two Michelin stars and, as mentioned, it was named the world's best restaurant in 2010 and 2011.

A Nordic movement

The establishment of Noma was essentially a process involving a lot of different people, first and foremost partner Rene Redzepi. Claus' role was primarily to support Rene based on his experience as an entrepreneur: 'I supported him and helped with finance, building the website, recruiting staff, creating the first menus, chose the graphic designer, took care of the contractual relationships with the owners of the premises, but probably most important,

CASE STUDY (continued)

I brought together all of the Nordic food-intelligence . . . Ministers from Norway and Denmark, etc. even people from the Nordic food industry . . . to discuss how everyone could share our vision.' Claus simply chose to invite ministers, top officials from the Nordic food industry, journalists and famous chefs for a symposium to articulate the idea of Nordic cuisine. The participating chefs were set the task of defining a manifesto for the new Nordic cuisine, formulated as 10 commandments.

The manifesto would be launching a whole new movement – a movement with many different members (cooks, consumers, politicians and business people from all the Scandinavian countries). The movement came together to promote Nordic food culture based on the manifesto's words. The Nordic Ministers for Food were also part of the movement, launching a 'New Nordic Food Programme' based on the manifesto. This programme allocates funds to organisations and individual people who develop, produce or market products in accordance with the manifesto.

So, a restaurant and the concept on which it was founded has become a Nordic movement. Through the movement, Claus fulfilled his mission of creating a platform for a Danish / Nordic food culture. One that is not all about frozen vegetables, minced meat and frying margarine, but a food culture that promotes the uniqueness, the origin and quality of Nordic cuisine.

Dancing around
Reflecting on the creation of his entrepreneurial ventures, Claus relates how he cooks to how he creates organisations: 'There are many similarities. The way I love to cook is without a recipe or a definite plan. I love to go somewhere, for example, Hungary, and see which vegetables are in the garden; what meat is available and what's in the fridge. Then I dance a little, thinking about what I can do and what I know. On the way I interact a little with the surroundings – and that's also how I do business. I listen to people; I talk to my employees. If I have a dishwasher who is good with flowers, I would be stupid if I didn't ask him to arrange the flowers. If I meet someone who wants to build a dairy and it could be bigger and better if we did it together, then I would be attracted. So I build businesses in the same way that I cook: I dance around, see what happens and try to feel the energy.'

Similar thoughts are expressed in an interview with the *CBS Observer* in 2008. Claus Meyer explained: 'I've never made many plans. My plan has been to be open to the outside world, so you can't just rush past the opportunities that present themselves. I think this has been good for my dream because I have always been open to new paths, but it has not necessarily been good for the individual companies. Growth comes from planning and financing. I have not planned and I have not taken loans and this means that everything has gone very slowly. If I had done things differently, I could probably have experienced much faster growth.'

However, the larger the Meyer group became, the more Claus experienced a need to professionalise and structure its organisation. He set up a professional board, but mostly it functions as a provider of inspiration. He likes to retain control himself. 'The Board supports me

CASE STUDY (continued)

in having a well organised company with the right skills in the right positions relative to what we want to do. Who should be the leader? . . . I do not know much about building large organisations. I didn't want to have a big organisation, but now I have one . . . I hope that I am a good priest and a visionary person and that all employees want to follow my footsteps. But I'm not the classic leader.' The Board often advises Claus to think more about making money, but he has a larger vision of his entrepreneurial activities than financial goals.

Your immediate interpretation

How do you understand the organising process that Claus talks of? Here are some questions that may help you to reflect on the story in terms of organising.

- You are a stand-in teacher in an eighth grade class (15-year-olds) at a state school. Based on Claus' story, your task is to explain to the class what an organisation is and how organisations are created. What do you tell the class?
- You draw a timeline on the blackboard that gives the class an overview of Claus' progress. You get a reaction. One of the boys in the class asks you: 'When do you know that the entrepreneurial process has led to the establishment of a new organisation?' What is your answer?
- A girl in class is also curious. She asks: 'Why do you think that Claus didn't start by establishing Noma, which is really the opportunity that truly realises his mission in life?' Do you have a good answer?

Theories on entrepreneurship

As you know, organising opportunities is the subject of this chapter. The literature offers many different interpretations of what organising involves. Some believe that the organising process is a conscious, deliberate process that plans for and aims to achieve a predetermined and predictable goal – a successful organisation. In this way the entrepreneur is seen as a kind of rational architect who organises the process and the opportunity optimally through planning. This interpretation seems to be widespread in society, among politicians, educators, consultants, banks, etc., and it reflects what we would call a planning perspective of organising.

However, the literature also contains an alternative view of the organising process, which we call the improvisation perspective of organising. This perspective emphasises that in many cases the entrepreneur starts out with no clear goal as to what organisation he wants to create, and even if the entrepreneur starts out with a clear goal, this can change because the future, environment, etc. are not predictable but are changing and insecure. The latter becomes particularly clear if you think about how the entrepreneur often finds himself in an organisational situation where the parameters of the opportunity, such as market demand structure, customer group, prices, competition, etc., are not yet known, because entrepreneurship is fundamentally about creating something new – creating the future (Shane 2003). The improvisation perspective argues that since there is so much uncertainty associated with entrepreneurship, planning makes less sense. Instead, the entrepreneurial process is, in practice, characterised by entrepreneurs feeling their way forward, constantly reconsidering their environment, asking others for advice and finding resources along the way, which constantly opens up new opportunities and goals. It's basically about improvisation. Only through many and unpredictable small steps is a new organisation realised. Together, the planning and improvisation perspectives represent a paradox:

Planning or Improvising

What is an organisation?

In organisation theory, it is often assumed that the organisation is something that already exists. However, the focal point of entrepreneurship is the organisation-in-creation, and hence the emergent organisational processes that lead to a new organisation being created (Katz & Gartner 1988, Gartner et al 1992). Nevertheless to understand what the organisation process involves, it is first and foremost worth looking at what characterises an organisation. An organisation is, in itself, an incredibly broad and ambiguous concept, and numerous perspectives are used to define an organisation (March & Simon 1958). This perhaps is because organisations are in many ways obscure entities, processes and structures that we take more or less for granted as they are around us all the time, and shape us as we shape them. Some of the perspectives of an organisation place weight on the organisations' formal structures, common rules, administrative procedures, frameworks and goals. Others focus on the more informal, process-oriented, interactive, social and human dimensions in their definition of an organisation (Morgan 1997). As an example of the latter, Weick (1995) offers an interesting suggestion for the individual and social cognitive sense making processes that lead to a new organisation being created. Katz and Gartner (1988) refer to McKelvey's (1980) definition of an organisation that provides both structural and process-oriented dimensions. An organisation is a 'myopically purposeful [boundary-maintaining] activity system containing one or more conditionally autonomous myopically purposeful subsystems having input-output resource ratios fostering survival in environments imposing particular constraints.' (Katz and Gartner 1988: 430)

Formal organisations are relatively easy to identify whereas informal organisations can be much more imperceptible.

Berger and Kellner offer a different definition of an organisation: 'Every human organization is, as it were, a crystallization of meanings, or, to vary the image, a crystallization of meanings in objective form.' (Berger & Kellner 1981: 31) Organisations are thus organised communities consisting of actors, resources, knowledge, etc., where the glue that holds it all together is commonly held and generally accepted opinions and perceptions among stakeholders about why they appear as objective structures, systems, norms and logics. These control the stakeholders' opinions and actions whilst also being shaped by them.

One can also argue that organisations are basically about a kind of group formation where individuals are not just random people who gathered on a pedestrian street. On the contrary, the individuals interact in the organisation to achieve a common goal.

> At first a primitive organization emerges from cooperation between individuals who wish to pool their efforts to achieve a common goal, such as bringing a new product to market. This primitive organization has not got a structure in the technical sense of the term because cooperative effort is more a result of individual motivation than it is an organizational achievement. However if the primitive organization is going to survive beyond its initial project it will develop an elaborated social structure and become an organization in the usual sense of the world. (Hatch 1997: 177)

In the process of moving from a primitive to an elaborated organisation, individuals come together through a series of processes that establishes:

- More formalisation: it is framed by some common rules and physical limits
- More complexity: underlines the need for administrative functions, linking activities
- Clarification of objectives: aimed at a specific overall goal.

Source: Fayolle (2003: 41).

Figure 5.2 The development of a new organisation

Organisations can therefore be said to be a framework for any kind of concerted social and human action. However, because starting a new organisation involves basically only one, or a few entrepreneurs, you might not immediately think about social unity. Nevertheless, parallel to the organising of the entrepreneur's opportunity (designing a logo, pooling resources, exchanges with clients, etc.), the entrepreneurial opportunity develops from being attached to the entrepreneur to becoming an accepted social organisation, which also involves other actors in addition to the entrepreneur. The involvement of other actors can be seen as a prerequisite for entrepreneurial organisation. 'People construct organisations to accomplish things they cannot do on their own.' (Aldrich 1999: 75) The many actors involved require further formalisation, direction, and thus structure. The starting up of a new organisation thus takes shape through a lot of different actors' interactions. The more actors involved in the process, the more complex it becomes and the greater the demands for the organisation-in-creation to be formalised in relation to objectives and administrative processes.

What does organising involve?

We see organising as a process that is about creating a new organisation over time. Inspired by Fayolle (2003), we have divided the development of a new organisation into five phases. The phases cover getting an idea, evaluating and shaping it into a real opportunity, conceptualising the opportunity of an entrepreneurial project so that it can be exploited by making the opportunity of a new emergent organisation actually happen, which in turn and over time becomes increasingly stable in its design. This chapter focuses mainly on the fourth phase. The last phase is outside this book's sphere of interest. As we established in Chapter 1, this book divides the entrepreneurial process into three phases, namely: 1) opportunity creation, 2) opportunity evaluation, and 3) opportunity organisation. This classification is generally in line with Fayolle's thoughts. Figure 5.2 illustrates the five phases mentioned.

As the five stages are described here, the entrepreneurial process appears as a linear and progressive process. However, Fayolle's point about the phases is to show that there may be feedback from later phases to earlier ones.

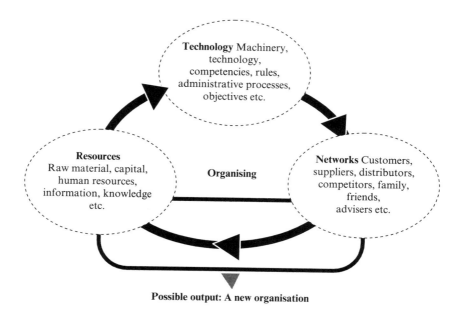

Source: Inspired by Jones (2007).

Figure 5.3 The organising components

Furthermore the development phases do not necessarily occur in that order. For example, some entrepreneurs will establish a formal organisation before they have evaluated whether the idea represents a real opportunity. Finally, the process may stop at a certain stage without a new organisation ever being formed.

As such, Fayolle's phase model shows that the organisation does not consist merely of a single step – going from a situation 'without organisation' to a situation 'with a new organisation'. On the contrary, one can talk about a series of fluid organisational steps on the way towards a new independent organisation or organisational unit within an existing organisation. Since there is a smooth transition from the 'without organisation' to the 'with a new organisation' situation, it is difficult, in practice, to determine when the organisation is formed. Is it when the external funding is secured? When the first bill is paid? After the first sale takes place? When the organisation is formally registered with the authorities?

Whilst Fayolle's model provides an overarching vision of how we can understand the organisation in terms of the entrepreneurial process as a whole, Figure 5.3 shows some elements of the organisational efforts the entrepreneur must make to realise his opportunity in the market.

The figure illustrates that the organisation requires resources in terms of raw materials, capital, human and social resources, information, knowledge, customers, etc. Chapter 6 examines the resource challenge in more detail.

Acquisition of resources requires the entrepreneur to act and interact with the environment, since it is rare that he or she already possesses the necessary resources. This makes the formation and development of networks a critical factor. As Aldrich said: 'All nascent entrepreneurs draw upon their existing social networks and construct new ones in the process of obtaining knowledge and resources for their organizations.' (Aldrich 1999: 81) Relevant actors in these networks include customers, shareholders, suppliers, distributors, competitors, advisors, family, friends, etc. The network challenge is set out in Chapter 7.

A third important factor in the formation of an organisation is the establishment of technology, in a broad sense, so that inputs can be transformed into products and services with the use of resources. Technology refers to machinery, buildings, control systems, etc.

In the final organisation these three components are in place; a resource base, a technology and a network are all established. In the early phase, the task for the entrepreneur is to establish these conditions: to accumulate resources, to establish the technology, to develop the network: definitely not an easy task. There are a multitude of diverse activities to be deployed simultaneously. As an illustration of the complexity, Aldrich (1999) refers to a US study that points to 17 key activities as being relevant in the entrepreneurial process. The activities are shown in Figure 5.4. The list should not be taken to mean that all entrepreneurs carry out all listed activities. Every organisation is unique, or in other words, organising is not a generic route, to be marched again and again by the same entrepreneurs (Gartner 1985). Instead the processes vary 'vastly in their characteristics as do the entrepreneurs who create them' (Bhave 1994: 224).

The activities that are most representative of the individual entrepreneur can be closely linked with the country in which a business is started. Data from the World Bank, an international bank which provides financial support to developing countries around the world, shows that there is a big difference in how easy it is to start a business (World Bank, www.doingbusiness.org, last accessed 22 May 2012). Depending on how business-friendly the regulations are in a country, it may be easier or harder for an entrepreneur to start-up. Ease of start-up is, is measured, among other ways, by comparing different countries' procedures (number of procedures to complete before starting),

Source: Inspired by Aldrich (1999).

Figure 5.4 Crucial activities in the start-up process

time (number of days to wait before acceptance to start), cost (percentage of the Gross National Income per capita) and minimum capital (minimum capital requirement) to open a new business. For example, according to the Doing Business 2010 report, Australia ranked third on the first sub index 'Starting a business' behind only New Zealand and Canada. In Australia there are two procedures required to start a business which take on average two days to complete. Further the official cost is 0.8 per cent of the Gross National Income per capita, and there is no minimum capital requirement. By contrast, in Guinea-Bissau which ranked among the worst (183rd out of 183) on this same sub index, there are 16 procedures required to start a business taking 213 days to complete. The official cost is 323.0 per cent of the gross national income per capita, and a minimum capital investment of

1006.6 per cent of the gross national income per capita is required (World Bank, Doing Business 2010 report).

Organising is not always a success

Organising does not always lead to the establishment of a new organisation. Often the entrepreneur chooses to abort the process. The GEM survey results from 2010 show that there is a diminishing participation during the entrepreneurial process, from having the intention to start a new organisation to actually starting-up or already having established a new organisation. The study shows for example that in the United States, whilst 7.7 per cent of Americans intend to start-up, only 4.8 per cent have taken concrete steps to do so and only 2.8 per cent actually runs a fledgling (less than three and a half years old) organisation (Kelley et al 2011). The same fall-off pattern is also found in other countries such as Denmark, Germany, Sweden and the United Kingdom, although there are variations in the number of respondents who have the intention of starting-up, have taken concrete steps or are already running a start-up.

The figure obviously raises the question: why is there so much failure in the entrepreneurial process? Overall, Brush and Manolova (2004) point to various barriers such as weak knowledge, opportunity identification, product/service development and the ability to develop systems and structures. In addition problems of legitimacy occur, barriers in relation to creating relevant networks and the ability to identify and develop an attractive resource base. Finally it is pointed out that risk can be a key issue. So that we can get a closer look into the reasons why entrepreneurial organising ends, it makes sense to distinguish between the processes that, according to Fayolle's (2003) model – see Figure 5.2 – lead to a 'stable organisation' and the processes arising once such an organisation is established. The barriers, which the entrepreneur specifically meets in the process towards a 'stable' organisation are, according to Brush and Manolova (2004), divided into two main categories: personal challenge (getting suitable health insurance, balancing time and lack of mentors) and social challenges (being taken seriously and receiving support) (Brush and Manolova 2004: 280).

When considering perceived barriers associated with the post-establishment period, it is crucial, according to Levie et al (2011) to note that organisational efforts are not only terminated for negative reasons or venture failure, such as bankruptcy. Often an organisation is closed down on the basis of more voluntary and positive considerations. Maybe it was not the intention, from the beginning, that the organisation should persist for a longer period

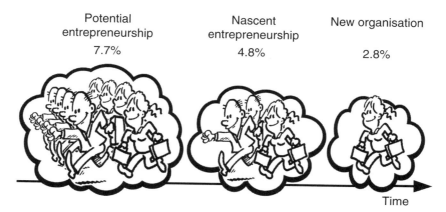

Potential entrepreneurship 7.7%

Nascent entrepreneurship 4.8%

New organisation 2.8%

Time

Note: Potential entrepreneurs: percentage of those aged 18–64 who expect to start a business within three years.
Nascent entrepreneurs: Percentage of those aged 8–64 who are currently involved in setting up a business they will own or co-own.
New organisation: Percentage of those aged 18–64 who are currently an owner-manager of a new business (max 42 months old).

Source: Kelley et al (2011).

Figure 5.5 The diminishing participation during the entrepreneurial process in the USA (% of population)

than to exploit temporary market opportunities or achieve a desired sale. Alternatively the organisation may be closed down because the entrepreneur simply gets a better job offer, or it no longer meets the entrepreneur's needs when he or she is looking for new challenges. In a GEM study Bosma et al (2008) focused on why entrepreneurs within the past 12 months had closed down an organisation. Here the results show that about one third of organisations have actually been continued in a different form or with other owners. The change should thus be recorded as a continuation rather than an exit. In a discussion of failure, Levie et al (2011) refer to studies showing that as little as 4–5 per cent of the businesses close due to legal bankruptcy or insolvency. Other reasons included a resale, voluntary closure, illness, retirement, etc.

Seen in this light, Wickham's (2004) point about the importance of understanding success and failure as being subjectively determined also makes sense. This means the entrepreneur's experiences of success or lack thereof in the entrepreneurial process, must be seen in light of the entrepreneur's expectations, motives and objectives. If these are not met, the entrepreneur will probably consider the process to be a failure. For example, if an entrepreneur's objective is to improve the balance between work and family life, then success is when this balance is realised. Another entrepreneur may be more motivated by economic growth. For him the key to success is not the creation of a 'balanced life', but the making of profits.

Organising can be planned

Now it is time to look more specifically at how the organising process might proceed by looking deeper into the two perspectives that we introduced earlier: the planning and improvisation perspectives. Let's start with the former.

The planning perspective in entrepreneurship has its roots in classical management theory where manufacturing organisations are seen as entities, created by the manager to achieve predefined goals. The manager builds and operates the organisational machine using tools such as rational analysis and planning (Hatch 1997). Thus, the perspective suggests that the organising is intentional, rational and considered, and the process of organising can be driven by analysis (competitor analysis, customer analysis, etc.) and planning. Finally it can be steered towards a specific goal. So, the perspective assumes that the entrepreneur has a clear picture of the goal (the organisation) that he or she wants to achieve, right from the start.

Sarasvathy (2008) talks of the planning perspective's vision of the organisation as a causal process in which the entrepreneur has to ask himself the question: 'What must I do to achieve the desired goal – a successful organisation?' The challenge for the entrepreneur is now to choose the optimal strategies, resources, networks, etc., that enable him to achieve the best possible result. Through analysis, rational and objective decision making (where he seeks to maximise benefits and minimise the drawbacks), he is able to make those choices and produce a plan, which he predicts will result in goal achievement. The entrepreneur focuses on the dimensions of the organisational process, which he believes to be predictive and enable him to control the course of events (Sarasvathy 2001).

It is assumed that the entrepreneur has almost complete information, clear preferences, and an available adequate resource base, and that the entrepreneur makes a plan with set steps for the entire organisation from the beginning. He plans before taking action. This last point highlights how the entrepreneur, in preparing the organising process is separated from the activities and challenges along with the risks associated with organising. That planning can be separated from the action, also points to the presupposition that the environment is more or less stable and transparent. The reason is that the planned process is expected to be relevant, in terms of the environment, at the time of implementation. Consequently, the planning perspective only makes sense, if we assume that the future – or at least important aspects of the future – is predictable, that the entrepreneur's goals and preferences are clear, and that the environment is independent of the entrepreneur's actions. The logic behind this causal thinking is that to the extent the entrepreneur can predict the future, he or she is also able to control the future and thereby reduce the uncertainty and risk associated with organising (Sarasvathy 2008).

To illustrate the planning perspective Sarasvathy (2008) describes a cook creating a meal. Rationally, the chef starts by choosing the menu, which he or she will prepare. Then, the cook finds a recipe that he or she can follow in preparing the food. The next step is purchasing the ingredients that the recipe suggests, and then the meal can be created. The process 'starts with selecting a menu as a goal and finding effective ways to achieve the goal' (Sarasvathy 2008: 74). Figure 5.6 illustrates this process.

The recipes, which the entrepreneur can use to create a new organisation are many. The literature recommends that first and foremost the entrepreneur answer questions such as: what is the goal, vision and mission of the organisation? How will the entrepreneur organise and manage the organisation, including issues such as number of employees, organisational procedures, management style, organisational structure, etc.? How can the entrepreneur achieve organisational 'lift-off' in terms of strategy, marketing, growth, internationalization, etc.? The answers can be built into the business plan model, which is discussed in Chapter 8.

Organising is all about improvisation

Entrepreneurs are, however, rarely faced with predictable environments and they have by no means complete information about the future, clear preferences about goals or unlimited resources, which the planning perspective seems to assume. The organising process is simply too complex and unclear, and it will only show its true nature through the entrepreneur's actual activities and struggles to understand the goal, gain access to and control over resources, establishing an organisation, etc., and even then the nature and direction of the organising process will take new forms. These thoughts are captured by the improvisation perspective on organising.

This perspective emphasises first and foremost that the entrepreneur cannot, in advance, articulate a clear goal of the organisation or a plan for achieving his or her objective. Instead, an entrepreneur needs to give up control and build on the often-limited resources that he or she has available right now. The entrepreneur must look to the present situation and current opportunities and find new directions along the way to transform this opportunity into

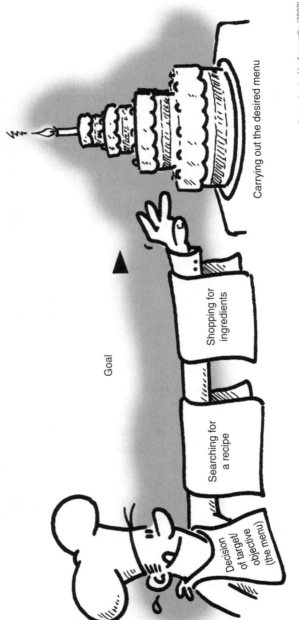

Decision of target/objective (the menu)

Searching for a recipe

Shopping for ingredients

Goal

Carrying out the desired menu

Source: Inspired by Sarasvathy (2008).

Figure 5.6 The planning perspective

a new independent organisation or organisational unit within an existing organisation. The perspective is based on the idea that a bird in the hand is worth more than two in the bush (Sarasvathy 2008). In other words, make use of what you have when organising instead of starting with the ultimate goal. The entrepreneur's starting point should be based on what is sure and not on a dream of achieving a Bill Gates level of success that he or she may never achieve.

Sarasvathy (2008) uses the term 'effectuation' to capture the logic behind the improvisation perspective's approach to organising. According to the effectuation-mind the organising is characterised by the entrepreneur asking himself: 'What effects can I achieve with the resources I have?' Thus: 'What do I do right here?' Whereas the entrepreneur's challenge in the planning perspective was to choose the most optimal strategies, the entrepreneur's challenge when entering an improvised scene is to create the organisation through the exploration of possible combinations and modifications of the available means. It requires an open approach to organising, where the entrepreneur involves others because it is through interaction with others that he or she can gain access to new resources, which can help to create larger and more valuable organisations. To a great extent, the involvement of others generates a dynamic organisation; because the entrepreneur must at all times behave flexibly, creatively and experimentally with the varying inputs, that interaction with others give rise to. The organisation may end up with several different outcomes that cannot be predicted in advance.

Sarasvathy (2008) illustrates the effectuation perspective by once again relating organising to the preparation of a meal. The cook begins the improvisation process by looking in kitchen cupboards to find out which raw materials, ingredients and tools he or she has available. Then the cook designs possible meals that can be created from the ingredients found. It is a process characterised by improvisation, where the cook has to feel his way and try out different combinations. Actually, the meal is often developed in parallel with the cook preparing it. The cook 'starts with a given kitchen, and designs possible, sometimes unintended, even entirely original meals with its contents' (Sarasvathy 2008: 74). The process may thus end up in vastly different meals that you could not have predicted in advance. It is the many small steps involved in looking into the cupboard and trying out the available resources that creates the menu. The result of this process can only be seen in retrospect – when you look back and see what actually happened. Figure 5.7 illustrates this process.

Improvising: What meals can be created?

An innovative meal is the result

Available means (ingredients & tools)

Source: Insprered by Sarasvathy (2008).

Figure 5.7 The improvising perspective

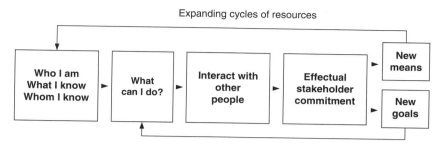

Source: Sarasvathy (2008: 101).

Figure 5.8 Clarification of the improvising perspective

Sarasvathy (2008) elaborates on how the organising process evolves in light of the improvisation perspective. Improvisation is often connected with a random process, but as illustrated in Figure 5.8, it is nevertheless possible to identify features that characterise improvisation. Sarasvathy (2008) argues that entrepreneurs typically have three resources available as they enter the organising process, namely, insight into: 1) 'Who I am' 2) 'What I know', and 3) 'Whom I know.' From these resources the entrepreneur assesses, what possible actions he or she can implement, which the entrepreneur often only becomes aware of through interaction with others. Sometimes the interactions lead to these others becoming attached to the emerging organisation, such as in the role of investor, advisor, partner, customer, etc. The many new actors who are involved in the entrepreneurial process also means that new means and thus resources and objectives become part of the entrepreneurial process and that opens new potential avenues for activities on the part of the entrepreneur.

Organising: planning or improvisation?

The paradox in this chapter is whether the organising progresses as a planned process, or whether the organisation is more improvisational in character. The following table summarises the core of the paradox.

In the planning perspective, the goal is therefore determined in advance and the key issue for the entrepreneur is: 'What can I do to achieve the desired goal?' It is assumed that the entrepreneur through rational decision making, analysis, control, generic recipes and planning can shape the organisation towards the desired goal. Process predictability is high, since it is assumed that the environment is fairly stable and transparent, the entrepreneur's preferences are clear, and the goal is given.

On the other hand, the focal point of the improvising perspective is that resources are limited, so the entrepreneur's starting point must be based on

Table 5.1 The paradox: Planning or improvisation

	Planning	Improvising
Starting point	The target is given	The means are given
Crucial question	"What can I do in order to achieve the desired effect?"	"What can I do with these means?"
The role of the entrepreneur	A rational architect	An improvising creator and social agent
Crucial activities	Analysis, planning	Small steps, interaction
Predictability of output	High	Low

the question 'What can I achieve with the resources I have?' What kind of organisation can he or she create? By being open in the organising, focused on 'here and now' feeling one's way and interacting with other players, the entrepreneur forms an organisation based on the means that he or she has available and additional resources that are gradually added to the organisation as a result of the entrepreneur's involvement with others. The predictability of the organising process is low as it is available resources, the participating actors, the many small steps and social interactions that shape the organisation.

Sarasvathy's thoughts on improvisation dominate this chapter, and it is important to conclude by mentioning that she does not see planning and improvisation as 'either-or'. According to her, elements of both planning and improvisation can be identified in any organisation. However, Sarasvathy (2001) assumes improvisation processes to be more frequent and useful in understanding the uncertain, risky and unpredictable conditions that are often the hallmark of entrepreneurial situations.

A theoretical interpretation

And so back to the chapter's beginning, where you met Claus Meyer and heard his organising story. We will now offer an interpretation of the story firstly from a planning perspective and then we'll shift the focus to the improvising perspective.

The planning perspective

A planning-based interpretation of Claus' story is in many ways difficult, because the story is simply better aligned with the improvising perspective. However on closer inspection planning and calculation are also present in the story.

Firstly, Claus has a long-term mission and therefore a goal. It is within this framework that he improvises. There are then certain business types and areas that he will not get involved with because they are inconsistent with the mission. This indicates that Claus is partly rational in his organising and that this is somewhat controlled by the question: 'What can I do to achieve the desired effect?' For example, in Noma, one can say that Claus identifies an appropriate business partner who has knowledge of haute cuisine and experience in the gourmet industry to achieve his initially established objective. Together they create an output that fulfils that goal.

The story also raises the question of whether Claus perhaps plays (at least in part) on his image and brand as 'missionary' which is, so to speak, above mundane calculation and goal-oriented behaviour. It is certainly a fact that at one point in time he chose to study at Business School, specializing in starting and developing businesses, where he must have heard a lot about the rational models, economic management and the like. This education must have given him the business acumen and analytical tools that can be used selectively to create new organisations. Of course, he says: 'I've never worked with plans', but it can be understood in the sense that he has not produced actual business plans before starting-up. However, he has obviously thought strategically and thoroughly considered the steps he takes.

Finally it is worth noticing that Claus at some point chooses to make use of a professional board. The board support him in developing a structured and focused organisation: 'The board supports me in having a well organised company with the right skills in the right positions relative to what we want to do.' He is probably aware that traditional, rational organisational leadership is not his strong point, and to compensate for this he will establish a board that can rein in his desire for improvisation. This decision also indicates that Claus thinks and plans rationally in his organising activities.

The improvising perspective

Although there are elements of planning in the story, we can't ignore that it is predominantly told in the spirit of the improvising perspective. Claus' approach to entrepreneurship is oriented towards improvisation. In many ways he keeps away from planning or at least he tries to minimise that side of things.

The improvising perspective is demonstrated by the fact that Claus from the outset had no clear intention of where he wanted to go with his organising activities. Instead, his starting point was the means that he had with him right from the time when he started his student-business. A key motto seems to have been: 'we started in the easiest way'. In this way he has, step-by-step, created a complex of food-based companies with a focus on quality. So, we are also talking about an organising process that had no predefined goal or strategy. Based on a lot of small actions and interactions an output that no one could predict was created, along with some results that were never sought after. As Claus says: 'I've never wanted a big company', but all the same he ended up with one. Claus is aware of the unpredictable nature of organising. For example, as he says about the Nordic cuisine: 'how the new Nordic movement will end up is not something I can explain. We will know that in about 10–20 years.'

Claus' story clearly illustrates that he has a social and interactive personality and how, by involving others, being close to them and getting them to feel a connection with his organising activities, Claus constantly creates new things. As he says: 'Better to win a small victory with the people you love than reaching for a distant goal.' Claus seems to be an expert at mobilising resources, through interaction with others, for the organisations he has helped to develop. But Claus also understands the need to involve other stakeholders in a broader sense. This shows in the story of the symposium he organised of ministers, CEOs and the like.

However the improvisation perspective is probably best illustrated by how Claus compares the entrepreneurial organising process to cooking. He says he dances about the food, and he draws on the resources available to him when he cooks. He lives, so to speak, in accordance with Sarasvathy's (2008) theory of entrepreneurship as an improvisational process, focusing on the means available.

Finally, one can ask: 'Why didn't Claus start with establishing Noma, which is really the opportunity that truly realises his mission in life?' This can also be explained using the improvisation perspective. At the beginning Claus hardly had the necessary skills and resources to start Noma. He had yet to gain legitimacy as an entrepreneur in his environment, sufficient experience or cooking skills, and above all, he had not met the people who have contributed to the opportunity creation. A lot of small steps had to be taken before Claus was ready to realise his mission.

Testing the theory

Think of what you have learned in the chapter and try to review some of the exercises below. This will help you gain an increased understanding of organising for entrepreneurship.

 EXERCISES

1 **Put yourself in focus.** Think back to the process that you went through when you had to choose your course of study. Draw a picture of the process and reflect on whether planning perspective, improvising perspective or a combination thereof, can best explain the process.
2 **Elevator pitch.** Identify two or three advantages and disadvantages of the planning and improvising perspectives respectively, as seen from the entrepreneur's point of view. Next write out an elevator pitch (see Chapter 1), where you first 'sell' the improvising perspective and then the planning perspective to an audience.
3 **'Both-and' exercise.** Sarasvathy (2008) believes that elements of improvisation and planning can both be found in the entrepreneurial organising process. Start by choosing a case (possibly one of the cases that are presented in this book) and analyse the case study in light of the two perspectives. Can both perspectives be identified?

 LITERATURE

Aldrich, H.E. (1999) *Organisations Evolving*, London: Sage.

Allen, K.R. (2006) *Launching New Ventures: An Entrepreneurial Approach*, Boston: Houghton Mifflin Company.

Berger, P. L. and Kellner, H. (1981) *Sociology reinterpreted: An Essay on Methods and Vocation*, New York: Doubleday Anchor.

Bhave, M.P. (1994) 'A Process Model of New Venture Creation', *Journal of Business Venturing*, 9, 223–242.

Bosma, N., Acs, Z., Autio, E., Conduras, A. & Levie, J. (2008) 'Global Entrepreneurship Monitor 2008 Executive Report', London: Global Entrepreneurship Monitor Association.

Brush, C.G. & Manolova, T.S. (2004) 'Start-up Problems', in Gartner, W.B., Shaver, K.G., Carter, N.M. & Reynolds, P.D. (eds) *Handbook of Entrepreneurial Dynamics – The Process of Business Creation*, Thousand Oaks: Sage, 273–285.

Fayolle, A. (2003) 'Research and Researchers at the Heart of Entrepreneurial Situations', in Steyaert, C. & Hjorth, D. (eds) *New Movements in Entrepreneurship*, Cheltenham, UK and Northampton, MA, USA: Edward Elgar Publishing, 35–50.

Gartner, W.B. (1985) 'A Conceptual Framework for describing the Phenomenon of New Venture Creation', *Academy of Management Review*, 10(4), 696–706.

Gartner, W.B., Bird, B.J. & Starr, J.A. (1992) 'Acting As If. Differentiating Entrepreneurial from Organisational Behavior', *Entrepreneurship Theory and Practice*, 16(3), 13–31.

Hatch, M.J. (1997) *Organisation Theory*, Oxford: Oxford University Press.

Headd, B. (2003) 'Redefining Business Success: Distinguishing Between Closure and Failure', *Small Business Economics*, 21(1), 51–61.

Jones, G.R. (2007) *Organizational Theory, Design, and Change*, Upper Saddle River: Prentice Hall.

Katz, J. & Gartner, W.B. (1988) 'Properties of Emerging Organisations', *Academy of Management Review*, 13(3), 429–441.

Kelley, D., Bosma, N. & Amoros, J.E. (2011) 'Global Entrepreneurship Monitor, 2010 Global Report', GERA (www.gemconsortium.org, last accessed 21 May 2012).

Levie, J., Don, G. & Leleux, B. (2011) 'The new venture mortality myth', in Hindle, K. & Klyver, K. (eds) *Handbook of Research on New Venture Creation*, Cheltenham, UK and Northampton, MA, USA: Edward Elgar Publishing, 194–215.

March, J.G. & Simon, H.A. (1958) *Organisations*, New York/London/Sydney: John Wiley and Sons.

McKelvey, B. (1980) *Organisational Systematics*, Berkeley: University of California Press.

Morgan, G. (1997) *Images of Organisations*, 2nd ed., Thousand Oaks/London/New Delhi: Sage Publications.

Sarasvathy, S.D. (2001) 'Causation and Effectuation: Toward a Theoretical shift from Economic Inevitability to Entrepreneurial Contingency', *Academy of Management Review*, 26(2), 243–263.

Sarasvathy, S.D. (2008) *Effectuation: Elements of Entrepreneurial Expertise*, Cheltenham, UK and Northampton, MA, USA: Edward Elgar Publishing..

Shane, S. (2003) *A General Theory of Entrepreneurship: The Individual-opportunity Nexus*, Cheltenham, UK and Northampton, MA, USA: Edward Elgar Publishing..

Wickham, P.A. (2004) *Strategic Entrepreneurship*, Boston: Pearson Education.

Weick, K.E. (1995) *Sensemaking in Organisations*, Thousand Oaks: Sage Publication.

Section 3

The entrepreneurial content

6

Resources

In order to carry out the entrepreneurial process, it is necessary to have access to a variety of resources (Alvarez & Busenitz 2001). The entrepreneur needs money, knowledge, materials, energy, enthusiasm, motivation, staff, help from friends and family, etc. The list of resources that may be necessary to implement an entrepreneurial process is virtually inexhaustible, but the necessary resources and the combination thereof are dependent, in each case, on the situation. We will go, in detail, into how all these different types of resources can be categorised.

Many have argued that the acquisition of resources is among the major factors that distinguish traditional management behaviour from entrepreneurial behaviour. As managers operate within an already established business context, they usually have access to the necessary resources. Their behaviour is then characterised by attempts to streamline and optimise the use of these resources. In contrast, entrepreneurs often have no, or very few, resources. However, instead of accepting these resource constraints entrepreneurs are characterised by their ability to exploit opportunities regardless of their access to resources. As Stevenson and Jarillo put it: 'entrepreneurship is a process by which individuals . . . pursue opportunities without regard to the resources they currently control' (Stevenson & Jarillo 1990: 23). Accordingly, entrepreneurs act in spite of the fact that they may, here and now, lack essential resources. So, whilst managers act with what they have, entrepreneurs act in spite of what they have. In this chapter we will introduce you to the entrepreneur's identification and use of resources.

Entrepreneurship in practice

We start this chapter with a story of entrepreneurship and resources. It's a story about the organisation Logopaint (www.logopaint.com, last accessed 21 May 2012), which was founded in 1997. In 2007 the organisation had a turnover of nearly US$2.6 million. In 2011, Logopaint has approximately 25 employees and has sales offices in several places around the world.

CASE STUDY

The idea of 3D carpets

(Devised by the authors)

Logopaint supports itself by optimising advertising and sponsorship in sport. They even state on their website: 'The company's general goal was and still is to optimize advertising in sports and sponsoring'. They want to be the best in their niche and they are trying to achieve this through increased product value, delivery, experience and professionalism. They try to differentiate themselves primarily by taking responsibility for their products from start to finish. 'We want to make it easy and efficient to work with us. We take responsibility for our products, and ensure quality before, during and after delivery, so the client experiences that we see our products through to the end'.

The organisation mainly provides two different products for sports: 3D carpets and 3D barrier boards, which today are found in more than 50 countries worldwide and used in more than 500 football clubs, including Bayern München, Juventus and FC Barcelona, and are bought by customers such as Coca Cola, Toyota, etc. The products are used for many different sporting events such as football, handball, volleyball, auto racing, basketball and ice hockey. The most unique product is the first of these products – 3D carpets (Figure 6.1 shows an example: they are located – rolled out – just behind the goal line next to the goal on a football field). Through the use of specially developed computer software, the writing on the carpets appears to stand up when seen from a camera angle without this actually being the case, providing companies with more effective branding and advertising of their services in connection with various sporting events.

Figure 6.1 Logopaints 3D carpets

CASE STUDY *(continued)*

There are several different stories about how the idea for 3D carpets arose and nobody knows, several years after they were first launched, which story is actually right – it may well be a combination of parts of several versions. One story focuses on the notion that the idea occurred more or less by chance, when one of the characters from the start-up team was standing on the top of a ladder and noticed that the font on carpets is perceived and looks different from different angles, especially at heights. 'It's almost as if the writing sometimes stands up' was the realisation at that time.

This surprise made the team look more systematically at how writing on carpets (i.e. parallel to the ground) looks from different angles. Several of the start-up team had an educational and experiential background of working with computer science and mathematics at a high level. This knowledge was crucial for development. They ultimately developed a formula that will calculate what different fonts look like from different angles. Their idea was that the formula could be used to streamline advertising, branding and sponsorship in sport. By laying carpets in different places in a stadium (for example, behind the goals in soccer, as shown in Figure 6.1), they could calculate how the writing should be designed in relation to the cameras in a stadium, so that when viewed on television the writing appeared vertical from the viewer's perspective.

The opportunity had quite significant advantages in terms of what was permitted in football stadiums at the time. There are, for example rules on how close signs, barrier boards and the like may be to the touchline for the safety of the players. With these carpets the safety distance is no longer a limitation. Sports people can just run over the carpets. It is suddenly possible for the various stadia to have an extra row of barrier boards beyond the one or two rows of boards that most major stadiums have. Furthermore, and perhaps most importantly, the new row of boards is in far the best place, since it is located exactly behind the goal line. The potential is huge; they know that. But how big? And how can they ensure that no other competitors quickly imitate their products? These are some of the thoughts that the team discuss assiduously in the start-up process.

Patenting: Arguments for and against

Even during the development of the idea they realised that the safest way to avoid imitation by competitors was to patent the idea. But the cost – both in terms of money and time – is enormous when applying for a patent and then you are not even sure of getting the patent, when you apply for it. Neither can you just apply for a single patent that is valid worldwide. Different countries and different continents have their own patenting systems. It is therefore quite costly if you want a patent covering most of the world.

The application for patents is particularly expensive for the start-up team, as they find it necessary to buy in assistance. No one in their family or circle of friends had sufficient knowledge or experience of applying for patents. Therefore they contacted various lawyers, specialists and patent agents specialising in patent applications, and these are very expensive.

CASE STUDY *(continued)*

Economically they were faced with a dilemma. On the one hand, they believed in the idea and the importance of the patent. This spoke in favour of applying for patents in as many parts of the world as possible. On the other hand they didn't have the financial resources required to apply for patents worldwide or even in several countries. They therefore needed to raise more funds if they were to go through with making a broad patent application. This consti-tuted a significantly greater risk if it all went wrong. If they failed to get a patent on the idea, or if the idea simply had no value on the market, all the funds would be wasted and the entrepre-neurs would suffer an economic blow. At the same time they ran a risk in applying for a patent in the sense that it would take much longer before they were ready to enter the market. In that time, potential competitors may be able to catch up with them or find other attractive tech-nical solutions.

A golden middle way

Logopaint's start-up team chose a middle ground and took out a patent in many countries, but with important exceptions. They did not patent in China, Japan, Portugal, Eastern Europe, the Gulf countries and others. Their criteria for selection of countries was first and foremost that the country had a known and conspicuous football league, and next that the patent system in that country was not a complete jungle. They encountered many different problems in the process, especially in legal battles with a South African company that had a similar, but not identical, patent already. Along the way, many of these legal problems were solved with license agreements, but in 2008 Logopaint acquired the South African firm, including their patent rights.

Despite the fact that Logopaint does not have patents in all countries, they are market leaders in all the markets where they operate. In the countries where they have a patent, they have 100 per cent market share, whilst they are content with about 80 per cent of the market where they have no patent. At Logopaint they have often discussed the significance of these patents. On this subject, Logopaints business development director says: 'We would not have been in the position we are in today if we did not have our patents – they gave us access to the market.'

Your immediate interpretation

What does the story tell you about resources? How would you immediately interpret it? The following exercises can help you form an understanding of the story.

- You are the keynote speaker at a conference. The topic is entrepreneur-ship and resources. Start with the Logopaint story and explain to the audience which resources are important to the story and the ways in which resources play a role in the entrepreneurial process.

- Your speech gives rise to a discussion about how to categorise the type of resources that are at stake in the story. What categories do you think are relevant?
- When you get home from the conference, you can't stop thinking about the day's discussions. You think generally about the resources that you believe are critical for starting a new independent organisation. Make a list of these resources.
- You meet one of your friends who has already started an independent organisation. In discussing the importance of resources for entrepreneurs he claims that it is always the idea that is crucial for the entrepreneur's success. If the idea is good, it's easy to attract the necessary resources. What do you think about this argument?

Theories of entrepreneurship

The Logopaint story is a good illustration of how entrepreneurs are constantly being confronted with resource issues. They constantly find themselves in situations where they must weigh up whether it is better to continue working with the resources they have readily available at any given time or alternatively spend their time and limited resources obtaining or developing new and greater resources to pursue their potential. In other words, should the entrepreneur focus on exploiting existing resources or on exploring new resources in the entrepreneurial process?

Balancing takes place in an uncertain context in the sense that decisions about resources must be made before knowing anything about the profits that can be achieved by exploring new resources and/or exploiting existing resources (Shane 2003). How entrepreneurial resource decisions are made are often based on the entrepreneur's expectations about the future.

By exploiting existing resources, the entrepreneur focuses on the effective implementation of his or her existing resource base to evaluate and organise the opportunity. The advantage is that the entrepreneur has control over his resources, and thus the risk associated with resource utilisation is relatively low. The disadvantage may be that focusing on existing resources limits the development potential because the existing resources set the framework determining what is possible. Conversely, the entrepreneur chooses to explore new resources. Here, the benefit is that new resources and combinations of resources can be a catalyst for creative development of the opportunity. The problem attached to this perspective is, among other things, that the entrepreneur does not possess the same control over resources. So, this chapter deals with the choice between exploiting existing resources and explore new resources, and thus the paradox:

> Exploit or Explore

From a market to a resource focus

Before we elaborate on the paradox, we will need to define what we mean by a resource: but first a little history. Theories about resources and their importance originate within the 'strategy' literature, which made a breakthrough in the mid 1980s and early 1990s; although Penrose's (1959) ground-breaking book *The Theory of the Growth of the Firm* had introduced the discussion much earlier. The discussion in the strategy literature focuses on how organisations create long-term competitive advantage. Although the debate has, of course, many different shades, it is primarily divided into two types of argument: the 'inside-out argument' and the 'outside-in argument'. The latter argument maintains that creating sustained competitive advantage comes through better positioning in the market and differentiation from your competitors. On the other hand, the inside-out argument claims that sustained competitive advantage is best established within the organisation through its unique combination of resources. The outside-in argument takes the market as its starting point and then looks into the organisation (hence, outside-in), whilst the inside-out argument is concerned firstly with the organisation's internal resources and then looks at the market (hence, inside-out). The discussion is therefore about whether sustained competitive advantage is created outside the organisation, in the market, or within the organisation, through its resources and capabilities.

However it is important to bear in mind that everyone agrees that both outside-in positioning and possession of unique resource combinations are crucial for obtaining competitive advantage. The disagreement lies in whether one should choose to focus on the unique resource combination in the long term, and adjust in the short term through market positioning, or whether market positioning is decisive in the long term, and that the necessary resources and capabilities must be acquired in the short term.

Within the entrepreneurship literature it is the inside-out argument that is particularly inspiring when resources are discussed. The argument also typically compares with Resource Theory, which we review next.

Resource theory

According to resource theory the best means by which both entrepreneurs and existing organisations gain sustained competitive advantage is through control of valuable resources. Although resource theory was originally developed with larger established organisations in mind (Wernerfelt 1984), it has also had great influence on entrepreneurship theory. Larger established organisations may have ownership of more resources compared to independent entrepreneurs: but what resources the entrepreneur directly owns may be less important than what resources he or she has control over (or has the opportunity to gain control over) (Stevenson & Jarillo 1990). It is therefore immaterial whether someone else owns a given resource that is needed by the entrepreneur as long as he or she has control over it and determines how it is put into use in pursuing the opportunity. Despite resource theory's frequent references to the established organisation, we will hereafter only focus on the entrepreneur.

Additionally, resource theory is built on two basic assumptions. First is the assumption that the actors in an industry are heterogeneous and therefore have unequal control over strategic resources (Barney 1991). They simply do not have access to, and control over, the same resources. The second assumption is that resources are not perfectly transferrable between actors (Barney 1991). This means that resources are not readily passed from one entrepreneur to another because the value of resources depends on the holder and the holder's ability to exploit them.

Based on these assumptions, it is Barney's (1991) view that entrepreneurs achieve sustained competitive advantage by having access to and control over resources that are both heterogeneous and immobile – more on this later.

The resource concept

Before we start discussing what characterises valuable resources in relation to creating competitive advantage, we should discuss what we really mean by a resource. There are many different definitions of what a resource is, but generally within resource theory, resources have a broad definition. Wernerfelt defines a resource as follows: 'By a resource is meant anything which could be thought of as a strength or weakness of a given firm. More formally, a firm's resources at a given time could be defined as those (tangible and intangible) assets which are tied semi permanently to the firm.' (Wernerfelt 1984: 172)

A similar focus to define resources as anything that helps entrepreneurs to perform, is seen in Barney's definition: 'firm resources include all assets, capabilities, organizational processes, firm attributes, information, knowledge, etc. controlled by a firm that enable the firm to conceive of and implement strategies that improve its efficiency and effectiveness.' (Barney 1991: 101) The resource concept thus covers an infinite number of resources that share the fact that they support entrepreneurs in pursuing opportunities through organising.

Valuable resources

The next question then concerns what makes a resource valuable. Barney (1991) writes that resources are heterogeneous and immobile in order to create sustainable competitive advantage. Wernerfelt says that valuable resources are to keep competitors at bay: 'What a firm wants is to create a situation where its own resource position directly or indirectly makes it more difficult for others to catch up.' (Wernerfelt 1984: 173) Here he introduces the concept of 'resource position', which is crucial. An entrepreneur's resource position is formed by the combination of resources over which they have control. Access to, and control over new resources, naturally changes the resource position.

However, access to and control over new resources that immediately seem to strengthen the resource position is not sufficient to ensure that a resource is attractive. The resources that are attractive are those that can help to create a barrier relative to a competitor's resource position. A barrier, in other words, to keep current and future competitors out of the game. On this matter, Wernerfelt writes:

> The general attractiveness of a resource, understood as its capacity to support a resource position barrier, is only a necessary, not a sufficient, condition for a given firm to be interested in it. If everyone goes for the potentially attractive resources and only a few can 'win' in each, firms will lose unless they pick their fights well. So firms need to find those resources which can sustain a resource position barrier, but in which no one currently has one, and where they have a good chance of being among the few who succeed in building one. (Wernerfelt 1984: 174–175)

Barney (1991) has developed some criteria that can be used to assess whether a resource contributes to such a barrier. On these criteria he writes:

> a firm resource must have four attributes: (a) it must be valuable, in the sense that it exploits opportunities and/or neutralizes threats in the firm's environment, (b)

Table 6.1 Evaluation of resources

Characteristics of the resource position				Competitive consequences	
Valuable	Rare	Imitable	Substitutable	Competition	Economic performance
No	–	–	–	Disadvantage	Below average
Yes	No	–	–	Disadvantage	Normal
Yes	Yes	Yes	–	Temporary advantage	Above average
Yes	Yes	Yes	No	Temporary advantage	Above average
Yes	Yes	No	No	Sustained advantage	Highest

Source: Inspired by Barney (1991).

it must be rare among a firm's current and potential competition, (c) it must be imperfectly imitable, and (d) there cannot be strategically equivalent substitutes for this resource that are valuable but neither rare or imperfectly imitable. (Barney 1991: 105–106).

Applying these criteria, one can build the model shown in Table 6.1. The table can be used to compare an entrepreneur's resource position with its competitive implications. So, whilst its primary function is to evaluate the combination of the entrepreneur's resources, it can also be used to assess the value of a single resource.

When the resource position is not valuable, the model predicts that the entrepreneur will be at a competitive disadvantage, perform below average and thus eventually be forced to close down. When the resource position is valuable, but not rare, competitive equality and a normal performance are achieved. The entrepreneur can achieve a better situation with temporary competitive advantage, where his or her performance is above average in two different ways, i.e. when the resource position is valuable and rare but can be imitated, or when the resource position is valuable, rare, imitable but not substitutable. Last, but not least, achieve sustained competitive advantage and the potential for peak economic performance arises when the resource position is valuable, rare and cannot be imitated or substituted.

A three-way split of resources

We have now discussed resource theory and what is needed for resources to be valuable and capable of providing entrepreneurs with sustained competitive advantage by creating a barrier through resource positioning. We have also defined what a resource is, but so far we have worked with resources in broad terms. We will now try to remedy this. We will not restrict the definition, but on the other hand we will divide the resources into a number of different categories.

There are numerous ways in which we may categorise resources. One way might be to divide resources into hardware (start-up capital, machinery, buildings etc.) and software (knowledge, social relations, rumour, reputation etc.). On occasions we can also distinguish between natural resources and intangible resources. This has historically been the case in economic theory with its emphasis on physical capital and labour, although in more recent times sociologists have also indicated the importance of other resources. Here, inspired by Coleman (1988), we categorise resources under the following headings:

- Financial resources
- Human resources
- Social resources.

Somewhat simplified, financial resources refers to the money that the entrepreneur has in his or her pocket, whether borrowed or their own. Human resources refers to the knowledge and skills that the entrepreneur (or team of entrepreneurs) possesses. Social resources are the benefits the entrepreneur enjoys through the use of personal contacts and acquaintances.

In discussing the tri-partite categorisation it should be mentioned that the concept of 'capital' is often used synonymously with resources in the literature. Thus, some talk about financial capital (financial resources), human capital (human resources) and social capital (social resources). This terminology follows a supply-logic where the supply is understood to be the resources that a person owns or has temporary control over (Stevenson & Jarillo 1990). Financial capital is a term that refers to the supply of financial resources at an entrepreneur's disposal. Similarly, human capital is a concept for the supply of human resources that an entrepreneur has available. Finally, social capital is a term for the supply of resources that the entrepreneur has available through his contacts. In this book we use the concept of resource rather than the concept of capital. Table 6.2 provides some specific examples of financial, human and social resources.

Financial resources

Although there are many different types of financial resources, it makes sense, in terms of this book's objective, to work with two main types: equity

Table 6.2 Three categories of resources

	Financial resources	Human resources	Social resources
Explanation	Capital supplied by the owners or external players	Intangible resources such as knowledge and experience	Resources provided by the entrepreneur's personal contacts
Examples	Equity capital (own money) Debt capital (borrowed money)	Education and training Experiences (business, start-up, managerial experience . . .) Engagement, motivation and enterprise	Entrepreneurial role models A large network Diverse networks Supportive circle of friends

and debt. Equity is the financial resources made available by the owners of an organization with the expectation of a say in decisions and future returns. Supply of equity can either be via owners' deposits of cash or other assets, or by the owners retaining a portion of the profits of the organization. Debt capital is the capital not provided by the organization's owners such as mortgages, bank loans, supplier credits, etc. Debt capital is often divided into what can be described as short-term debt and long-term debt.

Human resources

The list of examples of human resources is almost endless (Becker 1993). We will therefore only concern ourselves with a few. A human resource is inherent within people. Formal education may enable individuals to be more able to recognize opportunities and implement entrepreneurial processes, whilst more focused training – such as entrepreneurship training – should hopefully contribute positively to the entrepreneurial process. Experience also seems to play a significant role, although one can speak of many types of experience. The requisite experience is, of course, dependent upon the type of entrepreneurial process that you have to deal with as an entrepreneur. Typically, relevant work experience and previous start-up and managerial experience are types of experience that are essential to the successful implementation of entrepreneurial processes. Cognitive psychologists have also identified a wide range of cognitive abilities that seem to affect the entrepreneurial process positively and which can be regarded as human resources. Several of these we have already pointed out in Chapter 2.

Social resources

Social resources are somewhat different from the other two. Firstly, it is not a resource that a single person can possess in the way that they might with both financial and human resources. Social resources are something created in the interaction between people (Coleman 1988). They belong to the relationship between these people, but not the individual. In this way, social resources are something that entrepreneurs and intrapreneurs have access to through their personal relationships. Chapter 7 elaborates on examples of social resources and how they can be provided.

Differences and connections between resource categories

The interesting thing about the above tripartite division is not so much the division in itself, but the basic differences between the three types of resources. Some of the resources are reduced when used, while others actually multiply with increased use. For example, financial resources are reduced when they are used. Money can only be used once – unfortunately. However, it's not necessarily true for human and social resources. When the entrepreneur uses the knowledge gained from education, there is also a revitalization of knowledge that takes place, because it is being reproduced and possibly strengthened. It is commonly accepted that new knowledge is created when existing knowledge is brought into play in new contexts. For example, educational knowledge can contribute to the creation of new knowledge, and through its use, the human resource increases. This is often the case with social resources as well. When one interacts with the environment and one's personal contacts in an effort to provide valuable resources to implement the entrepreneurial process, that generates new knowledge in the relationship, which can be used later. Pushed to its logical extreme, one could say that people who never talk to anyone and don't know anyone will have difficulty getting hold of resources in their environment in comparison with individuals who frequently interact with their environment. One can therefore again conclude that the increased use of social resources may contribute to the further development of the resource.

The last thing we need to discuss about the tripartite division is the relationship between the three types of resources. It is interesting that the various resources can be transformed from one type to another (Bourdieu 1986). Social resources are often seen as the resource type that activates the other two (Burt 1992). For example, it is possible to use one's personal networks (social capital) to recruit new qualified employees (human resources) or to obtain financial resources. There are actually several studies that suggest that personal contacts, including friends and family, are by far the leading inves-

Table 6.3 International variations in financial, human and social capital

	US	Brazil	Sweden	China	Ghana	India
GDP per capita 2010 (2008 US Dollars)*	46,653	10,847	36,139	7,206	1,533	3,354
Mean years of schooling of adults**	12.4	7.2	11.6	7.5	7.1	4.4
Most people can be trusted**	39.3 %	9.4 %	68.0 %	52.3 %	8.5 %	23.3 %

Note: * World Bank: Human Development Index (http://hdr.undp.org/en/)
** World Value Survey (http://www.worldvaluessurvey.org/, last accessed 22 May 2012).

tor in the entrepreneur's start-up processes. However there are many other ways in which the three types can interact. You can buy advice on marketing (human resources), through use of your financial resources. Or you can use your knowledge of business plans (human resources) to convince a banker that you need more credit (financial resources).

International differences

It's no great surprise that there are large international differences in the average supply of resources available to individuals worldwide. Table 6.3 provides an insight into these differences. As a measure of financial capital, the table shows how GDP per capita varies from US$3,354 in India to US$46,653 in the USA in 2010. There are thus significant differences in average wealth. One way to measure differences in human capital is the average schooling of a country's population. Here again, the table shows great variation, whilst the US population goes to school for an average of 12.4 years, the average in India is just 4.4 years. Last but not least, the proportion of the population in a country that considers that people can be trusted is used as a measure of social capital. Here, Sweden ranks highest with 68 per cent of people believing that one can trust people, whilst Brazil and Ghana are at the bottom with only about 9 per cent believing that most people can be trusted. These indicators clearly suggest large international variation in financial, human and social capital. Furthermore, it should be noted that within each national context there can also be variations depending on the political, social and historical fabric of society.

Resource exploitation

Now back to the paradox. As mentioned earlier, the entrepreneur is faced with a dilemma in relation to identification and use of resources. The entrepreneur will assess whether he or she must continue working with and leveraging the existing resources that they have available or whether they must use their often limited resources to explore new resources. We are talking here about the paradox: resource exploitation versus resource exploration.

According to March, exploitation activities cover: 'efficiency, selection, implementation, execution' (March 1991: 71). This means that the entrepreneur uses the existing resource position through rational and systematic consideration of how he or she can most effectively select and deploy those resources so that they best support the opportunity.

Thus, resource identification and use is about strengthening an already given direction (Van de Ven et al 1999). This underlines the assumption that the entrepreneur has, in advance, a picture of the direction in which he or she will move. The entrepreneur, in other words, has a clearly defined goal for the resource use. The challenge is to maximise efficient use of existing resources to achieve the goal. Further, the perspective assumes that the entrepreneur knows, in advance, the value of a resource in terms of the entrepreneurial process. Resources are objective entities. They are what they appear to be. From the outset, the entrepreneur can point out which resources he or she must identify and use in order to realise the goal.

Given that the starting point is the optimisation of existing resources, the entrepreneur is presumed to have management and control of resource use in the entrepreneurial process: it reduces the complexity and risk associated with the process. On the other hand, the entrepreneur, as mentioned earlier, cannot be expected to move the opportunity in radically new and unexpected directions, as using existing resources limits the opportunity and its realisation. The resource exploitation perspective thus leads to a relatively stable and linear entrepreneurial process.

As the exploitation perspective in many ways excludes the identification and application of radically new resources and resource combinations and hence new ways to exploit opportunities, it reflects a short-term approach to resources. The reason is that the entrepreneur focuses on how he or she can improve in the light of the current resource position. This involves not thinking about how he or she can keep up with the continuous processes of change in future markets, where products, services and processes constantly become out-dated and/or obsolete and must make room for the new, which requires exploration.

Resource exploration

Usually the entrepreneur does not control, from the start of the entrepreneurial process, all the resources required to realise the opportunity. 'For most new ventures, an optimal set of organizational resources is not developed instantly but rather evolves, and changes over a period of weeks, months, and years' (Lichtenstein and Brush 2001: 41). The entrepreneur experiences resource constraints. Similarly, the entrepreneurial process is often dynamic and characterised by risk and complexity so the entrepreneur cannot easily assume that the existing resources are sufficient, or that he or she can predict in advance the value of resources in terms of the entrepreneurial process. In other words, resources cannot be taken for granted. For these reasons, the entrepreneur starting from a position of limited resources must explore and perhaps even create new resources.

According to March exploration activities include 'search, variation, risk taking, experimentation, play, flexibility, discovery, innovation' (March 1991: 71). Unlike the exploitation perspective, exploration is about expansion, flexibility, experimentation and expression, which may lead to the creation or discovery of new opportunities and countless new ways of evaluating and organising. Here the entrepreneur is not limited and focused on the existing resource position and its optimisation. Instead through play, proactive and open interaction with the environment, the entrepreneur attempts to create resources that can lead him or her in exciting new directions in terms of the developing entrepreneurial process. This is resource behaviour, where new boundaries are constantly tested.

That new boundaries are being constantly tested, naturally also means a more risky and unpredictable entrepreneurial process. The entrepreneur simply cannot predict how he or she will end up. Unpredictable resource identification and usage, as previously mentioned, makes it difficult for the entrepreneur to establish control over the entrepreneurial process. Especially because the entrepreneur must acquire resources, before the actual value of the opportunity is known it is in the interaction with the environment that the value of the resource is created. This means that the value is a result of how the entrepreneur actually utilises the resource in the entrepreneurial process.

The exploration perspective reveals a dynamic approach to the identification and use of resources. There is also a forward-looking and long-term perspective. The reason is that an exploratory entrepreneur is continually open to unexpected resources that can lead to radically new opportunities or ways to exploit them. In this way the entrepreneur is also better equipped to survive in the longer term with the future's markets requirement for continual change.

Sarasvathy's (2008) model presented in Chapter 5 gives an idea of how the entrepreneurial process can be seen as having a starting point in the use of limited resources ('Who I am', 'What I know', and 'Whom I know'). However, it is through interaction and exploration of the environment in the entrepreneurial process that entrepreneurs gain control over resources beyond immediate verification. Through exploration, new resources are constantly added that support the entrepreneurial process by being transformed into opportunities and organisations. Sarasvathy's (2008) theory can thus be seen primarily as an example of the exploration perspective's representation of the resource issue, despite the theory also having elements of resource exploitation.

A similar logic is found in Baker and Nelson's (2005) bricolage approach to resources. Overall, the bricolage concept refers to resource exploitation logic, because it is fundamentally about 'making do with what is at hand'. Nevertheless, the bricolage concept certainly contains elements of resource exploration, since the point is precisely that entrepreneurs are exploring and creating new resources through 'applying combinations of the resources at hand to new problems and opportunities' (Baker & Nelson 2005: 333). Here, the entrepreneur defies the environment and his own resource limitations and will sometimes get successful organisations to grow apparently from more or less nothing.

Resources: exploit or explore?

We have, above, discussed two different perspectives on how entrepreneurs can relate to resource identification and use. The discussion is summarised in Table 6.4.

The exploitation perspective thus argues that the entrepreneur should make effective use of existing resources that are available, whilst the exploration perspective holds that the entrepreneur should seek new resources based on the limited resources that he or she typically controls. The focus of the exploitation perspective is to 'improve effectiveness of your current situation', and this perspective is very much about stability and the short-term. The exploration perspective is more about the entrepreneur continually 'moving on' by interacting with the environment and creating new resources and resource

Table 6.4 The paradox: Exploit or explore

	Exploit	Explore
Resources	Existing resources	New resources
The entrepreneur's role	To use existing resources efficiently	To find and gain control of the new resources
Focus	To improve efficiency	To move
Changeability	Stability	Dynamics
Perspective	Short term	Long term

combinations. It is therefore directed towards something more long-term and represents a more dynamic approach to resources in entrepreneurship.

However, it is important to emphasise that entrepreneurs in practice can benefit from both perspectives. As March (1991) argues the discussion about exploitation and exploration is not a question of 'either-or' but rather a question of balance. March writes: 'maintaining an appropriate balance between exploration and exploitation is a primary factor in system survival and prosperity' (March 1991: 71).

A theoretical interpretation

Below are two different interpretations of the Logopaint story that started the chapter. In the interpretations the story is related to the above theory and interpreted from each of paradox perspectives.

The exploiting perspective

If you choose to look at the Logopaint story from an exploitation perspective, the focus will primarily be on how Logopaint attempted to optimise the use of their existing resources. The story is about the schism between financial resources and the application for patents. The first question that arises is what type of resources a patent represents. Is this an example of a monopolised human resource or a 'tied' financial resource base? The immediate impression is that a patent is closest to what we refer to as a human resource. The patent begins as knowledge in the form of the formula being developed. Later it becomes a patent, but the patent is really just a temporary monopolisation of the knowledge inherent in Logopaint's entrepreneurs from the outset. In terms of the exploitation perspective the patent therefore represents a crystallisation of existing resources, which were owned by the Logopaint entrepreneurs from the beginning of the entrepreneurial process.

Furthermore, from the exploitation perspective, the purpose of the loan capital appears to be for the optimisation of existing resources through patenting and not the development of new resources. The act of applying for the patent is, in itself, an indication of wanting to optimise what one already possesses and is good at. The Logopaint story focuses on improving the existing situation and provides no indication that the firm was attempting to 'move on' by simultaneously creating resources with which to create new opportunities that could create competitive advantage in the long-term in respect of future markets.

When the story is interpreted from an exploitation perspective, we can also argue that despite the fact that Logopaint obtained new capital to fund patent applications, they still felt that they were only working with those resources over which they had considerable control. Firstly, they sought patents only when they believed that the probability of success was greatest. They did not apply for patents in markets where they believed that the risk of their patent application failing was great. Thus, the financial resources used were under reasonable control. Secondly, they used the loan carefully without taking too great a risk that this capital might suddenly take control of them, for instance through loan conditions. One can thus argue that Logopaint primarily optimised the resources they controlled. They restricted themselves to applying for patents with the money they could control, despite the fact that some of this money was borrowed.

The exploring perspective

Logopaint's story can also be interpreted completely differently, i.e. from an exploration perspective. As is often the case in entrepreneurship, Logopaint had, at the start, basically no control over all the resources necessary to realise their potential. They were, in other words, left to explore the environment in order to generate additional financial resources. In connection with the exploration, the company focused on finding and increasing control over as many new resources as humanly possible. It can easily be imagined that Logopaint had, in some way a risk profile that prevented them from borrowing certain types of capital. It is very likely, but the story may still be interpreted to mean that they wanted patent protection in as many markets as possible.

Logopaint's limitations are primarily set by their ability to obtain the financial resources required to design and process patent applications. So when they chose not to apply for a patent in the Chinese market for instance, it was largely because they simply could not fund the application. It is not because they chose to limit themselves and stick to the resources they already had control over. So, it's the various markets, their risk profile and the associated potential capital that sets limits on the number of patent applications. In other words, Logopaint's strategy was to obtain as many patents as it was possible to borrow the money to fund applications for. By gaining many patents they could then explore opportunities in a larger geographical area, thereby opening the door to more new opportunities. This allowed them to move developmentally and create competitive advantage in the long-term.

The story's conclusion underlines how, as mentioned in the exploration perspective, resource value cannot always be predicted in advance. Logopaint is, in any case, doubtful as to whether the acquired patents create the value intended, as the company also ended up with a large market share in those markets where they have not acquired a patent for their product.

Testing the theory

Based on the above thoughts and discussions, you are ready to develop your own tests to understand resources and how they are part of the entrepreneurial process. The following are suggestions for exercises.

 EXERCISES

1 **Interview an entrepreneur.** Make a list of interview questions that seek to capture some of the central debates on the role of resources in entrepreneurship. Contact an entrepreneur, and interview him or her in order to test the theory presented in this chapter.
2 **The resource utilise.** Which innovative ideas can you come up with, to start leveraging your existing resources? Make a list of your existing resources, providing an overview divided into financial, human and social resources. Now try to combine these resources to come up with innovative business ideas that can facilitate an entrepreneurial process.
3 **Give advice to a friend.** One of your friends who is a trained electrician, and has always had a passion for design, tells you that he is working on an opportunity. He intends to design upmarket and expensive lighting. You have confidence that he has the skill to put the electronics, light and design together with the ability to make it special. Then he asks you for financial advice. He has saved US$50,000, and is willing to put up more. But, on its own, the US$50,000 is not enough. What should he do? What options does he have? And what is important to consider?

 LITERATURE

Alvarez, S.A. & Busenitz, L.W. (2001) 'The entrepreneurship of resource-based theory', *Journal of Management*, 27, 755–775.

Baker, T. & Nelson, R.E. (2005) 'Creating Something from Nothing: Resource Construction through Entrepreneurial Bricolage', *Administrative Science Quarterly*, 50, 329–366.

Barney, J.B. (1991) 'Firm resources and sustained competitive advantage', *Journal of Management*, 17(1), 99–120.

Becker, G.S. (1993) *Human capital: A theoretical and empirical analysis, with special reference to education*, Chicago: University of Chicago Press.

Bourdieu, P. (1986) 'The forms of capital', in Richardson, J.G. (ed.), *Handbook of theory and research for the sociology of education*, New York: Greenwood, 241–258.

Burt, R.S. (1992) *Structural holes – The social structure of competition*, London: Harvard University Press.

Coleman, J.S. (1988) 'Social capital in the creation of human capital', *American Journal of Sociology*, 94, 95–120.

Lichtenstein, B.M.B. & Brush, C.G. (2001) 'How Do "Resource Bundles" Develop and Change in New Ventures? A Dynamic Model and Longitudinal Exploration', *Entrepreneurship Theory and Practice*, 25(3), 37–59.

March, J.G. (1991) 'Exploration and exploitation in organisational learning', *Organisation Science*, 2, 71–87.

Penrose, E.T. (1959) *The Theory of the Growth of the Firm*, New York: John Wiley.

Priem, R.L. & Butler, J.E. (2001) 'Is the resource-based 'view' a useful perspective for strategic management research?', *Academy of Management Review*, 26(1), 22–40.

Sarasvathy, S.D. (2008) *Effectuation: Elements of Entrepreneurial Expertise*, Cheltenham, UK and Northampton, MA, USA: Edward Elgar Publishing.

Shane, S. (2003) *A General Theory of Entrepreneurship: The Individual-opportunity Nexus*, Cheltenham, UK and Northampton, MA, USA: Edward Elgar Publishing.

Stevenson, H.H & Jarillo, J.C. (1990) 'A Paradigm of Entrepreneurship: Entrepreneurial Management', *Strategic Management Journal*, 11, 17–27.

Van de Ven, A.H., Polley, D., Garud, R. & Venkataraman, S. (1999) *The Innovation Journey*, Oxford: Oxford University Press.

Wernerfelt, B. (1984) 'A resource-based view of the firm', *Strategic Management Journal*, 5, 171–180.

7

Networks

An entrepreneur without a network is like a fisherman without a fishing rod. In order to be successful, the entrepreneurial process requires the involvement of more than just the entrepreneur. Entrepreneurs involve a number of different people through the entrepreneurial process. These may be people closely connected to the organisation, including customers, suppliers, investors, auditors, etc. However, it might also include people who have a less visible, but equally crucial role in the entrepreneur's success. Here we might consider the significance of receiving free help and advice from experienced friends and family members along with the importance of emotional support and having the right 'backing on the home front'.

So, the social environment, of which they are a part, including the network they possess, influences entrepreneurs. Entrepreneurial decisions are made not in a vacuum, but rather in social contexts. In a ground-breaking article, Aldrich and Zimmer wrote: 'The approach we take, by contrast, focuses on entrepreneurship as embedded in a social context, channelled and facilitated or constrained and inhibited by people's position in social network' (Aldrich & Zimmer 1986: 4).

Entrepreneurship in practice

The music industry is loaded with entrepreneurship, networking and shifting careers. We now introduce you to a story about an entrepreneur who out of his interest in Hip hop music engaged in a number of entrepreneurial activities in collaboration with other people.

CASE STUDY

A hip hop entrepreneur

(Devised by the authors)

'I'm a pornstar baby baby baby pornstar ...' So sings an entrepreneur and musician who over many years made his way from being an underground hip hopper to a commercial and successful dance musician, primarily within the Danish market. It is the story of Mike Simonsen, who along with the two well-known and respected DJs, producer Ronnie NME Veiler and producer Kenn 'The Killer' started the dance group Cargo. Cargo's best-known hit is probably 'Pornstar'. It is important here to bear in mind that it's the story of Mike we are putting the spotlight on and not the group Cargo.

Mike, an otherwise ordinary boy, comes from a small provincial town in Denmark. During his early teenage years he became interested in hip hop music and the underground culture associated with it. At that time, hip hop was an underground culture in Europe that had not been noticed by the vast majority of European teens. It was a long time before hip hop groups like the Beastie Boys and Run-DMC in the late 1980s made their way into the European charts. The entire European wave was initiated by, among other things, two films called 'Beat Street' and 'Breaking'.

Before hip hop's commercial breakthrough, there was a small crowd of young Europeans who were heavily inspired by American hip hop culture. They made hip hop music, 'scratching' turntables and painting illegal graffiti at night in their local areas. Many of them were dedicated, living and breathing hip hop. To a great extent we are talking about an underground culture where very few are involved, but where those involved all know each other. Many of the early hip hoppers then became DJs in the discos and nightclubs across the country. Over time the hip hop culture grew much larger and more precisely in the footsteps of commercial successes like the Beastie Boys and Run-DMC.

Then it got serious

As Mike got older, it became clear to him that he wanted to be something 'in music'. He tried many different things throughout his youth, but everything can be related back to his dedication and passion for hip hop culture. At 22 years of age, he and a good friend and hip hop / DJ colleague started their own studio. It was a dream come true to be able to sit in his own studio, but at the same time they also had an ambition to get a record deal and put their hip hop music on the air. It was difficult, but they fought hard for several years with studio costs being funded through various ad hoc jobs such as production of radio commercials and various DJ jobs.

At some point they realised that they were stuck and not really moving forward; so they decided to close the studio and go their separate ways. They wanted new adventures and to explore other opportunities to break through. At this point Mike's ambitions had changed. From his earlier self-perception as a hip-hopper, he now had a wider view of himself as an

CASE STUDY *(continued)*

artist and rapper. This meant that he had become more open to other music styles and the commercial part of the music industry. Mike's ambition was now to become a successful musician without breaking the connection to his past and hip hop.

An opportunity is created

A few months before Mike and his partner closed their studio, Mike contacted two former acquaintances from the early hip hop period – Ronnie NME Veil and Kenn 'The Killer'. Both Ronnie and Kenn were by then recognised and respected DJs and producers who had long had commercial success on the Danish scene. Mike had not been in contact with Ronnie or Kenn for many years, but he remembered them from the earlier hip hop days and they also remembered Mike.

Mike wanted them to do a remix of Mike and his partner's latest attempt at a breakthrough – a song called 'What's the Matter in Paradise?' If they could get these famous people to remix their number, it would be easier to break through: but it never materialised, so they decided to close the studio and give up the song.

Instead, Ronnie and Kenn got Mike to rap for a number they were about to record. As often happens when talents meet by chance, there is creativity: in this instance a track called 'The Horn', a dance number in keeping with 1990s dance music. They decided to call the group Cargo. It was relatively easy for them to get the single 'The Horn' published by Scandinavian Record, mainly because of the reputations of Ronnie and Kenn. Nevertheless, the record company stipulated that their next single must be a big hit if they were to continue to release Cargo's records. Cargo's second single, to be called 'Loaded with Power', had to reach the top five in the 'dance chart'.

New strategy

As a reaction to the record company's requirements the team changed their strategy. They were all DJs with a relatively large network of colleagues. They also knew that the 'dance chart' acts as a guide to many of the decisions that record companies make. The 'dance chart' is a list of the dance hits that DJs across the country consider to be most successful on a weekly basis. So, it is the DJs – with all their semi-secret and non-commercial releases – who decide what is in the 'dance chart'. So, the 'dance chart' is not like other charts, which reflect the singles with the highest commercial sales. Of course those sales may be the result of the 'dance chart's' weekly list. The different DJs' votes are weighted according to how many people are on the dance floor when each song is played. This means that the DJs who play at the major venues have tremendous power over which songs will be voted for.

The three musicians in Cargo burned about 20 CDs with their new track 'Loaded with Power' and sent the CDs to the most powerful of their DJ colleagues encouraging them to vote the number into the 'dance chart'. The following week they entered the top 10, and the following week were in the top two. The single was later Grammy-nominated.

With the single 'Loaded with Power' placed in the 'dance chart' Cargo got a record contract for an entire album. The album entitled 'The Movie' sold 2,500 copies.

CASE STUDY *(continued)*

An opportunity is organised

However, this was not enough for Mike and Cargo. They did not think they had made enough of the musical material. Most of all, they were annoyed that the record company has not prioritised them in budgetary terms compared to other emerging groups. The commercial success was not satisfactory although, in the wake of the release, the group undertook an extended tour, primarily consisting of club venues.

At one point, the director of record company, who obviously has an impact on the prioritisation of new emerging groups, was replaced. The new director happened by chance to hear his young daughter singing 'I'm a pornstar pornstar baby baby . . . ' – the most famous song from the album 'The Movie'.

The director asked his daughter who she was listening to and of course she told him it was Cargo. According to Mike this event was decisive in the Director's decision to change the company's strategy and priorities for Cargo. Among other things Cargo were provided with a completely different and larger budget. At the same time the first album was re-launched, but now with a new cover and a new female frontman. Everything else remained exactly as before although the new album was called 'The Movie Goes Party'. Among other things, the larger advertising budget meant that commercials for the new album appeared on one of the largest national TV stations.

The new album debuted at number 13 in the Danish list of best selling records. The following week they were in sixth place and in the third week in seventh place. In all, the record spent six weeks in the top 20 of most sold albums and went gold platinum (25,000 records sold) within a month.

Figure 7.1 The dance group Cargo

CASE STUDY *(continued)*

A new chapter

After several years Cargo disbanded. Mike lived for a time doing different jobs including an apprenticeship as a graphic designer and then operating his own small advertising agency, whilst enjoying his DJ job at the weekends. At times he was also a professional DJ and had no other income. By chance and in connection with a DJ job he met Aba – a younger man with an interest and musical skills in dance music. They got together as a group AbaSimonsen (www.facebook.com/abasimonsen, last accessed 22 May 2012) and currently have great success with remixes and their own numbers in the Danish market. Their primary income is through gigs where payment is now considerably higher due to their well-known and popular remixes and tracks. They are currently working to move beyond Danish borders. So be aware – one day you may suddenly find them playing at your local club or on your local radio station.

Your immediate interpretation

What does the story of Mike and Cargo tell you about the importance of networking? What is your initial interpretation of the story? The following exercises can help you to form an understanding.

- Do networks play a role in the story? Make a list of the meanings attributed to network and 'networking' as expressed in the story. Discuss these meanings.
- How has Mike created his network? How has he used his network, and is there is a pattern in how he uses it?
- What does Mike's network look like? Does his network include many or just a few people? Are the people in his network similar or different? What other factors can be gainfully used to describe Mike's network?
- You have decided to start your own organisation and want to make sure that you get the most out of your network. What would you take into account in your attempts to 'network' and in creating the perfect network of contacts? Who should your network contain and how will you get in contact with them?
- You meet one of your friends. She is a successful entrepreneur. In discussing the importance of networking for entrepreneurs she declares that she was quite conscious and calculating in her use of networks, and that explains her success. What do you think of this argument?

Theories of entrepreneurship

The story we have just presented has many links to this chapter's topic, namely the theory of entrepreneurship and networking. The theory concerns how networks affect the entrepreneur's decisions and behaviour. However, that's about as far as any agreement on the subject goes because there is considerable disagreement about the importance of networking and the way entrepreneurs should network. In terms of these disagreements we can identify two fundamentally different perspectives on the significance of networks and how to approach networking. The two perspectives are reflected in the paradox: rational or embedded? One perspective discusses whether entrepreneurs can regard the network as a rational tool for deliberate and calculated use in order to succeed in their efforts to discover or create, evaluate and organise. This focuses on how networks can be changed and optimised depending on what resources the entrepreneur needs. The second perspective sees the network as a result of the entrepreneur's past. Networks are thus a consequence of the life that is led, and are thus something within which people are deeply embedded. The individual therefore has little possibility to manage and use the network efficiently. In other words, networks comprise uncontrollable conditions that the entrepreneur cannot change at will. Put another way, this chapter deals with the paradox of whether a network is a rational tool or a set of uncontrollable conditions within which the entrepreneur is embedded. In short, the paradox is:

Rational or embedded

Theory of entrepreneurship and networks

Theory of entrepreneurship and networks builds on and is a source of traditional social network theory. The traditional theory, originally developed in sociology, has since spread to several social science disciplines, including organisational and entrepreneurship theory. The central argument of social network theory is that the network influences individuals' behaviour. Lin (2001) mentions four main ways in which networks influence individuals' behaviour. Networks can help to:

- provide people with information that can be applied to the situations they face;
- influence other people in the network. Network relations have, so to speak, influence on the decisions and actions made;

- create social legitimacy for people within a network structure. People can then effectively gain access to resources through other individuals in the network vouching for them;
- develop and enhance personal identities. Individuals can strengthen their identity by interacting with others who wish to maintain their identity.

The theory of entrepreneurship and networks has primarily focused on the resources that can be provided through the network. Hoang and Antončič write:

> Interpersonal and interorganizational relationships are viewed as the media through which actors gain access to a variety of resources held by other actors. With the exception of work on the role of networks to access capital . . . most research has focused on the entrepreneur's access to intangible resources . . . A key benefit of networks for the entrepreneurial process is the access they provide to information and advice. (Hoang & Antončič 2003: 169)

The resources that can be mobilised through social networks are often referred to as social capital. Social capital refers to the means and resources, the entrepreneur enjoys through using his personal contacts and acquaintances.

Although social network theory has a long history, the interest in networking within entrepreneurship is somewhat newer. The first contribution dates back to Birley (1985), Aldrich & Zimmer (1986) and Johannisson (1988). These contributions can be seen as a backlash against the research characterised by, among others, the psychological tradition in which the entrepreneur was treated as an individual without regard for the environment within which the individual existed. On the contrary, as mentioned, the theory of entrepreneurship and networks considers an entrepreneurial network to be a medium through which the entrepreneur may gain access to different resources. In this way, the individual and the individual's environment function simultaneously in the theory of entrepreneurship and networking. In fact, the network's role is not only related to the start of a new organisation but is valid throughout the entire life cycle of the organisation (Hoang & Antončič 2003).

The heterogeneity argument

However, before we address the paradox, we must look more closely at different types of network arguments that characterise both sides of the paradox. For although there is consensus that networks play a crucial role for entrepreneurs, there is disagreement about what a good and efficient network looks like. The dissimilarity – or heterogeneity – argument suggests that differences among individuals in the entrepreneur's network and weak relationships between these are the most efficient network. This should be seen in relation to the argument for uniformity or the homogeneity argument, where it is argued that networks consisting of uniform (homogeneous) and strongly associated persons are most effective. This argument is presented in the following section on homogeneity.

The foundation of the argument for heterogeneity is that entrepreneurs obtain optimal access to valuable market information that they can apply through the entrepreneurial process by having networks that consist of diverse individuals with regard to their attitudes, values, jobs, experiences, skills, etc. Through these differences among the people of the network, the entrepreneur becomes, so to speak, the centre and bridge for information and increases the possibility of discovering or creating, evaluating and organising new opportunities.

The argument takes place at two different levels:

1. The relational level, which focuses on the relationship between the individual entrepreneur and his/her contacts. The relational level is illustrated in Figure 7.2 by the dotted box between the entrepreneur and his/her colleague.
2. In contrast, the network level includes all contacts the entrepreneur has in his/her entire network. The network level is illustrated in Figure 7.2 by the box around the entrepreneur's total network. Overall, Figure 7.2 illustrates the heterogeneity argument.

The relational level

At the relational level the heterogeneity argument is strongly inspired by – if one cannot actually say it comes from – Granovetter's ground-breaking article of 1973 on the strength of weak relationships. Granovetter defines the strength of relationships as follows: 'the strength of a tie is a (probably linear) combination of the amount of time, the emotional intensity, the intimacy (mutual confiding), and the reciprocal services which characterize the tie' (Granovetter 1973: 1361). So, the less emotional attachment, trust and reciprocity between an entrepreneur and his or her contact, the weaker the relationship. In Figure 7.2 a weak relationship is indicated by the dashed arrows between the entrepreneur and the entrepreneur's contacts (friend, customer, family member or colleague).

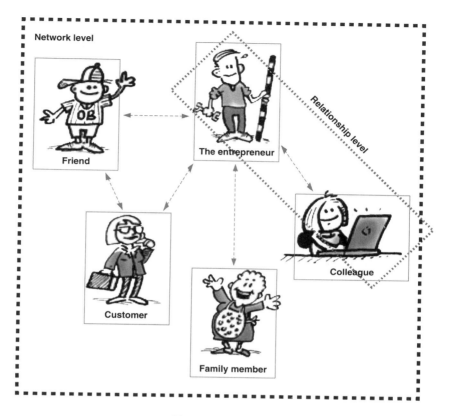

Figure 7.2 Weak relations and a heterogeneous network

Granovetter argues that the strength of the relationship affects the nature and value of the information that the entrepreneur gets from his/her contacts. According to him, one is more inclined to receive valuable information from the weak relationships because these relationships generally behave in other social networks than the entrepreneur himself and therefore possess different information. He thus believes that entrepreneurs with many relatively weak links and relatively few strong relationships have better access to valuable information and better ability to disseminate information about their options than entrepreneurs with relatively few weak relationships and relatively many strong relationships.

The network level

Burt (1992) backs up Granovetter's argument for weak relationships. He argues that the typical drawback of strong relationships is that they are often strongly related to each other and thus possess the same information. In this way having many strong relationships is unimportant because, through using the existing network, you already have access to the information that these contacts possess. Information one can receive from a strongly related contact can surely also be gained from other strongly related contacts in the network. For example, it is not necessary or more rewarding to have two uncles with experience in the consulting industry, if it is this area of business in which you want to become established. The advice offered by each of the two uncles is unlikely to differ significantly from the other, and the advice from one uncle and the contact with him will usually be enough.

At the same time, Burt (1992) raises the argument for the heterogeneity of the network level, where the entrepreneur's total network, meaning all the entrepreneur's contacts, is brought into focus. In this context, Burt talks of the importance of structural holes in the overall network and the opportunity for entrepreneurs to serve as a bridge between different parts of the overall network. Structural holes in a network occur when some individuals in the entrepreneur's network are not interconnected – do not know each other. The more people who do not know each other, the more structural holes there are in the entrepreneur's network. When there are some people who do not know each other, there will be people in the network who become key figures and build bridges between different parts of the overall network. They get access to what Burt calls non-redundant information, which is crucial in order to discover or create, evaluate and organise opportunities, i.e. information that no other contacts in the network possess. Figure 7.2 shows a network with a structural hole between the entrepreneur's family members, customers and friends and colleagues.

The homogeneity argument

The argument about homogeneity is almost the opposite of the heterogeneity argument. Here it is argued that dense networks are the best, where as many people as possible in the network know each other, and where the relationship between the entrepreneur and these people is strong. Weak contacts and heterogeneous networks consisting of many bridges therefore play no role in this argument. How can that be?

The starting point for disagreement between the homogeneity and heterogeneity arguments is basically what kinds of resources are considered to be important. The heterogeneity argument focuses on information and specifically market information primarily related to discovering or creating, evaluating and organising capabilities. The homogeneity argument however, focuses on resources, such as emotional support, sensitive market infor-

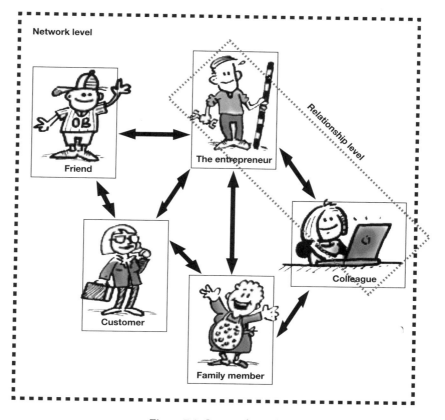

Figure 7.3 Strong relationships and a homogeneous network

mation and access to financial resources. From this perspective it is therefore about gaining access to the type of resources that are exchanged only
if both parties trust each other, spend much time together, have an emotional attachment to each other and where reciprocity exists between the
two parties: Granovetter's definition of what creates a strong relationship.
The homogeneity argument is strongly inspired by Coleman's (1988) work
on the relationship between social and human capital. As is the case with the
heterogeneity argument the homogeneity argument may also be explained
on a relational level and network level (see Figure 7.3).

The relational level

On the relational level, the homogeneity argument's point is that the entrepreneur needs contacts that he or she has strong and close relations with.
In such strong relationships, trust and mutual commitment between the

contacts are often established, increasing the likelihood that the entrepreneur will receive the necessary emotional support required under the otherwise sometimes chaotic and complex entrepreneurial process. People who are not close to the entrepreneur will probably not spend their time and energy on emotional support. The same applies to the resource-sensitive market information. There is information, e.g. about markets, that people only share with people they trust. Moreover, very sensitive market information, such as information on conflicts or research efforts in another organisation, can be crucial to successfully discover or create, evaluate and organise opportunities.

Regarding access to financial capital the homogeneity argument may also be used. Bygrave et al (2003) surveyed the relationship between entrepreneurs and their private investors across 29 countries. They found that 40 per cent of entrepreneurs' investors were close family members and a further 8 per cent were other family relations. Only 8 per cent of the entrepreneurs who received private investment obtained capital from a stranger. These results aroused great interest when they were published. Focus was directed away from the earlier primary concern about the availability of venture capital, which can be described as professional and risk capital as too many entrepreneurs may find it almost unattainable; impossible to get into their hands. The bold arrows between the entrepreneur and the entrepreneur's contacts (friend, customer, family member or colleague) in Figure 7.3 indicate a strong relationship.

The network level

At the network level there is also an argument for homogeneity. In their cutting-edge article of 1986 Aldrich and Zimmer wrote that entrepreneurs embedded in dense networks, where many people in the network know each other, are more likely – based on mutual trust – to increase the collective power to act. When individuals are strongly associated in a dense network there is an increase in the likelihood that they will act as a whole and with a common goal in mind. Such collective action can be crucial for the implementation of the entrepreneurial process.

People in dense networks are also generally more uniform in relation to attitudes, values, jobs, experiences, skills, etc. than the people in a network where few know each other. Therefore, one can imagine that the entrepreneur's contacts share the same passion for a particular hobby, which means that they know each other on a personal level. Because of the personal dimension of the network and the shared interests, the provision of emotional support and exchange of sensitive market information are also more likely in dense networks than in less dense networks. The box around the entire network in Figure 7.3 indicates the network level.

Effective networking is situation-dependent

We have now discussed two opposing arguments about what an effective network should look like when the entrepreneur battles his way through the entrepreneurial process, namely the heterogeneity argument and the homogeneity argument.

Immediately, both arguments appear to hold water: there is sense in them both. Both arguments also seem to hold true empirically. Various studies have, each in their own way, supported the heterogeneity and the homogeneity arguments. The explanation for these opposing arguments, making sense individually and being empirically supported, lies in the fact that social networks are dynamic (Larson & Starr 1993). Entrepreneurs meet and confront various challenges throughout the entrepreneurial process, and each of these requires access to different resources. Some resources are acquired most effectively through diverse social networks with many structural holes and weak relationships with people, while other resources are procured through dense networks where there are strong relationships between the characters.

The effective network therefore depends on the situation the entrepreneur is in. The challenges determine which resources are in demand, and hence which network the entrepreneur should aim for. Lin (2001) expresses this synthesis between the heterogeneity argument and homogeneity argument as follows: 'For preserving or maintaining resources (i.e. expressive actions), denser networks may have a relative advantage ... On the other hand, searching for and obtaining resources not presently possessed (e.g., instrumental actions), such as looking for a job or a better job, accessing and extending bridges in the network should be more useful.' (Lin 2001: 27)

There are several different models, primarily life-cycle models, that attempt to describe how the entrepreneur's network evolves with the advancement of the entrepreneurial process. In the very early stage when the entrepreneur is looking for an opportunity, the entrepreneur needs non-redundant market information to either create or discover a new opportunity. Therefore the entrepreneur is interested in a network consisting of many diverse people, a network with many structural holes, and where the entrepreneur has weak relationships with people (Klyver & Hindle 2007). When the

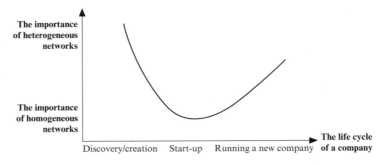

Figure 7.4
Heterogeneous and homogeneous networks across the lifecycle of an organisation

Source: Klyver & Hindle (2007: 26).

entrepreneur has identified an opportunity and is about to start the organisation, completely different resources are suddenly needed. During this stage there is a demand for advice and support to help with taking the final decision to start and also perhaps a need for capital injection. Therefore the aim is to utilise a closer network consisting of many strong relationships, including many family members (Evald et al 2006).

After the organisation has started, and the enterprise moves forward, some of the people in the network are replaced. In this phase it is essential for the entrepreneur to become established in the market, and the entrepreneur therefore needs access to market information again. Therefore the network will once again switch to a network consisting of many diverse people, a network with structural holes and a network with more weak relationships to, among other things, new contacts (Evald et al 2006).

So, we can see that the network changes throughout the entrepreneurial process and these changes can be attributed to the problems that confront the entrepreneur, and thus the resources that the entrepreneur needs. Figure 7.4 illustrates this graphically.

However, the efficiency of the network depends not only on the company's life cycle, but on a number of other factors such as industry, gender, culture, etc. Klyver et al (2008) discuss whether the network should be understood as just universal and generic regardless of context, or whether the network should be understood in close interaction with the context. They show how the network plays a different role for entrepreneurs in 20 different European countries. A number of studies centred around Howard Aldrich's work have also tried to find similarities and differences between the way entrepreneurs use and apply their network. Concluding a review of these studies, Dodd and Patra (2002) wrote 'in summary, the results from this series of linked (although not methodologically identical) studies indicate some homogeneity, suggesting a degree of generic universal entrepreneurial behaviour, and some heterogeneity, highlighting the importance of cultural differences.' (Dodd & Patra 2002: 119)

So, the conclusion must be that although the network is important for entrepreneurs in all contexts and cultures, there are crucial differences in how networks are used and how networks operate.

Networks seen as a rational tool

So far we have discussed two different types of networks, heterogeneous and homogeneous, each of which have their merits depending on the various challenges the entrepreneur encounters during the entrepreneurial process. But what we have not dealt with is whether entrepreneurs use and apply their network in a rational and calculated manner or whether the network is more akin to something that controls and limits the entrepreneur's opportunities. This is the paradox about whether the network is a rational tool, or whether entrepreneurs are (for better or for worse) embedded in their network.

From a rational perspective, the entrepreneur is considered to be a goal-oriented actor who chooses his characters in the network based on who is expected to contribute the best and most important resources in relation to the implementation of the entrepreneurial process. It is a simple case of rational and arithmetical calculation to decide on who it pays to get involved with. The characters in the entrepreneur's network are thus 'supporters' who will each bring resources into the process such as councils, funding, or more intangible resources like legitimacy.

According to the rational perspective, the relationship between entrepreneurs and the people involved will often be concrete (i.e. supportive), emotionally neutral, quasi-contractual and short-sighted. People are selected with care, but are also carefully dropped again once they no longer support the process in the best possible way.

The rational perspective of networks is widespread among researchers, politicians, consultants and entrepreneurs. Networking events are an entirely natural thing today and networking has become a natural part of many other events. There are a number of speakers and consultants who focus on the importance of networking. Stephanie Speisman (Speisman 2011) is a coach and has, among other things, formulated 10 popular tips for successful business networking. Her advice largely reflects a rational approach to networking, although some of it more than other parts. Among the most rational advice in terms of assumptions are the following:

- Ask yourself what your goals are in participating in networking meetings so that you will pick groups that will help you get what you are looking for.
- Have a clear understanding of what you do and why, for whom, and what makes the way you are doing it special or different from others doing the same thing. In order to get referrals, you must first have a clear understanding of what you do that you can easily articulate to others.
- Be able to articulate what you are looking for and how others may help you. Too often, people in conversations ask, 'How may I help you?' and no immediate answer comes to mind.

Speisman's advice reflects an intention to utilise the network's potential in the most efficient way, at the same time considering the network to be something that can be controlled through planning and careful organisation.

Keith Ferrazzi (http://www.keithferrazzi.com, last accessed 22 May 2012) is among the best-known of the networking consultants and advisors. His motto is 'Business is human. Relationships power growth'. He believes that success is self-determined, but that it can only be achieved through the help of others. In his popular book *Never Eat Alone: And Other Secrets To Success, One Relationship At A Time* he outlines how personal networking should be undertaken in order to achieve success (Ferrazzi 2005). Among his three most famous pieces of advice are:

- Don't keep score: it's never simply about getting what you want. It's about getting what you want and making sure that the people who are important to you get what they want, too.
- 'Ping' constantly: the ins and outs of reaching out to those in your circle of contacts all the time – not just when you need something.
- Never eat alone: the dynamics of status are the same whether you're working at a corporation or attending a society event – 'invisibility' is a fate worse than failure.

Ferrazzi's understanding of networks is another illustration of a rational approach to social networks and an example of networks being considered and treated as an adjustable tool.

Embedded in networks

As we have already mentioned, there is also a different perspective, namely the embedded perspective. The embedded perspective goes one step further in terms of social embeddedness and the socialisation of human behaviour. The rational perspective recognises the influence of the social surroundings, but retains a belief that people govern themselves and determine what these social surroundings look like. This is not the case with the embedded perspective. The embedded perspective goes one step further in terms of social embeddedness and socialisation and is more sceptical about the ability of people and entrepreneurs to be rational and calculating in selecting the network that suits them.

Whereas the rational perspective focuses on the entrepreneur's opportunity to choose, the embedded perspective focuses on the network being something that is carried forward from the past. Networks are bounded by history – they are a result of the life you have led and the people you've met and interacted with. According to this perspective, the entrepreneur cannot actively select a network in relation to the problems he or she faces without there being consequences. Rather than being something that can be chosen or not chosen, the network is given from the past. For example, for many entrepreneurs there is a need to discuss with and involve their spouse in the crucial decisions to be made during the entrepreneurial process. Many of these decisions can also have a decisive influence on future family life, including for example, economy, leisure and working hours. These entrepreneurial decisions cannot be considered and taken in isolation. Thus, the spouse, whether supportive or not of the entrepreneurial process, becomes involved and has a decisive influence in many cases.

In the embedded perspective, networking is regarded as something that is created and maintained through all life's activities, and it cannot be identified and isolated in relation to specific challenges such as the start-up of an organisation. Social networking is something that is created holistically through the activities a person performs. Similarly, a network is the result of a person's past activities. A person's network is a result of the life that is led, and thus there are some who have large, diverse networks. Others, however, have less and dense, homogeneous networks: not because they have chosen it, but because the life they have led has resulted in it.

The embedded perspective and the rational perspective hold different views as to the nature of relationships. In the rational perspective relationships were described as being specific (i.e. supportive), emotionally neutral, quasi-contractual and short-term. The embedded perspective describes relationships as broader (both supportive and obstructionist), emotional, trusting, mutually binding and long term.

Table 7.1 The paradox: Rational or embedded

	Rational	Embedded
View of the entrepreneur	Goal-oriented, rational player	A socially embedded player
View of the networks	A rational tool	Ungovernable condition
View of the relation	Concrete, emotionally neutral, contract like and short-termed	Diffuse, emotional, trusting, reciprocally binding and long-termed
Focus	Effective networks	The facilitating and restricting qualities of the network
The importance of social contexts	Low	High

The embedded perspective is somewhat more sceptical in relation to the network's positive impact on the entrepreneurial process. That it may be the case is not rejected – not at all – but it stresses that the network can also act as a barrier to entrepreneurs' progress through the entrepreneurial process. Aldrich and Zimmer wrote the following in their famous article: 'The embedded nature of social behaviour refers to the way in which action is constrained or facilitated because of its social context.' (Aldrich & Zimmer 1986: 4)

The consequence of devoting oneself to the embedded perspective is that you can no longer consider the network as a tool to be used in isolation in relation to specific activities. Networking is, however, something that is embedded and brings some structure that defines and constrains the opportunities you have to network. The network becomes something that controls us rather than being something that we control and therefore we can say that for better or for worse entrepreneurs are embedded in their network.

Network: rational or embedded?

We have now discussed the two different perspectives on the nature of entrepreneurial networks. They are illustrated in Table 7.1.

The rational perspective describes the entrepreneur as a focused and rational actor who considers the network as a tool. The relationship between the entrepreneur and the people in his/her network are concrete, emotionally neutral, quasi-contractual and short-term. Research within this perspective seeks to identify and determine what the most effective network for entrepreneurs looks like. The rational perspective gives low priority to the social context compared to the embedded perspective. The main criticism of the rational perspective from the view of the embedded perspective is that the entrepreneur is under-socialised. This means that the social context is not given sufficient importance in describing the entrepreneur's actions. In contrast, the entrepreneur is seen as having more power over his/her own behaviour and decisions, than may actually be realistic.

While the rational perspective can be criticised for being under-socialised, the embedded perspective is criticised for the opposite, namely being over-socialised. This means that the embedded perspective does not give adequate consideration to the entrepreneur's own actions, but primarily focuses on how decisions are externally determined by the social context. One can therefore say that the embedded perspective places a higher priority on importance of the social context.

Over-socialisation means that the embedded perspective considers the entrepreneur as a socially embedded person who, with his/her network, has to deal with uncontrollable circumstances. The relationships between the entrepreneur and the people in the network are broad, emotional, trusting, mutually binding and long term. The role of research is, according to the embedded perspective, to clarify how the network promotes and/or limits entrepreneurs.

A theoretical interpretation

Below are two different interpretations of Mike's story that began this chapter. In the interpretations, the story is linked to the theory and focuses on the paradox: rational or embedded?

The rational perspective

If you choose a rational interpretation of Mike's story, the focus will be on how Mike consciously, rationally and in a calculative manner uses his network in his efforts to become a successful musician. These are many facets to deal with. Firstly, one can argue that Mike and his partner in the music studio chose each other as partners, hoping to obtain various benefits. Initially it may have been to reduce or further share the economic costs and risks. However, another advantage that may have played a crucial role was that they possess different skills and thus collectively offered a better product. 'Together' they believed that they were something special. Therefore, they both have some clear advantages and motives for joining forces with each other. They choose each other, but as time goes by they each eventually recognise that they have not quite reached the point where they wanted to be and they begin to doubt whether the team and the partnership is right for them. They therefore unanimously chose to go their separate ways. We might say that here they have taken a conscious decision to 'drop' each other.

Another situation that illustrates the rational network approach is the way Mike initially selects Ronnie and Kenn to remix their 'What's the Matter in Paradise', and subsequently how Ronnie and Kenn want Mike to rap on their number 'The Horn'. They had probably discussed which of their contacts would best help them with this rap. They had screened the market for rappers and contacted those that they think can best give them what they need.

However, the situation where we can see the most rational behaviour is the way in which Cargo as a group used their network to secure a record deal. They had a product / album, but were only guaranteed a recording contract if their second single was a great success. So, they deliberately changed their strategy and in a calculated and intelligent way they used their network to legitimise and promote their product. By getting the single 'Loaded with Power' into the 'dance chart' through their network of Danish DJs they convinced a record label of the group's value, and they got a contract for an entire album. Here we are talking about a decidedly instrumental approach to the network where the network was used to achieve the objectives that the entrepreneurs had in mind.

The embedded perspective

Mike's story can however, also be understood completely differently, namely from an embedded perspective, which focuses on networks as uncontrollable conditions. It may well be that in some situations he has deliberately used his network to promote his own interests, but overall the network that he uses is the result of his life. The contacts that he uses during the course of his career are, for the most part, contacts or people he got to know many years back in his early hip hop period. These are the people he has created relationships with, without having, at that time, any kind of calculative intentions. For this reason, these contacts proved to be decisive many years in later life. The common past, and the confidence built up in its wake, means that those people later in life have a soft spot for each other. Therefore, they want to help each other – not to get something in return, or because they owe each other anything, but rather to celebrate the relationship and the past.

Mike had not seen many of the people that had been around him in the earlier hip hop period for many years. When he met them, it was about hip hop and love of the underground culture. At that time, no one thought about whom it might be prudent to know in the future if you wanted to make a record. In any case, if some had thought so, it would have probably been impossible to predict who ended up in powerful positions. One can therefore say that the network that turned out to be conducive to Mike's music career was created under a completely different agenda, and with completely different intentions.

Perhaps one can't exactly say that Mike's network has limited his career, as the story has unfolded here in this chapter, but maybe one can say that Mike's past life, and the network that resulted from it, set and defined the limits and possibilities for him as a dance musician. We might ask whether he would have had the same success with the same talent but without a past as a hip hopper.

Testing the theory

Based on the above thoughts and discussions, you are ready to develop your own attempts to understand the entrepreneurial network and how it influences the entrepreneurial process. The following are suggestions for investigating the topic.

 EXERCISES

1 **Interview an entrepreneur.** Make a list of interview questions that seek to capture some of the most important discussions about how networks work. Contact an entrepreneur, and interview him or her in order to test the theory presented in this chapter on entrepreneurial networks. Based on this, express your opinion on this paradox: rational or embedded?

2 **The film 'The Social Network'.** Watch the movie 'The social network', a film about the start-up process of Facebook. What is the network view portrayed in the film? Is it consistent with a rational or an embedded view on social networks? How would the story have been if social networking was not part of it?

3 **Keith Ferrazzi.** Go to http://www.keithferrazzi.com. Study the various pieces of advice Ferrazzi gives about networking and assess how similar advice would sound from an embedded perspective. What do you think of Ferrazzi's advice? Does it make sense and will it promote entrepreneurial performance?

4 **Describe your own network.** What does your network look like? Is it small, large, heterogeneous, homogeneous, etc.? How many relationships from your childhood, youth, adulthood, etc.? How strongly attached are you? Do the people in your network know each other? Why do you think your network looks the way it does?

LITERATURE

Aldrich, H.E. & Zimmer, C. (1986) 'Entrepreneurship through social networks', in Sexton, D.L. & Smilor, R.W. (eds) *The art and science of entrepreneurship*, New York: Ballinger, 3–23.

Birley, S. (1985) 'The role of networks in the entrepreneurial process', *Journal of Business Venturing*, 1, 107–117.

Burt, R.S. (1992) *Structural holes – The social structure of competition*, London: Harvard University Press.

Bygrave, W.D., Hay, M. & Reynolds, P.D. (2003) 'Executive forum: A study of informal investing in 29 nations composing the Global Entrepreneurship Monitor', *Venture Capital*, 5, 101–116.

Coleman, J.S. (1988) 'Social capital in the creation of human capital', *American Journal of Sociology*, 94, 95–120.

Dodd, S.D. and Patra, E. (2002) 'National differences in entrepreneurial networking', *Entrepreneurship and Regional Development*, 14(2), 117–134.

Evald, M.R., Klyver, K. & Svendsen, S.G. (2006) 'The changing importance of the strength of ties throughout the entrepreneurial process', *Journal of Enterprising Culture*, 14, 1–26.

Ferrazzi, K. and Raz, T. (2005) *Never eat alone: And other secrets to success, one relationship at a time*, New York: Currency Doubleday.

Granovetter, M.S. (1973) 'The strength of weak ties', *American Journal of Sociology*, 78, 1360–1380.

Hoang, H. & Antončič, B. (2003) 'Network-based research in entrepreneurship – A critical review', *Journal of Business Venturing*, 18, 165–187.

Johannisson, B. (1988) 'Business formation – A network approach', *Scandinavian Journal of Management*, 4, 83–99.

Klyver, K. & Hindle, K. (2007) 'The role of social networks at different stages of business formation, Small Enterprise Research', *The Journal of SEAANZ*, 15, 22–38.

Larson, A. & Starr, J.A. (1993) 'A network model of organisation formation', *Entrepreneurship Theory & Practice*, 17, 5–15.

Lin, N. (2001) *Social capital – A theory of social structure and action*, New York: Cambridge University Press.

Speisman, S. (2011) '10 tips for successful business networking', available at www.businessknow-how.com/tips/networking (last accessed September 2011).

8

The business plan

Many entrepreneurs need a business plan, and many have also made one. However, there are also entrepreneurs who have prepared a business plan without actually needing it, and without actively making use of it. The business plan has become the major focal point of many textbooks and courses on entrepreneurship, with its importance being drummed into the heads of entrepreneurs. There is, however, much to suggest that the business plan's role and significance is more complicated than it may appear.

The business plan may have an important role in the planning of the entrepreneurial process, both internally in relation to the entrepreneur himself and externally in relation to third parties such as investors. However the business plan also plays other important roles that are more symbolic and provide legitimation in relation to the environment. At the same time there are some who argue that the business plan may in fact impede the entrepreneur's creativity. You will be introduced to these topics and issues in this chapter.

Entrepreneurship in practice

Here's a case study written by Thomas Cooney and Anita Van Gils about Michael, who in 2010 started Mobitrix – a medical software business – and about how Michael employed his business plan in the process.

CASE STUDY:

Mobitrix: a start-up company in the medical software industry

(Devised by Thomas Cooney and Anita Van Gils)

On a sunny Sunday afternoon in May 2011, Michael was sitting in the garden of his home. His thoughts would occasionally stray to the challenges that faced his business and to the major decisions that must be taken in the weeks ahead. He had established a business plan for

CASE STUDY *(continued)*

Mobitrix nine months previously, but the current business situation looked completely different. He could not help wondering how he should proceed with his business idea and with his plan!

Before starting his own business, Michael had been working for more than 10 years with different software companies in the medical sector. As a product manager, he was primarily responsible for the interface between the needs of the company's clients and the development of appropriate technical software solutions to meet those needs. This meant that both he and the software entrepreneurs frequently had to be imaginative to work around the distinctive challenges that each job would bring. In addition to this role, Michael also monitored the implementation of the different projects in the hospital setting. It was during the time that he spent on these projects in medical labs that Michael spotted several opportunities for product development.

One of these opportunities arose from concerns for patient safety. Medical caretakers are responsible for providing the correct medication to the patients (specifically with regards to blood transfusion), but many stories exist of errors that could have been prevented if the carer had access to correct and up-to-date information through the right software solution. Because Michael was very Apple-minded, and generally a first-mover in trying out Steve Job's newest creations, he had been considering how the iPhone, iPod and iPad could add value in creating mobile solutions for the health care business for some time. He pitched his idea to his bosses, but they did not see how these opportunities could fit in with their current portfolio of software products. Michael became increasingly frustrated with the lack of innovativeness in the companies' activities and plans, until eventually he woke up one night in a hotel room and started writing the first pages of a plan to start his own business as the many different possibilities and ideas rushed through his mind.

Mobitrix, a one-person business activity, was established in September 2010. Educated as a medical laboratory technologist with a Masters in biomedical technology, Michael soon realised that his business experience was very limited. As he had close contacts with entrepreneurship teachers at the School of Business and Economics at Maastricht University, he evaluated the possibility of collaborating with students on the development of a business plan. Bart, a medical engineering graduate taking a Masters in 'International Business in Entrepreneurship and Small Business Management', welcomed the opportunity to combine his medical and business expertise, and so began supporting Michael in researching and writing a business plan. For Michael, the development of a business plan helped him to put fine detail to his ideas and to evaluate the viability of the many possible market entry options that lay before him. He first had to decide on a business model: would he deliver his products to medical equipment companies, medical software companies or to the hospitals themselves? He felt that the programming of the software would need to be outsourced, so selection criteria for suppliers had to be established. Michael and Bart discussed financial projections extensively, made an initial projection of the break-even point and decided that no external investment was needed at that time as the money required for the software development could be covered

CASE STUDY *(continued)*

from Michael's own funds. Finally, they decided on a first important goal – they aimed at presenting Mobitrix's first product concept at the Medica Exhibition (the world's largest medical technology exhibition) which was to be held in Dusseldorf in November 2010.

During those first months of activities, many unexpected issues arose that required Michael's immediate attention. For example, while planning the first software developments, Michael accidentally discovered a scanning accessory that was developed for iPhone and iPod Touch, and which would perfectly fit the hardware requirements needed for the development of an application (app) that could solve the patient safety problems. Michael believed that putting barcodes on blood bags, medicines and on each patient's hospital wristband, and then scanning those barcodes with the mobile device, would almost certainly decrease the number of medical errors currently occurring. After carefully writing the software specifications and the functional design, Michael outsourced this first software development project to a company in Sri Lanka. Although the cooperation went smoothly, the development time was much longer than was planned.

Eventually, Michael and Bart managed to have their first app completed before the Medica Exhibition. While the final users for this app would be hospital personnel, Michael and Bart decided that the best strategy was to target their product for sale to medical equipment manufacturers and software companies. Initial reactions at the exhibition were very good, both from their targeted client segment and from end users. Mobitrix received visitors from very diverse and sometimes very large companies (including Philips Healthcare, GE Healthcare, Tieto, Panasonic, etc.), and Michael and Bart were usually asked highly focused questions. A later analysis of their interactions at the Exhibition showed that the leads generated consisted of 43 per cent of C-level functions (CEO, CTO, CFO), of which 70 per cent indicated an interest in

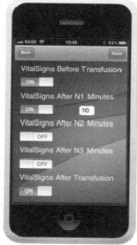

Figure 8.1 Delivering health care through an iPhone

CASE STUDY (continued)

having apps developed for them. Michael collected more than 100 business cards from people that showed significant interest, and secured at least five serious leads from medical and software companies that needed to be followed up. Moreover, shortly afterwards, the first app that they had produced was accepted by Apple's app store. Although the selling price of this app was just 3.99 Euro, for the owner it was a pilot project to test if he could manage the whole process. Meanwhile, a new software app for bedside registration was also in development in India, and this project would use the first app that they had produced.

In the months following the Medica Exhibition, Michael contacted all of the people that had shown interest at the exhibition, and he completed several interesting meetings. For example, one contact was with an Italian technology company that produces smart blood refrigerators. As their product covered the whole process from lab to nurse, but lacked the additional bedside registration, Mobitrix's software seemed to be a perfect fit. A second promising contact was with a Swedish company that produces haematology cell imaging solutions. Yet another contact was with a hospital ICT manager who saw the demo app and was surprised by the quality and speed of the barcode recognition. These people were interested in getting access to the improved barcode recognition functionality in their apps. Despite these meetings, no cooperation agreements could be developed. Several companies indicated a preference to postpone their investments in mobile solutions until the summer of 2011. For the software companies the major problem related to the integration of the proposed apps with existing systems.

Although Michael realised that starting up a venture is a bumpy ride with many highs and lows, the existing lack of follow-up projects really made him doubt the viability of his general business idea. However, as he was positive that the opportunity was recognised by the medical personnel, he persisted in pitching his idea. But instead of targeting his products at medical equipment or software companies, he started making appointments with doctors in hospitals to demonstrate his mobile solutions. These visits persuaded him yet again about the potential of the product, as doctors were very enthusiastic about the viability of his idea, and even offered suggestions for other apps that needed to be developed. Michael then convinced a team of doctors in a Belgian hospital of the added value of his product, and they decided to start a pilot project with him. Michael realised that this was an important breakthrough, as it created a reference project that would also increase his credibility with other clients. Unfortunately, the implementation of the project could not begin until he convinced the IT personnel and the management team of the value he could add to the processes in their hospital. Therefore, he needed to carefully prepare a presentation for this group, as they would probably use different decision-making criteria from the doctors.

But there are other issues that cause Michael to reflect on the actions that he has taken in recent months. The medical team in the pilot hospital has indicated that they are unable to do business with a one-person company, as service must be guaranteed even when an entrepreneur becomes sick or has an accident. For reasons such as this, Michael has been contemplating the benefits of partnering with a larger company. Should he then update his business

CASE STUDY (continued)

plan in order to prospect for these partners? In his initial version of the plan, the first sales were estimated to be realised in December 2010, while five months later, the venture really was still in the pre-sales state. Besides, in the plan, much more software development had been planned, but this was postponed, given the longer development time of the first two projects. As he expected to start with the first pilot project, it could also be the ideal moment to find some external financing. He definitely needed a change to his business plan for such a purpose. However, he wondered how he could write a business plan which on the one hand was sharp, goal-oriented and convincing to potential partners and, on the other hand, sufficiently flexible to absorb surprises and take advantage of new opportunities.

Your immediate interpretation

What does the story tell you about Mobitrix and the importance of business plans? How do you immediately interpret the story's twists? The following exercises can help you interpret the story.

- How does Michael use the business plan during Mobitrix's start-up period? What purpose does it serve? Do you get the feeling that he places a high priority on a written business plan?
- Does he have a written plan, or is it about more about loose ideas and thoughts that are not necessarily written down? Do you think it is important that the business plan is written down and specific rather than being just at the idea and thought level?
- You have decided to start your own organisation, and you have been advised to write a business plan before you start up. What should such a plan include, how long should it be, and how should it be developed?
- You meet one of your old friends from school. She has just graduated with an MSc in International Business. She is now considering starting her own organisation, where she and her partner will advise small businesses who want to start exporting to China. During their studies, both your old friend and her partner have devoted a lot of time and effort to China. They have been on several trips, have undertaken a semester's internship in China and have written their thesis on the subject of exporting to China. They claim they have a very good knowledge of the subject and that they also have the necessary contacts to make a start. They therefore believe that it is a waste of time to write a business plan. What do you think?

Theories of entrepreneurship

The Mobitrix story is closely related to the main topic of this chapter, i.e. the business plan. In many ways the story discusses business plans and how the entrepreneur describes and communicates his recognition of and plans (both ex-ante and ex-post) related to, the generation, evaluation and organisation of a new opportunity. This represents description, in a structured form, of the entrepreneur's insights and plans in relation to Chapter 3 on the emergence of opportunities, Chapter 4 on the evaluation of opportunities and Chapter 5 on the organising of opportunities.

There are many definitions of what constitutes a business plan. On their website, the US Small Business Administration defines a business plan as follows: 'A business plan precisely defines your business, identifies your goals and serves as your firm's resume. Its basic components include a current and pro forma balance sheet, an income statement and a cash flow analysis. It helps you allocate resources properly, handle unforeseen complications, and make the right decisions.' (www.sba.gov, last accessed November 2011).

Those who promote the importance of a business plan are often supporters of the planning perspective as opposed to the improvisation perspective (as discussed in Chapter 5). They believe that organisational processes can be controlled and see the business plan as an important management tool for implementing the entrepreneurial process as painlessly as possible. Conversely, there are others who view the business plan more sceptically; namely as a curb on creativity. They argue that entrepreneurs are pressured into a certain mind-set through the business plan's structure, and that their otherwise crucial creativity is reduced. The paradox in this chapter is therefore whether the business plan is a:

Management tool or creativity curb

The business plan: context, content and process

Before discussing the paradox further, we will concentrate on some other fundamental factors that relate to the business plan. The discussion about the business plan is often equated with the concept of planning. 'The plan' is the content or output of a 'planning process', called 'planning'. Planning takes place within certain limits and conditions as 'context'. This separation is illustrated in Figure 8.2 (De Witt & Meyer 1998).

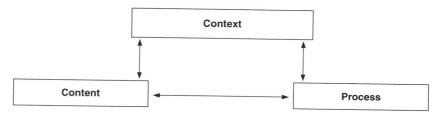

Source: Inspired by De Witt & Meyer (1998).

Figure 8.2 The plan context, content and process

As the figure illustrates, the three dimensions are connected and influence each other. One can therefore imagine that in some industries (contexts) the requirement for the business plan and the planning process is greater than in other industries. Honig and Karlsson (2004) found, for example, that entrepreneurs in the production sector are more likely to produce a business plan than entrepreneurs in other industries. They explain that the tendency arises because production-based industry has a planning approach. New entrepreneurs are therefore more willing to produce a plan and imitate the tradition in order to achieve legitimacy and gain the understanding of the other actors and stakeholders.

One can also imagine that the need for, and relevance of, a business plan varies according to the degree of uncertainty in the actual idea and the context within which it occurs. The need is probably limited in very simple and traditional small businesses such as shops and craft businesses where the uncertainty is relatively low. Likewise, the planning approach is of limited relevance and value in connection with business ideas that are radically innovative, such as Skype and Google (Sarasvathy 2008).

One may also imagine that having a need for a high level of venture capital (context) will impose different demands on the business plan's content than if the entrepreneur can personally finance his organisation's start-up. Here, additional detailed information on financial matters will be required. Alternatively, one may envisage that people with different backgrounds (contexts) have different needs for business plans. For example, some individuals have an education where planning plays a major role (for example, engineers, business economists or production planners), whilst others have an education where more creative processes have held pride of place (for example, designers or music teachers). These people will probably have different needs when it comes to planning and writing things down in specific business plan structures. There is a myriad of different contexts that may affect both the requirements of the business plan and how the planning process can take place.

However, the process can also affect the content, and the content can influence the process. One could for instance imagine that a particular way of doing things will lead to restrictions in the content itself. If, from the outset, the entrepreneur decides to ignore recommendations from an advisor, to involve various key stakeholders in the planning process – including actors, local communities, financial advisers, family members – one can easily imagine that some of the critical comments they have regarding the project will be completely ignored and will not appear on the final written plan (content).

One can also imagine that if the entrepreneur takes a predefined table of contents as the starting point for his business plan, it will influence the process because using an index as a starting point, can in itself lead to a structured analytical approach (process).

Written document or thought process

It has often been discussed whether it is the business plan as a written document that is crucial or whether it is the thought and planning process that is essential. Shane tries to capture the discussion this way: 'The entrepreneur formulates a plan, in mental or written form, for the organizing process . . . the planning then leads to organizing activities.' (Shane 2003: 221)

The arguments for the plan as a written document are that the entrepreneur obtains clarity on the decisions to be taken in relation to the supply of products, on which markets to become involved with and what constitutes the organisation's competitive advantage. Additionally, the plan as a written document can be important in relation to communication with an external third party such as banks, investors, customers or suppliers. Furthermore, the written document also plays a role in terms of internal communication and reflection. The business plan can be used in communicating with new employees: as a foundation in the socialisation of desired behaviour, and communication of organisational goals, but the plan may also, in other ways, contribute to the maintenance and possible strengthening of the entrepreneur's motivation. Baker et al (1993) cite three main reasons for the written business plan being better than the informal, unwritten thought process for small businesses:

1. The written plan ensures critical thinking.
2. It can be used in both internal and external communication.
3. It can serve as internal control of company development.

They found this third feature of the plan to be the most important function for most small businesses.

However, there are also people who argue that the very act of writing down the plan is often unnecessary and that the important thing is the right thought process. It's the process of thinking that provides clarity regarding the organisation's objectives and how they can be fulfilled. Ultimately, it is the process that provides motivation, not the written plan. Market conditions, technological possibilities, regulatory and numerous other factors related to the organisation's environment change so fast today that the written business plan becomes out-dated almost before it is finished. Therefore, continual rethinking is crucial.

However there is a further argument against the written business plan, an argument that specifically applies during the start-up of an organisation. People about to exploit an opportunity are often short of time and resources. For them it's about getting the opportunity realised through the organisation as soon as possible, so that cash flow is initiated and the organisation can begin to earn money and pay wages. The longer the process takes, the greater the financial risk run by the entrepreneur, and the greater funding required for the start-up. They are, therefore, busier with getting the organisation started up and entirely operational rather than sitting around devising long-term strategic plans. David Madié, co-founder of Start-up Company and later Growth Company which has offices in both Copenhagen and New York, has previously stated:

> Proponents of writing a business plan will reply, that it never can be detrimental to have a good plan. But actually, it can. The big problem with the business plan is all the time spent on it – maybe 100 hours or more, leading to several weeks of work . . . The worst is not the time and energy spent on writing worthless business plans. The worst thing is, what the time could otherwise be spent more wisely on tasks, which could increase its chance of survival, growth and ability to obtain financing from either banks or investors. (Madié 2007: 34–35; translated into English from Madié's original Danish text).

There is thus a lively debate about whether it's the plan in written form or the thought process that is decisive for completion of the entrepreneurial process. A debate where there are rational arguments on both sides. It's not all entrepreneurs who write a business plan. In Shuman et al's (1985) study of INC 500 companies, they concluded that 49 per cent of the companies developed a business plan during their start-up process. In a recent study, Delmar and Shane (2003) concluded that 40 per cent of the Swedish companies they studied had a written business plan.

These studies show that the preparation of a business plan is widespread, but it may be even larger than the percentages show, because the definition of a business plan is unclear. As a rule one tends to think of a fully developed business plan with detailed product descriptions, budgets and market analysis, typically a document of 10–20 pages. However, there may also be a more concise document, often called a concept statement, which primarily and succinctly describes the likely demand from future customers and the value proposition associated with the new product or service (Barringer & Ireland 2008). In addition, a PowerPoint presentation or other visual material has a similar effect for the entrepreneur and business development as a written format. Business plans may therefore have different formats that may be relevant at different stages of venture development, or in relation to various stakeholder groups.

Planning

Before jumping into the discussion of the business plan's content and its associated paradox, we will briefly discuss some issues about the close relationship between planning as a process and the business plan as output. There will therefore, as previously indicated, be parallels in this section to the discussions that you dealt with in Chapter 5 on the organisation of opportunities.

During a planning process, there are some critical factors that one should be aware of in connection with the development of a business plan. These factors are critical to ensuring that the business plan will work as intended. Kuratko and Hodgetts (2004) combine these factors into four main factors:

- Goals must be realistic
- The plan must provide commitment and dedication
- The plan must include milestones
- The plan must be flexible.

It is crucial that the targets set are realistic both externally with stakeholders, including for example, potential investors or lenders, and internally in relation to their own motivation. If the targets are unrealistic and not adequately thought through, it is difficult to attract investors or lenders. At the same time it is difficult to maintain the motivation to get through the entrepreneurial process when one can see that the goals are unrealistic and unattainable. It is also important that the plan contains some milestones by which various activities must be completed and show how these activities are interrelated. This makes it possible to check whether one is in step with the timing of the plan and thus on track. Last but not least, it is crucial that the plan is flexible. This may be a little inconsistent with the planning milestones. To

Table 8.1 Three examples of the contents of a business plan

Kuratko & Hodgetts (2004)	Schilit (1987)	Business Plan Journal
Executive summary	Executive summary	Executive summary
Business description	Background and purpose	Company analysis
Marketing	Objectives	Industry analysis
Operations	Market analysis	Customer analysis
Management	Development and Production	Competitive analysis
Financial	Marketing	Marketing plan
Critical risks	Financial plans	Operations plan
Harvest strategy	Organisation and management	Management team
Milestone schedule	Ownership	Financial plan
	Critical risks and problems	Appendix
	Summary and conclusion	

implement the entrepreneurial process is a relatively complex, difficult and unpredictable process and it may therefore be important to create room for changes along the way.

The plan's content

A plethora of advice exists on what a business plan should contain. Often these suggestions are shown as the table of contents proposed in the business plan. However, despite these numerous proposals for the content of the business plan, which are almost presented as universal, the only credible universal advice is that the business plan must be adapted to the opportunity, the situation and the target audience of the plan. Of course how different types of opportunities are best described in a business plan will vary. The situation concerning the opportunity also has great influence on how the business plan should fit together. For example, one might imagine that entrepreneurs with ambitions towards export and growth would have to structure their business differently from an entrepreneur who simply wants to establish him or herself locally. Finally it is natural that different audiences (be they bankers, investors, customers, suppliers, accountants, etc.) will have different requirements for the information in the business plan.

That said, Table 8.1 illustrates three examples of what the contents of a business plan might look like.

The three different proposals should be considered as separate suggestions for solving the same problem. There is nothing that speaks more for one than for another, unless the possibility of the situation and target group of the business plan is taken into account. Furthermore, there is some overlap between the three proposals, all of which have sections on management, finance and market conditions.

As you can see, there are many different views on what the contents of the business plan should be. The essential thing in determining a given plan is to think through what type of information is crucial in the specific situation. Below is some advice that may be helpful in the preparation of the plan. The recommendations are some of the proposals Kuratko and Hodgetts (2004) come up with. The business plan should:

- Not be too long
- Be oriented toward the future
- Avoid exaggerations
- Clarify critical risk factors
- Identify the target group
- Be written professionally (in the third person)
- Catch the reader's attention and interest.

The business plan as a management tool

Now we will deal with the paradox and discuss the two seemingly opposite perspectives. One perspective sees the business plan as a management tool and the other sees the business plan as a curb on creativity. We begin by discussing the business plan as a management tool.

This view of the business plan is by far the most commonly held and follows a rational logic, where the business plan is seen as a means to manage and plan for an organisation's future. Wickham (2004) describes the business plan as a entrepreneurial tool targeted to exploit opportunities, and Delmar and Shane argue:

> Business planning helps firm founders to undertake venture development activities because planning facilitates goal attainment in many domains of human actions . . . Specifically, we argue that planning helps firm founders to make decisions more quickly than with trial-and-error learning; and to turn abstract goals into concrete operational activities more efficiently. (Delmar & Shane 2003: 1166)

According to Delmar and Shane (2003), the use of business plans has three major advantages:

1. First, the business plan and planning process can be used to make decision making faster by identifying missing information before the (financial) resources are tied up.
2. Second, the business plan is a tool for managing supply and demand of resources in such a way as to avoid bottlenecks.
3. And finally, the business plan is a way to identify the activities that must be initiated to achieve the targets set within the timeframe.

Schilit (1987) also sees the business plan as a management tool:

> What is a business plan? Essentially, it is a vehicle to: 1) Assess the current and future state of an organization and its environment; 2) Delineate long-range and short-range objectives based on this assessment; and 3) Develop appropriate action guidelines to achieve these objectives. It is clearly the result of diligent market research and sound financial projections. (Schilit 1987: 13)

When one looks at the business plan as a management tool, it can be traced back to a conviction that the future can be predicted. March (1997) speaks of some pre-conditions that must be present before planning, in its perfectly rational sense, can be undertaken:

- Knowledge of alternatives
- Knowledge of consequences
- A consistent preference ordering
- A decision rule.

When the business plan is seen as a management tool, it is built on the assumption that the entrepreneur is familiar with the various future alternatives, such as the ways in which he imagines that the market can develop, and also that he is able to realise the consequences of the alternatives. What does it mean for the entrepreneur, if the market develops according to the different alternatives? And subsequently over time, the entrepreneur maintains a consistent set of preferences for these alternatives and thus makes a rational choice. Although some are very critical of these assumptions, proponents of the business plan as a management tool are often convinced that although the assumptions are only valid to a certain degree, it always makes sense to try to steer their way through the entrepreneurial process rather than wandering indecisively and unwittingly through the process.

Proponents of the business plan as a management tool are not necessarily immoveable in their belief in the above assumptions. They just lean more towards management than towards random behaviour. Many of them are actually critical of the approach in relation to the previously mentioned preconditions set out by March (1997). Proponents of the business plan often admit to bounded rationality (Simon 1947), where people and therefore entrepreneurs are considered as individuals who are unable to collect and process full information to predict and control their future completely rationally. People and entrepreneurs try to act rationally, but their behaviour remains rationally bounded, partly because they cannot grasp all the information present, and partly because they cannot analyse and treat it sufficiently rationally. Proponents of the business plan also recognise that it is not possible to determine the consequences of various options completely. Finally, they recognise that people, and therefore entrepreneurs, do not have consistent preferences over time. What an entrepreneur wants at a specific time can easily change later on.

Proponents of the business plan as a management tool are not naive in relation to the assumptions on which they base their beliefs. They are aware that people can only act with bounded rationality, but they still recognise the importance of planning and the importance of the business plan in managing this process.

The business plan as a creativity curb

There are empirical studies showing that planning has no positive impact on entrepreneurs' performance. Honig and Karlsson write: 'We found that those who wrote business plans were no more likely to persist in nascent activity as compared to non-planners.' (Honig & Karlsson 2004: 43) These studies have led to discussion of other logics of human behaviour. The logic that characterises the planning approach and vision in the business plan as a management tool is what might be called the logic of consequentiality (March & Olsen 1989). It's about predicting and prioritising based on the entrepreneur's preferences compared to the alternatives with the most profitable consequences in the future. However, there are indications that other logics can also be in play.

It is possible that some entrepreneurs are using previous experience (experience-based logic). They simply use the experience they have in the past to carry out the entrepreneurial process anew. Here, one can envisage that the knowledge from experience that comes into play is, in many ways, intangible and hard to describe. Nevertheless, it can still be of critical value to the entrepreneur. Several empirical studies show that entrepreneurs, who have previous start-up experience, are more likely to succeed than entrepreneurs who start an organisation for the first time. It could be that the effectiveness of experience-based logic can match the benefits of the logic of consequentiality.

One can also imagine that some entrepreneurs simply mimic what other entrepreneurs have done in the hope that this behaviour will again prove to be effective. Or they do it because it is expected from their environment. Honig and Karlsson write specifically about these environmental expectations, which almost force entrepreneurs into a planning approach:

> It appears that new organizations do not write business plans to improve perform-
> ance, rather, they do so in order to conform to institutionalized rules and to mimic
> the behaviour of other ... In sum, we propose that new organizations plan because
> they are reacting to how they are expected to plan, because they imitate other
> successful organizations in their fields that plan, or because they are told to plan.
> (Honig & Karlsson 2004: 43)

There are then many things that speak against the benefits of the business plan as a management tool, but we have still not discussed the greatest of them all. We have considered some reasons for writing a business plan and some of the logic that drives entrepreneurs, but we have retained a degree of optimism in the business plan. Even if the plan is seen as something that one writes in order to satisfy demands from the environment, the plan plays an important role in the entrepreneurial process.

However, some people think that the business plan has an inhibiting effect on the entrepreneur's creativity. They argue that when entrepreneurs start working with business plans, they are squeezed into a structured and logical form of thinking that spoils creativity. It is strategic thinking that is important in the planning process, and this requires a much higher degree of creativity than the logics of consequentiality and rationality.

Successful planning requires that the entrepreneur thinks 'out of the box' and breaks with the existing dominant paradigms in the market. It requires creativity and lateral thinking (De Bono, 1992), and creativity and structure do not go together. Creativity is therefore spoiled if you begin to work with business plans, which deliberately structure the process. The famous painter Picasso once wrote: 'Every act of creation is first of all an act of destruction.' This quote illustrates the importance of breaking with the existing dominant paradigms for creating new opportunities rather than filling some existing structures, which is what planning is fundamentally about. Another quote by Kierkegaard also illustrates the importance of creativity and a break with the existing: 'He who follows in the footsteps of others, never gets in front.'

Table 8.2 The paradox: A management tool or creativity curb

	Management tool	Creativity curb
What is the business plan?	Tool for planning	Creativity curb
Logic	Logic of consequentiality	Other types of logic (experience logic; imitation logic)
The importance of business development	Rationality over creativity	Creativity over rationality
Focus	Consistency	Break with the existing
Metaphor	Science	Art

Opponents of viewing the business plan as a management tool are opponents precisely because they prioritise creativity over the logic of consequentiality in the entrepreneurial process. It is not because they ignore and fail to appreciate logic and rationality. They just think that creativity is more important. They see entrepreneurship as art, where opportunities are, to a greater extent, generated and utilised as a result of a creative and intuitive process than as a logical and rational process. Ohmae, one of Japan's best known writers in strategic thinking, writes:

> My message, as you will have guessed by now, is that successful business strategy result not from rigorous analysis but from a particular state of mind. In what I call the mind of the strategist, insight and a consequent drive for achievement, often amounting to a sense of mission, fuel a thought process which is basically creative and intuitive rather than rational. (Ohmae 1982)

Business plan: management tool or creativity curb?

We have now discussed the business plan context, content and process and additionally we have discussed a paradox about the role of business plan for the entrepreneur, i.e. the business plan as a management tool or the business plan as a brake on creativity. The discussion is summarised in Table 8.2.

The first perspective, i.e. the business plan as a management tool, sees the business plan as a means to plan the entrepreneurial process. Here, the logic of consequentiality is followed, which gives logic priority over creativity in its importance for business development. The focus is on consistency in the analysis undertaken and the recommendations proposed and planning is thus considered as a science.

The second perspective, on the other hand, sees the business plan as a curb on creativity and thus on the entrepreneur's ability to complete the entrepreneurial process. It argues that planning is often based on other logics, and there may be other reasons to write a business plan rather than following a traditional logic of consequentiality. Here creativity has priority over logic. It's about breaking with the existing and thinking laterally about how players in the markets already think. It's about thinking 'out of the box'. Therefore, planning is considered to be more of an art than a science, and a business plan is considered more of a hindrance than a help in implementing the entrepreneurial process.

A theoretical interpretation

Below are two different interpretations of the Mobitrix story, which began this chapter. In the interpretations the story is linked to the theory above.

The management tool perspective

The immediate interpretation of the Mobitrix case study can easily follow the management tool perspective where the business plan is considered as a means to manage and plan the evaluation and organisation process of the business opportunity. Although Michael acknowledges that many things did not evolve as he expected, one could, according to the management tool perspective, easily imagine that the whole thing would have been even worse without planning and the scheduling process.

Firstly, there is nothing in the management tool perspective that doesn't accept that a business can be flexible – just as Michael also finally realises at the end of the case study. Various unforeseen events can change the premises of a business plan that will then require the plan's adjustment. It is quite common in relation to the management tool perspective to accept continuous adjustments to the plan in accordance with the development of the business opportunity.

In this way the case study provides a good illustration of how the process and the plan may affect each other. Additionally the case study shows how the context in terms of different audiences and purposes for the business plan will require different content within the plan. The latter is clearly illustrated when Michael is considering updating the plan to attract potential new partners.

Secondly, one can say that because the real business situation does not develop according to the business plan, this is not an argument against trying to control what can be controlled. It may be poor planning or poor execution of the plan's activities that explains why the plan and reality are not identical. It may also be that things would have turned out even worse without the plan. The plan has, after all, given Michael some milestones to aim for in trying to develop a sustainable business. The plan has ensured consistency and targeted behaviours.

The creativity curb perspective

In the creativity curb perspective it is understood as fact that the business plan and business opportunity do not develop in line with each other; quite different from the management tool perspective. Here we will consider this fact just as a sign that the business plan lacked the ability to predict the future and give the entrepreneur the necessary input on goals and actions.

The business plan that Michael prepared in the early stages of business start-up is now nine months old and totally out of touch with how things look in reality. Many unexpected things occurred along the way that Michael had not anticipated; including the scanning accessory developed for iPhone and iPod Touch and a longer development time in Sri Lanka than expected.

According to the creativity curb perspective, these unexpected events mean that much time and resource is used to predict an unpredictable future. This time and these resources could have been used far more productively to develop the product or contact different types of stakeholders, including investors, suppliers and not least potential customers. One could also easily imagine that the plan has given Michael a picture of reality and the future, which later becomes difficult to deviate from – even when it turns out that the picture described in the business plan does not hold true.

The case outlines Michael's frustrations over the plan's inadequacy in predicting the future more than the pleasure of the positive developments that have taken place. Disappointment over the lack of interest for follow-up at the Medica exhibition in Düsseldorf clearly shows how the energy is channelled in a negative direction when the plan does not hold true – energy that could probably be used more creatively to think in new and different paths about how the business could be developed.

There are also several situations in the case study which suggested that various unexpected events are crucial for changes in the business opportunity. It is in this way that a creative response to unforeseen events contributes to the development of business opportunities rather than a long-term plan.

Testing the theory

Based on the above thoughts and discussions you are ready to develop your own attempt to understand the business plan's impact on the entrepreneurial process. The following are suggestions for investigating the topic.

 EXERCISES

1 **Interview an entrepreneur.** Create an interview guide with interview questions that contains two main parts. The first part focuses on the overall benefits entrepreneurs may experience in connection with the use of business plans. The second part contains the disadvantages and problems that an entrepreneur may face with the use of business plans. Then contact an entrepreneur, and interview him or her in order to test the theory presented in this chapter on business plans. Based on this, create your opinion on this paradox: a management tool or creativity curb?

2 **Interview a banker / investor.** Do you know a banker or others who deal with investments in new business opportunities on a daily basis? Interview them about how they evaluate a business plan, what information they want and how they want it designed.

3 **The perception in the media.** Go to a library and find a database of print media. Search the term 'business plan'. You can choose to make your search broad or narrow, either by choosing a short or long period of time, or by choosing that the term 'business plan' should be included in the headline of the article or not. Read and then analyse the articles, and sort them according to their view of the business plan. Based on your analysis draw a conclusion about how the general view of business plans are in your country. Does it tend to view the business plan as a management tool or as a curb on creativity?

4 **Create an outline for a business plan.** Do you have a small idea that you are fiddling around with? If so, then search your social network to see if you know someone who is thinking of starting his or her own organisation. Next, try to make a more detailed outline of what a business plan for this opportunity should contain and to whom it should be addressed. You can then, when the outline is finished, continue working and write a complete business plan.

 LITERATURE

Baker, W.H., Addams, H.L. & Davis, B. (1993) 'Business planning in successful small firms', *Long Range Planning*, 26(6), 82–88.

Barringer, B.R. & Ireland, R.D. (2008) *Entrepreneurship: Successfully launching new ventures*, Pearson: Prentice Hall.

Business Plan Journal, www.businessplanjournal.com (last accessed 22 May 2012).

De Bono, E. (1992) *Using the power of lateral thinking to create new ideas*, London: Harper Collins Publisher Ltd.

De Witt, B. & Meyer, R. (1998) *Strategy – Process, content, context*, London: Thomson.

Delmar, F. & Shane, S. (2003) 'Does business planning facilitate the development of new ventures?', *Strategic Management Journal*, 24, 1165–1185.

Honig, B. & Karlsson, T. (2004) 'Institutional forces and the written business plan', *Journal of Management*, 30, 29–48.

Kuratko, D.F. & Hodgetts, R.M. (2004) *Entrepreneurship – theory, process, practice*, Mason: Thomson.

Madié, D. (2007) 'Farvel til forretningsplanen! Start af virksomhed kræver handling', *Iværksætteren*, 7, 34–36.

March, J.G. (1997) 'Understanding how decisions happen in organisations', in Shapira, Z. (ed.) *Organisational decision making*, Cambridge: Cambridge University Press, 9–32.

March, J.G. & Olsen, J.P. (1989) *Rediscovering institutions: The organizational basis of politics*, New York: Free Press/Macmillan.

Ohmae, K. (1982) *The mind of the strategist: The art of Japanese Business*, New York: McGraw-Hill.

Sarasvathy, S.D. (2008) *Effectuation: Elements of Entrepreneurial Expertise*, Cheltenham, UK and Northampton, MA, USA: Edward Elgar Publishing.

Schilit, W.K. (1987) 'How to write a winning business plan', *Business Horizon*, September–October, 13–22.

Shane, S. (2003) *A General Theory of Entrepreneurship: The Individual-opportunity Nexus*, Cheltenham, UK and Northampton, MA, USA: Edward Elgar Publishing.

Shuman, J.C., Shaw, J.J. & Sussmann, G. (1985) 'Strategic planning in smaller rapid growth companies', *Long Range Planning*, 18(6), 48–53.

Simon, H.A. (1947) *Administrative behaviour*, New York: The Free Press.

Wickham, P.A. (2004) *Strategic entrepreneurship*, London: Prentice Hall.

Section 4

The entrepreneurial context

9

Intrapreneurship

As promised in Chapter 1, we are now going to introduce you to intra-preneurship. In simple terms, intrapreneurship covers the phenomenon of entrepreneurship within the context of an existing business. Within this context, new opportunities are discovered or created which need to be evaluated and organised. The result may be new organisational units, strategic reorientation or innovations within the existing organisation. The driving force is still, as with starting up an independent organisation, based on a single individual or a group of people, often called 'intrapreneurs'.

However, intrapreneurship is very different from entrepreneurship. The existing corporate environment places certain conditions on the entrepreneurial process. The individuals who discover or create, evaluate and organise new opportunities within an existing corporate framework are dependent on the existing company accepting the presence of the new. The intrapreneur is thus constrained by the context of the firm. At the same time, however, the intrapreneur positively draws on the many diverse resources that are present in the existing business. Furthermore, it seems that the characteristics of intrapreneurs are in many respects similar to those of entrepreneurs (Bager et al 2010). This chapter provides you with an understanding of what intrapreneurship is and how the entrepreneurial process is created and run within the context of an existing business.

Intrapreneurship in practice

What follows is a story about intrapreneurship in a global company written by William B. Gartner and Ann Højbjerg Clarke. Since 2004 this corporation has attempted to foster new intrapreneurs among its staff and launch new innovative ventures by means of an internal business case competition.

Man on the Moon – a business case competition in a global company

(Devised by William B. Gartner and Ann Højbjerg Clarke)

Founded in 1933, the Danfoss Group is a family-owned corporation headquartered in Nordborg, Denmark and with operations in over 100 countries. Danfoss competes across global markets covering eight business areas: refrigeration and air conditioning, heating, frequency converters, industrial automation, water controls, high-pressure water solutions, geared motors and solar energy. In 2009, net sales for Danfoss exceeded 3.4 billion Euros, and the company employed over 25,000 people of whom fewer than 6,600 were based in Denmark.

Around the turn of the century, the Danfoss top management team realised a paradox existed between ways and incentives to develop incremental and radical innovations at the corporate and divisional levels of the organisation. At the corporate level, the creation of a centralised research and development centre could lead to the creation of radical innovations. However, such innovations were unlikely to be connected to business strategies within any of the existing divisions. By their nature, radical innovations are something different from the daily business of the divisions and therefore difficult to foster. Without direct links to a division's current operations and markets, radical innovations invented at the corporate centre were not likely to be pursued by the divisions. At the divisional level, the metrics of efficiency and profitability required a focus on existing customers, existing suppliers or other existing relationships so that innovative activities would aim at improving existing products or market shares, i.e. incremental innovation rather than radical innovation. The development of radical innovations required the investment of resources in new technologies and new markets which, in the short run, would not produce profits or efficiencies in each division's operations and markets. So, radical innovations were not pursued at divisional level. However, since most of the Danfoss divisions operated in mature markets with low growth and revenue, the future of the company required growth through the development of new products and markets. The primary question, then, for the top management team was: 'How might Danfoss go about creating new opportunities for growth while maintaining efficiencies and profitability in current markets and products?'

In 2004 Danfoss initiated a completely new organisational structure for pursuing incremental and radical innovations at the same time. The structure involved two primary parties:

1 The Danfoss divisions, focused at existing markets and products through incremental innovation
2 The creation of Danfoss Ventures and the Danfoss Entrepreneur Park.

CASE STUDY *(continued)*

Danfoss Ventures would aim at radical innovations measured in terms of whether the innovations were new-to-market or new-to-company. The Danfoss Entrepreneur Park would support local entrepreneurs from inside and outside the corporation that have viable business ideas, which could benefit from the competences Danfoss already have, but which fall outside of Danfoss' current business scope.

The Man on the Moon competition is created

In order to generate both incremental and radical innovations within the Danfoss Group, the top management team decided, in 2004, to hold an annual internal competition for the creation of new businesses named 'Man on the Moon' (MOM), a title inspired by President J.F. Kennedy when he spoke of sending a man to the moon and returning him safely to the earth:

> I believe we possess all the resources and talents necessary. But the facts of the matter are that we have never made the national decisions or marshalled the national resources required for such leadership. We have never specified long-range goals on an urgent time schedule or managed our resources and our time so as to insure their fulfilment. (J.F. Kennedy, 25 May 1961)

Not only would such a competition be likely to identify innovations that the company might pursue, but the process would also identify employees within the company with intrapreneurial potential. These individuals could then be provided with skills and support to enable their intrapreneurial activities to occur within the company. While the company appeared to lack employees with intrapreneurial skills that could work with novel technologies and markets, managers at Danfoss were convinced that these entrepreneurial employees *did* exist within the company, but they had to be identified and encouraged to try. It was thought that there would then be a new career path for Danfoss' employees, a new path for intrapreneurs in addition to the traditional career paths for managers and specialists.

Danfoss sought a process that would identify these new intrapreneurs and then establish a

Figure 9.1 A playful man on the moon

CASE STUDY (continued)

talent pool that could later be used in their new established venture unit. Furthermore, they acknowledged that, in order to create such a pool, they needed the attention and commitment of the top management team; otherwise the initiative would die as employees would not be encouraged to take risks. During the process of developing this programme the venture group began to see this project as a human relations and culture change programme and, in addition, as a way to identify new business proposals with great potential.

From the beginning the goal of MOM was to 'aim high', the thinking being, 'we cannot do this in half measures as then we will never pull through'. It had to be world class. Consequently, the first competition had a budget that was quite large, especially in relation to Danfoss Ventures' own budget. Furthermore, in order to develop the competition and train the participants, Danfoss Ventures worked with researchers from American and European universities as well as external venture capitalists.

The Danfoss Venture division set the guidelines for team formation and rules for the contest, endeavouring to emulate the conditions of a start-up as closely as possible. Teams consist of two to five members. In order to cover vital aspects of a venture, different competencies have to be represented in each team, for example marketing, finance, engineering and distribution. The teams are free to utilise any contacts and resources, both inside and outside the Danfoss Corporation. Teams will be working on their business proposal in addition to their regular jobs. The organisers of MOM believe that those who aspire to become intrapreneurs within the corporation are willing to give +100 per cent to their work *and* venture efforts. By working on both projects and current jobs, without complaining, the MOM contest reveals who is really ready to put in the extra effort to engage in intrapreneurship. It is also important that the company's divisions where these employees work do not lose productivity because these individuals are involved in the MOM competition.

The MOM competition consists of the following phases:

1   The yearly MOM starts with a global invitation to participate. An important part of the competition is a top-management invitation to employees across the entire corporation.
2   Based on a strategic and operational assessment of the proposed business idea's potential by Danfoss Ventures, a number of promising teams are selected to join the next stage of the competition.
3   The selected teams participate in a two-day workshop that includes training in: team-building; venture creation concepts, skills, tools and activities.
4   One month later teams submit a summary of their business proposal and deliver a short presentation in front of a jury which evaluates these projects. Normally half of the teams gain access to the final stage of the contest in which they receive one day of business coaching as well as mentoring from Danfoss managers. These mentors assist projects through the Danfoss system, ensuring that the teams are not held up by Danfoss policies and procedures. Teams are also given funds for expenses (e.g. travel, reports, and consultants) and training.

CASE STUDY *(continued)*

5   After six more weeks, the finalist teams present their ideas and business proposals to the Danfoss top management team. The top three teams are awarded the opportunity to participate in an MIT entrepreneurship course in January/February the following year.

6   In a post-contest evaluation by Danfoss Ventures, all business proposals are assessed for further funding. The venture group also evaluates whether it is appropriate to place the project in an existing division or in the Danfoss-incubator unit. They also evaluate in which country the project is likely to be exposed to the most favourable conditions.

The MOM organisers do not expect participants in the competition to finish developing their ideas into specific products or services. Given that the competition lasts only three months, it is impossible to develop a finished product or service. Instead, participants are expected to state their business case clearly along with critical assumptions about the technology used. Winners should also clearly outline the areas that need to be investigated to determine whether the product or service is truly viable and profitable in the short and long term.

The MOM outcome

For the first competition held in 2004, three projects (nine participants in total, all from Denmark) were selected to participate in the final round in front of the Danfoss top management team. All participating projects were given funding of US$200,000 to continue the development of their ideas. Two of these projects are still running and one of these projects has entered the market. In the second competition held in 2005, there were 90 inquiries from Danfoss employees that resulted in 40 applications; 20 individuals were interviewed, and 12 people were selected to participate in the competition (coming from Denmark and India). Four teams competed and two of these projects were funded. In 2006 there were 44 participants in 10 teams (from Denmark, China, India, France and Germany) of which four were funded. Each of the 10 projects had a business potential of over US$20 million. Three of these projects were absorbed by other divisions within Danfoss; two were shut down; and five are being developed further. Since 2006, the competition has stabilised at this level, engaging about 50 individuals yearly, divided into 10–15 venture teams. So, over the years a huge number of Danfoss employees have gained entrepreneurial experience and competence from this competition. In 2010 Danfoss decided to close down and reorganise some of its venturing activities, but MOM continues.

As the outcomes of the venture development competition vary from the successful creation of 'spin-ins' (projects that are absorbed into established Danfoss divisions); 'spin-outs' (projects that often are funded by outside investors and then sold-off); and 'stops' (projects that fail), the Danfoss Group sought to provide various pathways and incentives for employees who choose to be involved in these entrepreneurial ventures. All employees involved in the venture creation process had the opportunity to stay with their new ventures, and, if successful, earn bonuses based on the valuation of the project (either as an external exit or as an internal venture as valued by its profits to a division). Employees could also opt to

CASE STUDY *(continued)*

return to their respective divisions if they didn't want to continue with venture development efforts. When projects failed, managers could return to their divisions or find opportunities to work with other ventures.

The assumption that Danfoss had many entrepreneurial employees proved to be correct and MOM proved to be an efficient means of identifying these talents. Whilst not all MOM venture projects were successful, the venture competition did provide opportunities for employees at Danfoss to realise their intrapreneurial talents and direct the Danfoss Group into potential high growth markets through the development of radical innovations.

Your immediate interpretation

What does the story tell you about Danfoss' experience with intrapreneurship in general? How would you immediately understand the development process historically? The following exercises can help you create an understanding of what is at stake in the story, and thus how you can comprehend intrapreneurship.

- Think about some of the challenges that confront Danfoss in their attempts to foster intrapreneurship within the organisation by way of the Man on the Moon competition. Then, prioritise the challenges depending on what you believe are most critical in relation to understanding intrapreneurship.
- Now, you should try to tackle and solve the challenge to which you accorded highest priority in the above exercise. First, put yourself in the place of an individual employee. How would he/she solve the challenge? Then adopt the role of the senior manager in Danfoss. How would the chief executive meet the challenge?
- Then reflect on how the two solutions found are influenced by each of the two roles you played. Did the two different roles make you handle the challenge differently? Why / why not?

Theories of entrepreneurship

Although the title of this section is 'theories of entrepreneurship', the focal point is the theory of intrapreneurship. This theory will help you gain an understanding of the mechanisms that must be discussed when new opportunities arise that are to be evaluated and organised within the framework of an existing company.

The theory of intrapreneurship can be broadly divided into two perspectives. One perspective holds that intrapreneurship is initiated and driven by top management. Creation of intrapreneurship is thus top-down. The argument for a top-down process is that support and action from top management is essential if intrapreneurship is to become a reality. It is senior management's constant attention and monitoring that creates momentum and success. The other perspective takes the view that successful intrapreneurship is created by people with the enthusiasm and self-confidence to drive intrapreneurship forward. Here, intrapreneurship is created bottom-up. The argument is that intrapreneurship can only be cultivated through dedicated and enterprising people who in their daily work discover or create the potential for renewal. In this chapter you will therefore discuss intrapreneurship in terms of the paradox:

> Top-down or bottom-up

Background story

Before thoroughly exploring the paradox, let's delve into the background of intrapreneurship. Overall, intrapreneurship is a phenomenon that apparently, is closely related to socioeconomic development. Birkinshaw et al (2002) argue that the interest of US companies in intrapreneurship has, in historical terms, been fostered by three waves of popularity from 1960 to 2002. The waves show that it is particularly during periods of positive economic development that intrapreneurship is placed on the agendas of existing firms with a good economic situation, providing room for them to pursue new opportunities. Such interest does not appear during periods of economic recession. Birkinshaw et al talk of the three waves of popularity:

> The first ended in 1973 with the oil price shock and the ensuing recession. The second began in the early 1980s . . . and came to an end in the late 1980s (again because of recession). The third wave began during the great 1990s technology boom, and it peaked in 2000 before falling steeply. The third wave was driven by a combination of new technologies and also a bubble economy. (Birkinshaw et al 2002: 10).

In connection with each of the three waves, an increasing number of existing companies showed interest in intrapreneurship. The question is whether the experience of the three waves of popularity will influence how a fourth generation of existing companies engage in intrapreneurship. In other words, the question is: 'whether organizations will have learned the lessons in making the idea work' (Birkinshaw et al 2002: 10). There are indications that companies have not necessarily learned, as the financial crisis in 2009 again led to more companies downsizing their intrapreneurial activities. The Danfoss case study is a good example of this.

Other factors besides socio-economic development may also help to inhibit work with intrapreneurship. Birkinshaw et al (2002) list the following factors:

- Most companies work with multiple objectives rather than a precise measurement of intrapreneurship.
- There is no adequate managerial support. The result is that the skills required to develop intrapreneurial ideas and opportunities will not be developed.
- Remuneration systems, such as shares to employees, are not being implemented. There is simply no carrot that motivates the team behind the new opportunity.

So there are apparently many potential obstacles which must be overcome when working with intrapreneurship. This includes potential rivalry between new ventures and mature business lines in a company (Evald and Bager 2008). So, what are the success criteria? Critical success factors seems to be: 'develop clear goals – and a structure to deliver on them ... build specialised capabilities ... separate venture units and parent firm ... committed sponsorship from the highest level' (Birkinshaw et al 2002: 12–15).

The prevalence of intrapreneurship internationally

There are few reports on intrapreneurship that compare the incidence of intrapreneurship between countries. A recent report by Niels Bosma, Erik Stam and Sander Wennekers (2008) presents the results of an international study of intrapreneurship (defined as: employees developing new business activities together with their employer), carried out in 11 countries. The results show that intrapreneurship is not a very wide-spread phenomenon: 'On average, fewer than 5% of employees are intrapreneurs ... its incidence in the adult population is, on average, significantly lower than that of early-stage entrepreneurial activity.' (Bosma et al 2008: 5) The result provides clear evidence that even though we see independent entrepreneurship and intrapreneurship as being very similar activities, it is independent entrepreneurship that constitutes a more frequent expression of entrepreneurial behaviour. However, there are significant differences between low- and high-income countries: intrapreneurs seem to be roughly twice as prevalent in high-income countries as in low-income countries (comparing 11 countries, of which Brazil, Chile, Ecuador, Iran, Latvia, Peru and Uruguay are defined as low-income countries and where the Republic of Korea, Netherlands, Norway and Spain are defined as high-income countries). In another study comparing Denmark with other countries, Hancock and Bager (2003) find that Denmark is a country where one finds a high number of intrapreneurs. Not only is there a high level (46 per cent of the total entrepreneurial activity in Denmark), but also levels are slightly increasing over time. Denmark thus occupies a rare leadership position in terms of using employees in large companies as a springboard to discover / create new opportunities, evaluate and exploit them when compared with a number of other countries. Anyway, getting back to the Bosma, Stam and Wennekers (2008) study, there are various explanations for why there are differences in the level of intrapreneurship between low- and high-income countries: 'First, the level of economic development has a positive effect on the presence of larger firms, which negatively influences the prevalence of independent entrepreneurship in an economy. Second, large organisations in high-income countries may be more open to entrepreneurial behaviour than large firms in low income countries.' (Bosma et al 2008: 5) Further, employees working in larger firms have relatively greater latitude in their daily work than is the case in other countries (Dobbin & Boychuk 1999).

A diverse concept

In terms of starting an independent organisation, the concept of intrapreneurship is a newer phenomenon than entrepreneurship. Therefore, intrapreneurship is not backed up by the same tradition that characterises entrepreneurship. Intrapreneurship is still a phenomenon in development. Even the term intrapreneurship is often debated because competing terms are used, such as 'corporate entrepreneurship', 'dependent entrepreneurship' or 'entrepreneurship in established companies' (Sharma & Chrisman 1999). We understand these terms interchangeably, but in this chapter use only the term intrapreneurship.

Branches in intrapreneurship

There are similarities between entrepreneurship as the start-up of an independent organisation and intrapreneurship. Both research fields are based on entrepreneurial behaviour and entrepreneurial activities, i.e. the activities that involve discovery or creation of opportunities and the evaluation and utilization of these through organising.

However, differences also exist. Whereas the process of creating something new in entrepreneurship involves all of the activities required to form a new independent organisation, intrapreneurship does not necessarily include all of the activities that an existing company is involved in. Intrapreneurship can thus appear as 'Dispersed' (= wide) or 'Focused' (= narrow) (Elfring 2005), which means that intrapreneurship can be both activities that involve all employees (dispersed), 'because each employee has the capacity for both managerial and entrepreneurial behaviour', or only involve a *few* employees (focused) who are considered to be particularly entrepreneurial. The Danfoss case study is a good example of a combination of the two, since Danfoss created the Man on the Moon competition, potentially involving all their employees, but at the same time puts its money on new ideas in a more focused way in their 'incubator' system through Danfoss Ventures.

But the most crucial difference between entrepreneurship and intrapreneurship is that entrepreneurship is the entrepreneurial process through which an individual or a group of people who are independent of connections to an existing business, establish one or more new independent organisations (Sharma & Chrisman 1999). On the other hand, it is characteristic of intrapreneurship that the process takes shape, when opportunities are developed by individuals or groups of people that are dependent upon a company's existing organisational framework (Collins & Moore 1970). Collins and Moore are among the first to divide the research in entrepreneurship into two main groups according to whether entrepreneurial activity is independent or dependent of an existing company (intrapreneurship). This is illustrated in Figure 9.2, which divides the intrapreneurship concept into three different branches.

The figure shows that intrapreneurship research is characterised by three different branches or trends. To begin with Guth and Ginsberg divide intrapreneurship into two major subgroups, namely: 1) formation of a new organisational unit and 2) strategic renewal (Guth & Ginsberg 1990). The formation of a new organisational entity may include a new project, a new company or a new division. By strategic renewal we mean an organisational change strategy that may include changing core competencies, resource uses and competitive parameters at project, corporate, divisional or group level.

In 1999 the division was further refined when Sharma and Chrisman added a third subgroup: innovation. The addition occurs because existing companies can create new organisational units, or change their strategies without necessarily having to innovate: especially if innovation is viewed from a strictly Schumpeterian perspective. Additionally, a larger organisa-

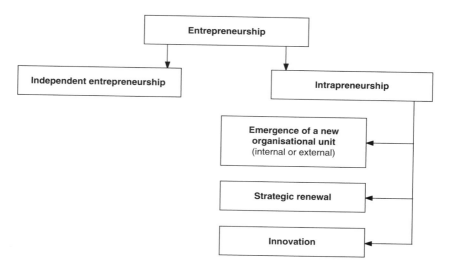

Figure 9.2 Ramifications in the research field of intrapreneurship

tion can innovate, without the other two elements necessarily being a part of the activity. For example, new combinations of knowledge occur without the combinations resulting in new units or strategic renewal. In most cases however, intrapreneurship involves all three aspects, as is the case in the Danfoss case study where Danfoss implements strategic renewal, innovates and creates new organisational units via the Man on the Moon competition and the incubator system.

The final refinement of intrapreneurship to which we will introduce you is that the formation of a new organisational unit can both be internal or external to an existing corporate organisational framework (Von Hippel 1977). The formation of a new organisational unit can occur internally, through the development of internal units such as new groups, projects or companies. The formation of a new organisational unit may also take place externally through the establishment of joint ventures and spin-outs. In the Danfoss case study both forms are combined, as Danfoss worked with spin-ins and spin-outs as a result of the Man on the Moon competition. In this chapter we confine ourselves to understanding intrapreneurship as creating new units internally. This is consistent with Burgelman's (1983a, 1983b) definition of intrapreneurship. He sees intrapreneurship as a process in which companies achieve differentiation through internal development processes. This focus really puts the paradox, 'top-down and bottom-up' on the agenda as internal intrapreneurship implies that innovation must either live side by side with the existing organisational structures, routines and strategies (focused intrapreneurship) or be adopted into the existing organisation structures, routines and strategies (dispersed intrapreneurship). The consequence of Burgelman's understanding that intrapreneurship is achieved through internal development processes can thus be very different processes according to whether intrapreneurship is assumed to be distributed across the whole organization, or if intrapreneurship is restricted to a particular unit or part of the whole organisation.

The degree of innovation in intrapreneurship

The forces and challenges that existing firms encounter in their establishment of intrapreneurship is dependent on the degree of novelty of the opportunities pursued. Are we talking about an option that is new to the existing organisation, new to the market or new to the world? The more the opportunity can be described as innovative, the more the existing business faces the challenge of creating a new market for that opportunity. This may result in the opportunity to be exploited, being associated with a high degree of risk and complexity.

On the other hand, the advantage in capturing an innovative opportunity is that the existing firm acquires clear differentiation and competitive advantage over its rivals.

To talk about the various degrees of innovation related to intrapreneurship we need to introduce the concept of incremental versus radical intrapreneurship. They must be understood as a continuum. The former refers to the idea that opportunities remain fundamentally the same, but are renewed gradually. Development of businesses therefore takes the form of a gradual process by which products, processes, etc. incrementally and slowly take new shape. This is the case for instance with the divisions in Danfoss, which itself stands for progressive innovations. At the opposite end of the continuum, radical intrapreneurship is concerned with how existing companies develop in leaps and bounds, coming up with potential opportunities that are completely different from existing ones. Here, the Danfoss case study is also illustrative, as Danfoss deliberately tried to establish an incubator system that has the opportunity gamble on more radical ideas (Clarke et al 2012). The difference between incremental and radical innovations is plotted in Figure 9.3.

The process behind intrapreneurship

So, what characterises the entrepreneurial process that lies behind intrapreneurship? There are obviously many different opinions on how this process progresses. Figure 9.4 offers one model.

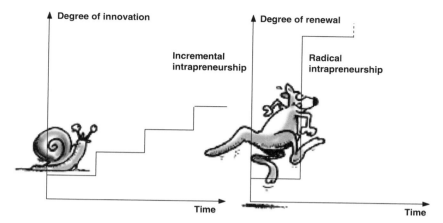

Figure 9.3 Incremental versus radical intrapreneurship

The figure shows what it takes for individuals or groups of individuals to take the initiative to undertake intrapreneurship, discovering or creating opportunities and perhaps ultimately translating these into concrete actions through evaluation and organisation. This figure focuses on what happens during the process behind intrapreneurship.

The figure particularly emphasises how intrapreneurship is a product of two factors, which are constantly interacting with each other, namely: individual characteristics and organisational characteristics. For these two factors to start interacting with each other there is often a catalyst or trigger event. 'The decision to act intrapreneurially occurs as a result of an interaction between organizational characteristics, individual characteristics, and some kind of precipitating event. The precipitating event provides the impetus to behave intrapreneurially when other conditions are conducive to such behavior.' (Hornsby et al 1993: 33) More specifically Zahra (1991) points to how the triggering event may, for example, be the development of new procedures or technologies, the replacement of management, a collaboration with, or acquisition of another company, a competitor's incipient takeover of market shares, efficiencies, changes in customer demand or economic changes. All this can lead to individuals in an existing company discovering or creating a new opportunity. The following explains the figure's content in more detail.

Individual characteristics

Over time, important individual characteristics have been shown empirically to influence the process of intrapreneurship. Many of the characteristics

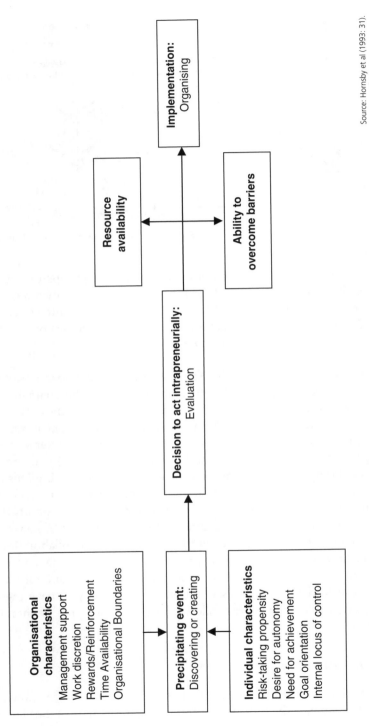

Figure 9.4 Intrapreneurship as a process

Source: Hornsby et al (1993: 31).

listed in Figure 9.4 are obvious, but two of them, deserve elaboration. These are the need for achievement and internal locus of control. The need for achievement is, as mentioned in Chapter 1, one of the first traits associated with entrepreneurs in the field of entrepreneurship research. As a natural consequence, this trait is also incorporated within the literature on intrapreneurship. People who prefer to be personally responsible for solving problems, setting goals and achieving them are considered to have high achievement needs. Achievement needs are then closely related to other factors listed as individual characteristics, such as goal-oriented behaviour and the need for autonomy. Control over inner feelings is a different type of character trait associated with the intrapreneur. This factor refers to individuals or groups of individuals feeling that they themselves have control over what happens in the process of intrapreneurship.

Organisational characteristics

In the case of organisational characteristics a number of factors play a crucial role. These are, in contrast to the individual characteristics, less obvious and are therefore examined in more detail. Management support includes, for example, rapid adoption of potential opportunities identified by employees, appreciation of those who present new potential opportunities, support of experimental projects and the availability of venture capital. Job autonomy covers employees' ability to independently plan work and an absence of destructive criticism of employees' mistakes. Within reward / reinforcement, there is consideration of personal challenge and responsibility, financial remuneration depending on performance and raising awareness of the potential opportunities that employees have developed within the organisational hierarchy. The time factor refers to the time that is made available for employees to hatch new potential opportunities through, for example, moderate workloads, removal of deadlines on all aspects of a person's work and support for time-consuming problem solving projects. Avoidance of rigid organisational boundaries is to avoid standard procedures for all work functions, reducing dependence on narrow job descriptions and rigid performance standards. All of these are assumed to be involved in promoting the process of intrapreneurship.

Activities in the process of intrapreneurship

If no obstacles arise in the interaction between organisational and individual characteristics, then according to the model, individuals or groups of people begin a series of activities. This can include preparation of business plans, market research and various meetings with the existing business concerning the size of venture capital support. In other words, a range of activities, for the purpose of evaluating the opportunity is set in motion. Is it ready for the market and how? If the necessary resources are made available and the range of organisational, socio-cultural, business administration and individual barriers are overcome, then the process of intrapreneurship can result in proper organising of the opportunity.

Top-down intrapreneurship

Now you know what the term intrapreneurship covers, and you know the key events in the process of intrapreneurship. However, this chapter's paradox indicates that there are two different perspectives of what creates intrapreneurship.

Overall, top-down processes are described as being characterised by the management within existing companies taking the initiative through the formulation of strategies, action plans and commencement of actual operations in the field. Intrapreneurship is thus implemented from the firm's upper layer and passed down into the system, which according to Figure 9.4 suggests that the organisational dimension dominates the process of intrapreneurship. Top-down intrapreneurship means a controlled process, which manages and controls its development. Last but not least one can expect a close relationship between the existing company's management, the intrapreneurs and the development of the potential opportunity.

From the top-down perspective this close relationship is considered to be appropriate. The relationship creates the opportunity for formal and informal coaching (Thornhill & Amit 2001). Furthermore the intrapreneurs have easy access to the skills and resources built up by the existing company over time.

Bottom-up intrapreneurship

Unlike the top-down perspective the bottom-up perspective focuses on the situation in which intrapreneurship is created as a result of employee initiative. Intrapreneurship thus grows in existing companies from scratch. Figure 9.4 suggests that the individual dimension dominates in terms of explaining the generation of intrapreneurship within the organisation. Instead of control, the bottom-up perspective emphasises greater autonomy, since the employees, through continuous innovation, break with the management's guidelines and plans. The bottom-up perspective assumes, in other words, a loose coupling between the existing corporate governance, the intrapreneurs and the potential opportunities that are discovered or created.

Figure 9.5 Top-down and bottom-up processes

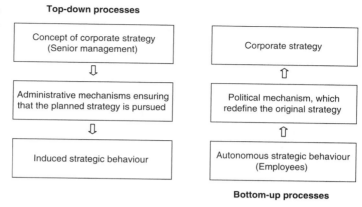

Source: Burgelman (1983a: 225).

Where the relationship between these actors is too close it is assumed by the bottom-up perspective to kill the entrepreneurial, dynamic working environment characterised by the team behind the potential new opportunity (Birkinshaw et al 2002). The reason is that it is explicitly or implicitly expected that existing corporate standards, structures, rules and values will be complied with when the new opportunity is being further developed (Day 1994). This can lead to a dimming of the creative development required for further development of the opportunity. A high level of autonomy in connection with intrapreneurship is therefore preferred.

Top-down and bottom-up

To clarify the difference between the top-down and bottom-up processes further, we introduce Burgelman (1983a and 1983b). He is concerned with how strategies of intrapreneurship emerge and are formed into larger existing businesses. Figure 9.5 shows the top-down and bottom-up perspectives in a single diagram.

As shown in the figure's left-hand side, the starting point for existing businesses is an articulate and official strategy, which informs the employees of the direction in which the company wishes to develop. To ensure that the employees in the existing company comply with the strategy, senior management can initiate a number of administrative mechanisms. As such, these mechanisms control the behaviour of employees so that they follow the direction identified in the strategy. These administrative mechanisms either motivate or punish employees to demonstrate the strategic behaviour that senior management wants. This is what Burgelman considers to be top-down driven entrepreneurial activities and processes.

Now the figure's right-hand side. Since most employees are at the operational level where day-to-day decisions are made, they are constantly faced with new potential opportunities for how challenges can be resolved, improved, or attacked quite differently from before. The new potential can sometimes differ dramatically from the planned and intended strategy. If the new opportunities prove to be successful, a series of political mechanisms start up. The political mechanisms can be discussions concerning existing strategy so that senior management is aware that there are alternative ways to solve challenges. 'Political mechanisms through which middle managers question the current concept of strategy, and provide top management with the opportunity to rationalize, retroactively, successful autonomous strategic behaviour.' (Burgelman 1983b: 1352) The existing firm's official strategy is thus reconsidered and the new opportunities are integrated. Here, according to Burgelman, it is a bottom-up process that creates and forms the official strategy.

However Burgelman's (1983b) main argument is that strategies for intrapreneurship emerge and are shaped by interconnected activities that people at different hierarchical levels in the existing firm attend to. A combination of the conduct and actions exhibited by top managers, middle managers and employees helps determine strategies for intrapreneurship. Strategies for intrapreneurship are not just either planned intentions that are created and shaped top-down, or strategies that emerge and take shape from the bottom-up. They are a result of both top-down and bottom-up processes. Actually it is a widespread assumption within the intrapreneurship literature that the balance between top-down and bottom-up processes is central to successful intrapreneurship. 'Many ventures fail because parent corporations provide the venture with inadequate support or autonomy. Paradoxically, to surmount this problem, some corporations grant ventures so free rein that the ventures incur large losses . . . how can corporations manage these extremes by providing autonomy while maintaining damage control?' (Simon et al 1999: 145)

How to create a balance

So, creating successful intrapreneurship is about finding a balance between top-down management and bottom-up initiatives (Heinonen & Toivonen 2008) and requires elements of both control and autonomy. Traditionally, the literature has focused on how larger companies can maximise the likelihood of the new opportunity's success through a high level of autonomy and thereby providing room for bottom-up processes. However there are several examples of how existing companies that give 'free rein' to their new projects

and companies have no guarantee of the venture's success. In fact, 'free rein' can be just as fatal for new opportunity's future as too much control through top-down processes (Block & MacMillan 1993).

However, Thornhill and Amit (2001) stress that the need for social acceptance, commitment and control from top management should be viewed over time. For the majority of new businesses the need for economic control diminishes as they mature. Social acceptance and the support of senior management will, however, remain important regardless of the age of the new venture. But there are few empirical results that run counter to this idea. Over time, some new firms experience a greater focus on financial targets whilst at the same time, senior management become less involved. These results also make sense because more financial independence often leads to greater financial accountability. Finally, a company that achieves both independence and accountability generally has less need for senior management to provide 'air cover'.

The question is: how can a balance be struck between the top-down and bottom-up processes? There are many approaches. Simon et al (1999) recommend that existing companies appoint three people to handle the new business and existing business interests when intrapreneurship is being implemented. The combination of three persons should ensure that, on the one hand, new companies have sufficient autonomy to develop. On the other hand, the combination also ensures continuous control of the new companies. The three persons are, firstly, a 'venture manager' for the new company whose task is to run the new company and ensure that it procures the resources required for it to develop. The venture manager's purpose is thus primarily to safeguard the interests of the new company. Next, a 'venture godparent' is appointed. Typically this will be a centrally placed person appointed by the existing business to help the new company in its development. The venture godparent's mission is primarily to protect the new business from existing corporate bureaucracy and ensure that the resources that are central to its development are provided. Finally, the existing company appoints a venture ombudsperson. Typically this will also be a central person in the existing business – for example a person from the existing company's management. This person's job is primarily to handle the existing business interests. This means that the investment that the new company reflects is continually assessed against the existing corporate interests. The roles that the three people fulfil are elaborated in Table 9.1.

Table 9.1 Key people in the balance between top-down and bottom-up processes

Venture manager	Venture godparent	Venture ombudsperson
Runs the venture: needs autonomy	Protects the venture from organisational resistance: helps provide autonomy	Monitors venture progress: balances need for autonomy and control
Develops innovative, high-quality products	Argues for a high level of support and against removal of support during corporate downturns	Decides markets to enter based on fit with corporation
Pursues aggressive strategies	Blocks corporate interference in day-to-day activities	Determines the number and size of ventures in the portfolio
Moulds a culture based on creativity and a bias to act	Opposes inadequate rewards and unjust punishment	Uses milestones to provide venture support and manager compensation

Source: Simon et al (1999: 157).

Intrapreneurship: top-down or bottom-up?

You have now been presented with the processes and mechanisms involved in the creation of intrapreneurship. In particular we can identify two perspectives, each of which emphasises the advisability of adopting either a top-down or bottom-up approach in order to achieve successful intrapreneurship. The two perspectives are summarised in Table 9.2.

Table 9.2 The paradox: Top-down or bottom-up

	Top-down	Bottom-up
Hierarchical level	Top level	Operational level
Source of initiative	Top management	Employees
The process	Controlled behaviour	Autonomous behaviour
Tool	Administrative mechanisms	Political mechanisms
Mechanisms for implementation	Control and minimal autonomy	Autonomy and minimum control

The source of the top-down perspective is at the top level of the organisation with the senior management being assumed to initiate the process of intrapreneurship. The process is a controlled process, ensuring that the official goal of management's plans and strategies are met. This takes place through various administrative mechanisms, such as various 'carrot and stick' approaches, thereby ensuring that the operational level listen to the senior level and understand the purpose of the official strategy. The success associated with the process of intrapreneurship is secured through control and minimal elbowroom. In contrast, the bottom-up perspective supports the idea that the operational level is the key to understanding how the process of intrapreneurship occurs. It is the employees who take the intrapreneurial initiative; the process itself is controlled by autonomous behaviour. There is room for sudden impulses and innovative opportunities. Instead of administrative mechanisms, the process is controlled through political mechanisms through which people seek to create space, resources and support for the bottom-up process in the organisation. However, the prerequisite for a bottom-up process is that management is restrained and provides space for innovation through elbowroom and minimal supervision.

A theoretical interpretation

In the following we give our interpretation of the Danfoss case study in light of the theory and the paradox presented in the chapter.

The top-down perspective

According to a top-down interpretation, we highlight the following in the Danfoss story. Over the years, Danfoss has experimented with various innovative approaches at the divisional and group level. At the divisional level small R & D departments have been attached to each division supporting the objective of creating innovation, and at group level a larger central research centre has taken care of innovation. Senior management in Danfoss has been dedicated in its efforts to support innovation, but have done so in different ways. Although the top leadership, through innovation strategies and associated administrative mechanisms, have got groups of their employees to comply with the two different innovation strategies, the results have not been satisfactory. Certainly, the innovation strategy to support radical innovation through a research and development centre at group level has resulted in radical innovations, but these have been so distant from the daily production in the divisions that this innovation has been poorly used. Moreover, the innovation strategy to support the divisions' own research and development of innovations also failed. No radical innovations have found a footing here, since the divisions' desires concerning what they innovated have been too narrow to fit directly into daily production – only incremental innovations have been achieved. However, the initiatives have convinced senior management that the staff involved in the activities have respected the various initiatives they have implemented. The administrative mechanisms have thus quite properly worked on controlling employee behaviour, but innovation strategies have lacked balance between the need for simultaneous incremental and radical innovations. After a period of years collecting experiences of how incremental and radical innovations are supported, the senior management then launched a system that supported both types of innovations simultaneously. The system included the Man on the Moon competition and the organisation of a venture company and an incubator environment.

When senior management launched the Man on the Moon competition in 2004, it did so with a certain amount of scepticism. There was anxiety about the system being launched and whether it was possible to really encourage the employees to think both incrementally and radically. However, a number of administrative mechanisms were implemented to monitor and back up intended and planned actions in accordance with the official strategy to ensure a steady course and inform employees what kind of behaviour they should exhibit. After a short test of the system senior management breathed a sigh of relief. The system worked and the administrative mechanisms they had put into play to control employees' behaviour also worked successfully.

On the basis of Figure 9.5, this can be interpreted as the administrative mechanisms operating and constantly keeping employees on track. The Danfoss story can thus be seen as an example of how intrapreneurship is constantly created top-down by senior management, who have an overview of what is needed for innovations to enhance the business of the group.

The bottom-up perspective

What if we look at the Danfoss story from a bottom-up perspective? This viewpoint would stress how it is only after several years with dedicated and ambitious employees that intrapreneurship was placed on the agenda of the senior management at Danfoss. The perspective will point out that it is the employees' own initiatives and commitment which ultimately convinces senior management that they are able to innovate both incrementally as well as radically and even at the same time.

The process at Danfoss, whereby senior management experimented with innovation at group and divisional level illustrates that the senior management had been unable to find out how they had to simultaneously create fertile ground for incremental and radical innovation. In cases of imbalance in the way innovation has been implemented at Danfoss, senior management has always taken action, but primarily in a lopsided/one-sided manner as they have focused on getting their staff to develop either incremental or radical innovation. Over the years, senior management began to see, through their employees' actions, that both types of innovation can occur simultaneously and that the combination of the two types of innovation is actually very useful for Danfoss: the existing business is constantly and incrementally renewed while Danfoss also ensures potential new business areas through more radical innovations that can evolve to become revenue sources, which are just as large as the 'old' business, in the future.

It is also why the senior management at Danfoss ultimately established the Man on the Moon competition, and even went a step further, establishing a venture department and an incubator environment. Senior management expected the Man on the Moon competition to draw on all employees' innovative capabilities throughout the organisation, whether this meant incremental or radical innovation. Moreover, the senior management also organised a venture department and an incubator environment for those employees who innovated more radically and therefore needed to isolate themselves from the rest of the company's everyday work in order to test the potential of radical ideas. Whilst they may have felt that they were on slightly shaky ground as initiatives started up and before they developed, the concerns and worries of the senior management were soon dispersed when employees exhibited enthusiasm and an overwhelming desire to participate in the Man on the Moon competition and other initiatives that were organised.

On the basis of Figure 9.5, this can be interpreted as individuals or groups of people with their autonomous behaviour having a positive effect on Danfoss' current and regularly changing innovation strategy. The Danfoss story can be seen as an example of how intrapreneurship is constantly created bottom-up before senior management shapes an official and intentional strategy.

Testing the theory

Now it's your turn to understand intrapreneurship. The following exercises are for inspiration.

 EXERCISES

1 **Offer a simultaneous bottom-up and top-down interpretation.** What happens to the Danfoss story, if you simultaneously try to identify the bottom-up and top-down processes? Which processes are in harmony with each other and which are in conflict with each other?

2 **Other companies that cultivate intrapreneurship.** Use the Internet to find material on other existing companies that make use of intrapreneurship. Search for words like 'intrapreneur' and

'intrapreneurship'. Next, discuss how different existing companies handle intrapreneurship, and in what areas they bear similarities to or are different from the Danfoss case study.

3 **Strengths and challenges associated with intrapreneurship.** On the basis of the material you have collected, you should now list the strengths and challenges that seem to characterise existing companies when trying their hand at intrapreneurship. What strengths and challenges recur regardless of size, age and industry association? Which seem to be specific to a small group of companies? Why is it apparently so?

4 **Introduce your new knowledge to a company.** Offer an invitation to or visit an existing company that would like to either experiment with intrapreneurship, or already have experience with intrapreneurship. Present the knowledge you have gained about intrapreneurship. Discuss with the company how best to handle intrapreneurship.

 LITERATURE

Bager, T., Ottósson, H. & Schott, T. (2010) 'Intrapreneurs, entrepreneurs and spin-off entrepreneurs: Similarities and differences', *International Journal of Entrepreneurship and Small Business*, 10(3), 339–358.

Birkinshaw, J., Batenburg, R.B. & Murray, G. (2002) 'Venturing to succeed', *Business Strategy Review*, 13(4), 10–17.

Block, Z. & MacMillan, I.C. (1993) *Corporate Venturing: Creating New Businesses within the Firm*, Boston, MA: Harvard Business School Press.

Bosma, N., Wennekers, S. and Stam, E. (2010) 'Intrapreneurship – An international study', Scales Research Reports H201005, EIM Business and Policy Research.

Burgelman, R.A. (1983a) 'A Process Model of Internal Corporate Venturing in the Diversified Major Firm', *Administrative Science Quarterly*, 28(2), 223–244.

Burgelman, R.A. (1983b) 'Corporate entrepreneurship and strategic management: Insights from a process study', *Management Science*, 29(12), 1349–1364.

Clarke, A.H., Evald, M.R. & Munksgaard, K.B. (2012) 'Exploring Open Innovation in a Comprehensive Innovation Setup', *International Journal of Entrepreneurship and Innovation Management*.

Collins, O.F. & Moore, D.G. (1970) *The organisation makers*, New York: Appleton-Century-Crofts.

Day, D.L. (1994) 'Raising Radicals: Different Processes for Championing Innovative Corporate Ventures', *Organisation Science*, 5(2), 148–172.

Dobbin, F. & Boychuk, T. (1999) 'National Employment Systems and Job Autonomy: Why Job Autonomy is High in the Nordic Countries and Low in the United States, Canada and, Australia', *Organisation Studies*, 20(2), 257–291.

Elfring (2005) 'Dispersed and focused corporate entrepreneurship: Ways to balance exploitation and exploration', in Tom Elfring (ed.) *Corporate Entrepreneurship and Venturing*, New York: Springer, 1–21.

Evald, M.R. & Bager, T.E. (2008) 'The problem of political rivalry among venture teams in corporate incubators: A case study of network dynamics in an advanced high-tech incubator', *International Entrepreneurship and Management Journal*, 4(3), 349–369.

Guth, W.D. & Ginsberg, A. (1990) 'Guest editors' introduction: Corporate entrepreneurship', *Strategic Management Journal*, 11.

Hancock, M. & Bager, T. (2003) 'Global Entrepreneurship Monitor: Denmark 2003', Copenhagen: Børsens Forlag.

Heinonen, J. & Toivonen, J. (2008) 'Corporate entrepreneurs or silent followers', *Leadership and Organisation Development Journal*, 29(7), 583–599.

Hornsby, J.S., Naffziger, D.W., Kuratko, D.F. & Montagno, R.V. (1993) 'An interactive model of corporate entrepreneurship process', *Entrepreneurship Theory and Practice*, 17(2), 29–37.

Sharma, P. & Chrisman, J.J. (1999) 'Toward a reconciliation of the definitional issues in the field of corporate entrepreneurship', *Entrepreneurship Theory and Practice*, 23(3), 11–27.

Simon, M., Houghton, S. M. & Gurney, J. (1999) 'Succeeding at internal corporate venturing: roles needed to balance autonomy and control', *Journal of Applied Management Studies*, 8(2), 145–159.

Thornhill, S. & Amit, R. (2001) 'A dynamic perspective of internal fit in corporate venturing', *Journal of Business Venturing*, 16(1), 25–50.

Von Hippel, E. (1977) 'Successful and Failing Internal Corporate Ventures: An Empirical Analysis', *Industrial Marketing Management*, 6(3), 163–174.

Zahra, S.A. (1991) 'Predictors and financial outcomes of corporate entrepreneurship: An exploratory study', *Journal of Business Venturing*, 6(4), 259–285.

10

Social entrepreneurship

In this chapter we look at entrepreneurship in another context, namely that of social entrepreneurship. As is the case when building an independent organisation or with entrepreneurship in existing firms (intrapreneurship), social entrepreneurship is about discovering or creating new opportunities and evaluating them in order to finally exploit those opportunities through organising. In that way there's not much new under the sun. However there are also differences between the forms of entrepreneurship that we have dealt with so far and social entrepreneurship. The goal of entrepreneurship in the private commercial sector is usually to create economic value for its owners – to make profits. In social entrepreneurship the primary goal is to create better conditions for people both locally and globally, while profit is merely a means to achieve social goals. Profit does not necessarily have to be the guiding goal. In other words, the guiding vision of social entrepreneurship is social and not economic in nature – although the second situation is also conceivable. It is precisely the balance between social and economic goals we discuss in detail in this chapter.

When we talk about social entrepreneurship, we apply a broader sense of the concept 'social' than one normally uses. We don't think only about the social sector and measures aimed at the socially disadvantaged. Social entrepreneurship can be created in many different sectors, through activities in the areas of culture and leisure, through relief efforts, aid and development projects aimed at people in the third world or by creating new commercial businesses that create better conditions for vulnerable groups.

Entrepreneurship in practice

In the following you will be presented with a parable, which is a short tale that illustrates universal truth. The parable is written by Kevin Hindle and can be taught in many contexts and interpreted in many ways. In this chapter the case illustrates how the distinction between 'for profit' and 'social' entrepreneurship is not an easy one to cope with.

The following parable refers to a community of indigenous entrepreneurship in the US. In common with nearly all indigenous communities in countries where they exist (Indians in the US, Aboriginal and Torres Straight Islander in Australia, First Nations in Canada, Ainu in Japan, Saami in Scandinavia, etc.) this community will be poorly resourced, probably on marginal land and the skills and educational levels of the members of this community will be lower than the average in the mainstream, all because of the massive disadvantage conferred on indigenous communities by the negative impact of colonial history. If the parable catches your interest then go to YouTube and listen to the video case by Kevin Hindle telling you personally about the idea of The Parable of the Teepee.

CASE STUDY

The parable of the teepee

(Devised by Kevin Hindle)

The Red Entrepreneur was making what the White Business Advisor called 'good money', but the Angry Group said it was very bad.

The business, called 'Redman Teepees', stood on a well-situated block of Reservation land leased from the Tribal Government, in an area zoned for commercial activity. Here, after some curves and go-slow warnings, the highway straightened again. The well-signed gas station, convenience stores, small museum and the casino were all designed to capture the attention of passing motorists, induce them to stop and spend a bit of time and money. A lot of cars, trucks and buses did stop on the commercial strip. A lot of drivers and passengers browsed the various stores. A surprising number bought teepees from the Red Entrepreneur. They bought them mostly as 'novelty items': something to put up in the back yard for the kids during summer maybe. They weren't that expensive, they kept the weather out, and they were 'a bit different'.

In the room the meeting was hotter than the air-conditioning could handle. The Elder listened patiently to the Angry Group. They spat venom at the Red Entrepreneur. The best of their speakers called the Red Entrepreneur a 'thief of our culture; a man who degrades our heritage by trivialising the collective home of our ancestors for the cheap amusement of those who stole our land and our pride. He takes what belongs to all, the knowledge, the symbolism, the majesty of the teepee and sells cheap imitations of it, keeping the money for himself. This is wrong and must be stopped.' The Good Speaker had a deep, resonant voice. His anger was genuine and his words had power. The Angry Group was loud in support and the Elder listened carefully.

When the Red Entrepreneur spoke his anger was only just under control. But out of respect for the Elder he managed.

CASE STUDY *(continued)*

Figure 10.1 Teepees are used in very hot and cold environments

'I don't know', said the Red Entrepreneur, 'what is more contemptible in this Group: their hypocrisy or their laziness. Is it OK for our tribe to earn money from a casino that has nothing to do with the history of our people, owes its existence to a mere quirk in the White Man's law and teaches our young people only how to wear green eyeshades and deal cards, making them cardboard people? And it is not OK to keep alive the skills of teepee building, giving real jobs and real skills to real people?

Because', said the Red Entrepreneur, 'let me tell you that I do not make and I do not train people to make "cheap imitations". My teepees are authentically made, of good materials and made well. My sweat is in them. My heart is in them. They are sold at fair value. What do you do all day? Nothing. When you give back your government welfare checks and do something constructive, I will listen to you. I will hear you better when you talk less and do more. Until then, your words lack the weight of conviction. I have gone to many classes – paid for by the Tribal Government I might add – to learn business skills and technical skills. Why teach these skills if you do not want people to use them. I have built a relationship at the bank. I train young people. I pay them well. I pay rent. I pay taxes. And you say I give nothing. I give you your welfare checks.'

The Angry Group got angrier. At first the Elder's quiet voice was hard to hear. But quickly the room fell quiet. It was a strange thing many remarked upon: the Elder's quietness. It somehow made you listen. Very strange. And he spoke.

'This Angry Group fills me with sadness. Where is your true respect? Your respect for the warrior and the artisan, traditions our Brother here so proudly represents. I have seen his work. His teepees are good: not good enough but I will come to that. First, I must ask you a

CASE STUDY *(continued)*

hard question. We are people of the plains. In the days of defending our land and our nation in the old way, who was nobler: the warrior who rode to battle or the people afraid of combat who stayed by the warm fires and talked of how bad the world had become?'

The Red Entrepreneur smiled as he listened, but the Elder wiped his smile away.

'Why do you smile? You have no grounds to be smug. Be careful how you use your pride. There are good people in this group and some of their anger is justified. Though it should not be anger it should be sadness. It is sad that you do not make a full teepee; a true teepee, though our skills are such that you could. I say "our skills" because this group is right to say that the *idea* of the teepee, the *soul* of the teepee, belongs to us all. This is a story your work should tell. In our tradition, though construction was similar, every teepee was unique because, painted on it, was the life story, the life and distinctiveness of the family it housed. In this Angry Group, I know, are two superb artists. Why do you not use their skill? Offer to your customers the chance to have their life story painted on their teepees. They will like it. They will pay more. You *do* sell too cheaply and you do not share enough. What extra you make from this, put it toward strengthening the language program that teaches our children the music of the ages. You do not speak our language and it is a shame that you do not respect this man, our Brother, who does – and speaks it majestically.'

Here the Elder directed his gaze and the gaze of all eyes to the Good Speaker.

'I have another question for you, Brother. Could you please write, for us all, the meaning of the teepee: its history, its role in the life and culture of our people? Write it well for two reasons. First, it is a great story and every buyer of a teepee must know it, understand it and, in doing so, they will come to understand us better. It is important work. Second, write it well because you will be well paid for your writing. No teepee will leave this reservation without your story, beautifully inscribed on parchment, being part of what the White Business Advisor might call the "product package". You will receive a payment every time a teepee is sold and you will deserve it because your words will add great value. They will be valuable to the buyers, enabling them to appreciate that the shelter they have bought is a noble thing, beautifully made and deep in significance as well as usefulness. They will add value to our community because every buyer will be keen to tell the story to all who see the teepee or share a night in it.'

And so it happened.

'Redman Teepees' changed its name. The White Business Advisor thought the new name, a name in the language of the people, 'made no marketing sense – and your new high-price, customization strategy will be the death of a good little business.'

The White Business Advisor was very wrong.

This was the birth – some would say re-birth – of a bigger, more profitable and growing business. The first customer of the re-born business was an Airline Pilot. He earned a lot of money and had a small property by the river where he loved to fish and invite his friends to stay. His story and his family history were carefully painted on the outside of his teepee. Where once, in the ancient days, the horse and weapons of a warrior might have been painted,

CASE STUDY *(continued)*

this man's life featured airplanes, his wife, his children and the fish that swam in the river he loved. It took a long time to finish this first teepee and it was very expensive. But the Pilot paid gladly and all summer the teepee was pitched on his land. It could be seen from a great distance. All summer it filled with a great variety of guests – who came to stay with the Pilot and his family. No-one who came into the teepee could resist reading the beautiful words inscribed on the sculpted buffalo-hide parchment which had pride of place as soon as they stepped inside. It told the story of the significance of the teepee in the life of the Tribe and how the concept of the teepee was not an old or dead thing but a vibrant tradition. A woman from Japan bought the next teepee. Artists from Japan came to join the artists of the Tribe and together their painting was truly beautiful.

Soon, from all over the world the volume of orders created the need for more artists, bigger premises, better training and all the things well known to go along with growing businesses.

The White Business Advisor was amazed. A national newspaper article and TV story ensured that demand outstripped supply dramatically. But the business will not compromise on quality. So, the opportunity will never be maximised. Once, this would have bothered the White Business Advisor but now, strangely, it does not. The Red Entrepreneur is very busy. The children's language school is flourishing. The Good Speaker has become a best-selling author. The Angry Group has changed its name to 'The Tribal Council for Cultural Dissemination through Native Enterprise'. (They have asked the Good Speaker to find them a better name and he is working on it).

The Elder smiled. But the smile soon faded to a look of deep concern because this good story was submerged in too much tragedy. More good stories are needed urgently. Still, there had been a little learning. And that was very good.

Your immediate interpretation

What does the story tell you about social entrepreneurship? The following exercises can help you establish your understanding of what characterises the phenomenon and determine where the line between social entrepreneurship and other types of entrepreneurship may be drawn.

- Imagine that you want to start a commercial organisation, primarily with a view to making a profit. List the factors you think would be likely to drive your commitment. Then imagine that you want to start an organisation, preferably with a social purpose, and once again list the motivating factors. Are there clear differences between the two lists? Try to explain the similarities and differences.
- Look again at the teepee parable above. Discuss whether and how the

story shows social entrepreneurship as an activity that creates better conditions for people locally or globally.

- Social entrepreneurship is about creating better conditions for people through the creation or discovery of new opportunities that are then realised through the process of organising. Express your opinion as to how innovative and imaginative the story is. Is the teepee story a good illustration of how new innovative opportunities are created? Is it, in your opinion, a requirement that social opportunities must, by their nature, be innovative in order to be able to speak about social entrepreneurship?
- Do you know of other examples of social entrepreneurship than the teepee story, where individuals or groups of individuals through the creation or discovery of new opportunities have improved conditions for people locally or globally?

Theories of entrepreneurship

As mentioned the main features of social entrepreneurship are similar to entrepreneurship that takes place in a commercial context. The main difference is that the driving force behind social entrepreneurship can often be a desire to ensure social justice, while entrepreneurship in a commercial context is directed primarily at profit (Johnson 2000).

There are a number of different perspectives on what social entrepreneurship covers. This chapter will focus on two perspectives that consider the social and the financial element of social entrepreneurship both as a means and as an end.

The first perspective on social entrepreneurship focuses on financial objectives as the ultimate goal and social objectives as a means to achieving financial goals. In other words, the focus of social entrepreneurship is to create a business and the social elements are a product in line with other commercial products. Since the ultimate goal is to create an economically sustainable and profitable organisation this kind of social entrepreneurship exists primarily in a commercial context, regardless of the social benefits produced in these organisations.

Perspective number two is primarily focused on social elements. Here, the social objectives are the ultimate goal, and any commercial exchanges take place only as a means of achieving social goals. Social entrepreneurship is therefore considered to be an activity that is fundamentally about creating a better world, and it takes place within what is often called the voluntary sector. The voluntary sector is so called because a substantial portion of the effort in these organisations comes from non-salaried workers. The voluntary sector is often referred to as the non-profit sector. In this chapter you will be introduced to social entrepreneurship in the light of the paradox:

> Business or a better world

Introduction of social entrepreneurship

Not many studies show how widespread social entrepreneurship is. A study of social entrepreneurship from the UK and one recently completed by the Global Entrepreneurship Monitor (GEM) in 2009 (Terjesen et al 2011) are the exceptions. Results from both studies are presented here to illustrate how different results for the prevalence of social entrepreneurship may be obtained, depending on how broadly the concept of social entrepreneurship is understood.

The prevalence of social entrepreneurship in Britain has been studied repeatedly (Harding & Cowling 2004, Harding 2006, Harding et al 2007). The latest survey from 2007 shows that nearly 1.2 million people in Britain were engaged in social entrepreneurship in 2005. Either the entrepreneurs were about to start a social activity (less than three months old) or led a fledgling social activity (between three and 42 months old). The start-up rate for social entrepreneurship is about half that of entrepreneurship as the building of an independent organisation (3.3 per cent of adults are active in social entrepreneurship compared with 6.1 per cent of those active in entrepreneurship to start up an independent organisation). In addition, a further 1.5 per cent of Britain's workforce operates well-established social activities which are more than 42 months old.

Social entrepreneurship thus seems to be a widespread activity in Britain. The impact of this on society is highlighted by calculations made by the UK government, which show that organisations with a social or environmental purpose account for a total turnover of £27 billion (Harding 2006).

The results from the UK indicate that social entrepreneurship in other countries can also be a major activity. The results from the GEM 2009 show that 'the percentage of the population that is explicit about its involvement in social activities varies considerably around the world'. On average it seems that 2.8 per cent of the world's working age adult population is involved in social activities. However the percentage ranges 'from 0.2 per cent in Malaysia to 7.6 per cent in Argentina'. The difficulty in capturing social activities is that variation is not only present across countries grouped by stages of economic development, but also by geographical region. 'Overall, very few consistent patterns of Social Entrepreneurship prevalence can be discerned at this point.' (Terjesen et al 2011: 3). However, it is possible to point out that forms of social entrepreneurship 'manifest themselves in different ways – from a pure non-profit model to organizations that marry philanthropy with business models.' (Terjesen et al 2011: 3) For example, the GEM study shows that it is possible to distinguish between companies which vary in the extent of their focus on social and commercial goals. Specifically, it is possible to distinguish between four categories:

> (1) Pure social entrepreneurial activity (where the individual launches or runs a social organization that has no commercial activities); (2) Pure commercial entrepreneurial activity (where the individual launches or runs a commercial organization that has no particular social goals); (3) Overlapping social and commercial entrepreneurial activity (where the individual launches or runs one and the same organization that is both commercial and social in nature); and (4) Simultaneous social and commercial entrepreneurial activity (where the individual launches or runs both a social and commercial organization which are different entities). (Terjesen et al 2011: 4)

The prevalence of social entrepreneurship reported in the UK and in GEM countries may however be debatable, because the volume depends greatly on the definition of social entrepreneurship used. As social entrepreneurship is an activity that has not yet been greatly explored, there is disagreement about how this phenomenon should be captured and defined. 'Social entrepreneurship . . . is not a tidy concept. Its untidiness has been argued to be a reflection of the way that the world is . . . It behooves anyone using the concept of social entrepreneurship to make clear the sense he/she attaches to it.' (Peredo & McLean 2006: 64)

In spite of disagreement about the definition of social entrepreneurship, there is however a widespread consensus that social entrepreneurship is about achieving social goals, thereby creating better conditions for people locally or globally. However, that's as far as any agreement goes. The disagreement is about what priority the social objectives have in relation to financial objectives.

Social entrepreneurship as a continuum

Table 10.1 clarifies existing perceptions of social entrepreneurship. The continuum contains two extreme perspectives of social entrepreneurship. One

Table 10.1 Perceptions of social entrepreneurship – A Continuum

	Priority of aims	The importance of commercial exchange and profit	Examples
A better world	The formulated, overall objective is entirely social (but subordinate financial objectives can be found)	Commercial exchange and profit are only created with the purpose of supporting the social objectives	Doctors without Borders (Médecins SansFrontières) (www.msf.dk)
	The formulated, overall objective is primarily social	Commercial exchange and profit are created for supporting social objectives and making the business financially sustainable	The Danish Merkur Bank (www.merkurbank.dk)
Business	The overall objective is entirely financial (but subordinate social objectives can be found)	Commercial exchange and profit are created for making the business financially sustainable	Vestergaard Frandsen (www.vestergaard-frandsen.com)

Note: All websites last accessed 23 May 2012.

Source: Inspired by Peredo & McLean (2006: 63).

defines social entrepreneurship as activities that are generally governed by social goals – a better world. The second understands social entrepreneurship as an activity in which social goals are present to some extent, but where business and therefore financial goals are the primary concern. In the centre is a third understanding of social entrepreneurship, which combines social and financial objectives in a more balanced relationship, although the social purpose is generally primary.

Creating a better world

One perspective shown in Table 10.1 strongly emphasises that it is only social goals that drive social entrepreneurship: 'At one extreme are those who hold that some goal(s) must be the "exclusive" aim of the social entrepreneur.' (Peredo & McLean 2006: 59) The perspective is also expressed by Dees:

> For a social entrepreneur, the social mission is fundamental. This is a mission of social improvement that cannot be reduced to creating private benefits (financial returns or consumption benefits) for individuals. Making a profit, creating wealth, or serving the desires of customers may be part of the model, but these are means to a social end, not the end in itself. Profit is not the gauge of value creation; nor is customer satisfaction; social impact is the gauge. (Dees 1998: 5)

The organisation Médecins sans Frontiéres (MSF, or 'Doctors without Borders') is an example of a voluntary, non-profit organisation that is in line with Dees' definition of social entrepreneurship. MSF is a 'private, international, humanitarian organisation that provides medical relief to victims of conflicts and disasters around the world' (www.msf.org, last accessed 23 May 2012). The organisation was founded in Paris in 1971 by a group of French doctors who years earlier had worked during the civil war in Biafra in Nigeria, as well as journalists who supported the idea of independent and cross-border relief in areas that no one else could operate in. As a result of frustration at the strict rules and bureaucracy during the civil war in Nigeria and as a consequence of the doctors' feeling of being able to act, they wanted an independent organisation that could provide global relief and put the humanitarian debate about international solidarity on the agenda. In 2011 the organisation had offices in 19 countries and projects running in more than 60 countries.

At the intersection of social and financial goals

Table 10.1 is a modified version of the above perspective, which emphasises that in social entrepreneurship, social and financial goals can be combined with each other; although the social objective has primacy. It is thus wrong to limit the phenomenon of social entrepreneurship to the voluntary sector because social entrepreneurship can also be created in the commercial sector. In practice, social entrepreneurship can therefore involve social and commercial considerations at the same time, making the boundary between the two sectors 'not only vague but porous' (Peredo & McLean 2006: 61). Social entrepreneurship can thus be said to: 'blur the traditional boundaries between the public, private and non-profit sector, and emphasize hybrid models of for-profit and non-profit activities.' (Johnson 2000: 1)

The argument for considering activities that combine social goals with financial objectives is that, 'a lack of financial resources or capital can constrain social entrepreneurship and restrict the ability of social entrepreneurs to create social capital.' (Thompson et al 2000: 330) Therefore, the definition of social entrepreneurship is not about limiting social entrepreneurship to a specific context. Instead, this perception of social entrepreneurship focuses on whether the activities that people set in motion create better social conditions or not. A world-famous example demonstrating that it is possible to balance social and financial goals is the case of the Grameen Bank. Grameen Bank is a hybrid form of organisation, because it can be interpreted both as belonging to the for-profit sector and not-for-profit sector: The founder of Grameen Bank, Muhammad Yunus, says: 'Grameen Bank is at the forefront of a burgeoning world movement towards eradicating poverty through micro-lending: The microloan concept can be described as 'a simple concept that anyone can participate in, and thus make a real difference in alleviating poverty'. The Grameen Bank was founded in 1976 by Muhammad Yunus, an economics professor, with the idea that lack of capital was the primary obstacle to productive self-employment among the poor. Today, the Grameen Bank has more than 2 million members, better than 90 per cent loan recovery rates, and has been replicated in more than 40 developing and developed countries (including the United States) worldwide (McKernan 2002). The Grameen Bank does not provide credit alone; they bundle noncredit services along with credit. These noncredit services provide programme members with vocational training, organisational help, and social development inputs aimed at improving health, literacy, leadership skills, and social empowerment (McKernan 2002: 94). The Grameen Bank tries to achieve a balance between the goal of creating a better world and creating a profitable economic business. The balance between social and economic goals is often called the double bottom line (Dees et al 2002: 173).

Social entrepreneurship as business

So far we have looked at two versions that agree that social objectives are more important than financial objectives in social entrepreneurship. The disagreement between them is illustrated by the degree to which they recognise the use of financial targets to meet social objectives.

However, there are also organisations where social objectives are not only blended with financial objectives, but are actually accorded a lower priority. The argument for also understanding this type of activity as a form of social entrepreneurship is that all activities which somehow improve people's social conditions are worthy of recognition, since this type of activity is ultimately instrumental in creating a better world (Austin et al 2006).

An example of a Danish organisation (which on one hand helps to create better conditions for people in the third world, but on the other hand does not hide the fact that the organisation is not an emergency aid project) is Vestergaard Frandsen. The products manufactured by Vestergaard Frandsen include, among other things, a mosquito net impregnated with chemicals that prevent the mosquito from flying and thus transmitting malaria. It is used, for example, in refugee camps. Additionally, Vestergaard Frandsen has launched a water-cleaning tool called LifeStraw. The suction tube is about 25 cm long and contains an advanced filter that purifies water. The filter makes it possible to drink from polluted rivers or ponds, which improves poor people's access to water significantly, especially in developing countries where lack of access to clean water is a major health problem. The CEO explains the balance between financial and social objectives:

> Our business is about 'doing business and doing good'. But business always comes first . . . You could say that we show that one does not preclude the other. But if the economy was of secondary importance, we might just as well hand over the keys to the Red Cross. There are plenty of problems in the world that call for more entrepreneurship. It is just a matter of rolling up our sleeves and getting started. (*The Economist*, 23 February 2007)

The emergence tradition and the opportunity tradition

So far in the discussion of social entrepreneurship we have mainly dealt with what is meant by the social element and with the weighting between the social and business elements. However, other discussions are essential. One of the things that we have discussed several times in this book is what is needed in order to describe something as entrepreneurial. In Chapter 1 we discussed two different traditions, each with their vision of what can be described as entrepreneurship: the emergence tradition and the opportunity tradition. According to the emergence tradition, the formation behaviour can be described as entrepreneurial if it relates to the formation of a new organisation, regardless of whether there is anything innovative involved. In contrast, the opportunity tradition considers behaviour to be entrepreneurial if it involves creation or discovery and exploitation of an innovative and ground-breaking opportunity, whether this results in a new organisation or not. This discussion also holds true in the theory of social entrepreneurship.

As with the emergence tradition Peredo and McLean define an activity as entrepreneurial if it is realised with social objectives in mind and results in the formation of a new organisation. 'Social entrepreneurship is sometimes understood merely as the initiation and/or management of a social enterprise.' (Peredo & McLean 2006: 58)

However, some also believe that behaviour can only be described as social entrepreneurship when it involves activities of innovative social value. This thinking is equivalent to the aforementioned opportunity tradition. For example, Dees underlines that social entrepreneurs are innovative: 'They break new ground, develop new models, and pioneer new approaches . . . Those who are more innovative in their work and who create more significant social improvements will naturally be seen as more entrepreneurial. The

Table 10.2 The paradox: Business or better world

	Business	A better world
Primary objective	Financial	Social
Sector	The for-profit sector	The voluntary sector/non-profit sector
Motive	To create a financially sustainable business	To create a better world and better conditions for people
The relevance of commercial exchange	Crucial for the success and development of the organisation	Supporting the primary social objectives
The relevance of social output	A product similar to other commercial products	The deeper purpose of creating social entrepreneurship

truly Schumpeterian social entrepreneurs will significantly reform or revolutionize their industries.' (Dees 1998: 4) In order for a new activity to be described as social entrepreneurship, that activity should be innovative and imaginative; it does not matter whether the activity involves the creation of a new organisation.

Social entrepreneurship: business or better world?

We have now discussed various perspectives of social entrepreneurship. These are brought together in Table 10.2.

We see from the table that the business perspective places emphasis on social entrepreneurship as an activity, which probably results in social benefits, but where the overall objective is financial; attempting to create a sustainable economic business. Here, it is the commercial exchanges which are considered crucial for success, and the social product is a product in line with other commercial products. On the other hand, the other perspective promotes the idea that the overarching objective related to social entrepreneurship is to create a better world. Financial targets are considered as ways to achieve the general social objectives. This type of social entrepreneurship belongs primarily to the voluntary sector, where the whole purpose is to create better social terms and conditions for the people. Besides these two perspectives there are innumerable variants, which to different degrees emphasise the relationship between social and financial objectives. This means that social entrepreneurship can actually take place anywhere in society. Activities do not take place solely within the voluntary sector or within the for-profit sector. There are countless hybrid forms of social entrepreneurship.

A theoretical interpretation

In the following we provide our interpretation of the Teepee case that we examined at the beginning of the chapter. The Parable of the Teepee can be taught in many contexts and interpreted in many ways.

This book talks about 'the business perspective' versus 'the better world perspective', but how can this case be interpreted from respectively a business perspective and a better world perspective?

The business perspective

The teepee case fits well with the business perspective. Whatever his passion for his native heritage, The Red Entrepreneur has a world view of business that is more connected to the White Advisor and mainstream attitudes to commerce than the Good Speaker, who genuinely regards the earning of individual profits as community property – the heritage, intellectual property of the tribe's intimate connection to the teepee as a cultural artifact – as anathema.

The Angry Group's reaction to the new teepee venture can be seen as a collective protest against its for-profit and individualistic character. Moreover, it is commercialising a product loaded with collective, cultural symbolism, thereby seen by protesters as a venture which profits from something which belongs to the entire community. The Angry Group therefore sees the venture as much more aligned with white individualistic business culture than with their indigenous culture and egalitarian values.

Even after the reform it is questionable if the teepee venture becomes social. We have to presume that the Red Entrepreneur still owns and directs the teepee venture, possibly as a sole proprietor but almost certainly as a principal shareholder. From the perspective 'a better world', this does not indicate that the teepee case is an example of social entrepreneurship.

The teepee case does not specify exactly what kind of business we are talking about after the reform and, for some scholars and practitioners, this is decisive when evaluating the 'social' character of any venture: how is it organised, was its mission statement changed, how is power distributed, how are profits allocated etc.? Has the venture fundamentally turned into a 'social enterprise' or is the 'social dimension' merely rather a smart way for the Red Entrepreneur to make more money for himself?

The better world perspective

The teepee case also fits well with the better world perspective. The reformed teepee venture especially can be seen as an example of social entrepreneurship. The reformed business definitely embraces a wider range of stakeholders than the individualistic, for-profit venture as it started out. It involves more community people, enhances the knowledge level in the community, revitalises traditions, creates new relationships with outsiders and shares some of the profits with community members not actually involved in running the business.

But even before the reform there are elements that speak in favour of a better world perspective. For instance the Red Entrepreneur defends himself by arguing that his venture has a positive community impact by employing and training young people and paying rent and taxes. He also argues that his teepees are of good quality and authentically made, paying due respect to indigenous traditions and culture. So, in his eyes it is not just an individualistic, for-profit business he is running, it is also a social enterprise in the sense that it is creating jobs and generating income in the community.

The teepee venture is definitely more socially oriented after the reform than in its previous individualistic, for-profit format. More of the community are involved and a school is supported, but the precise format is not outlined. Some would argue – this book does – that a fully-fledged social enterprise would have to consider a number of changes such as a new mission statement, specifying social goals, some kind of democratic rule, a changed ownership structure and new rules for profit distribution. In terms of overall sector position, such a deeply reformed social venture could then be said to 'belong' to the voluntary sector rather than the private for-profit sector.

For the author of this case, Kevin Hindle, the distinction between 'social' and 'individual' entrepreneurship is not seen as important. For Hindle the 'why' question – the motives and reasons for an entrepreneur starting a venture (for social good or personal profit) – is less interesting than the 'what, how and where' questions. 'What' and 'how' describe the entrepreneurial process (Hindle 2010b). 'Where' involves the vital importance of community factors to entrepreneurial process (Hindle 2010a). Whether you want to make a profit for yourself or be involved in an altruistic organisation for the benefit of others or anything in between, his argument is that you must do your best to understand the necessary mechanics of an appropriate entrepreneurial process; what will make the process 'appropriate' is a thorough understanding of the influence that community factors are likely to have on whatever it is that you want to achieve through your business. His diagnostic regime is a tool for facilitating that understanding. As such The Parable of the Teepee is a case that can be used beyond its indigenous specifics to demonstrate the highly generalisable analytical capabilities of Hindle's diagnostic framework for assessing how community factors are likely to affect any given entrepreneurial process. To further understand the 'diagnostic framework' concept go to YouTube and listen to the video case by Kevin Hindle, where the framework is summarised and applied to the teepee case.

Testing the theory

So, once again it's time for you to step into the entrepreneurial laboratory and try out another key topic in entrepreneurship, namely social entrepreneurship.

 EXERCISES

1 **Media coverage of social entrepreneurship.** Find a series of articles on social entrepreneurship in various newspapers. Next, discuss the different attitudes that characterise the debate about social entrepreneurship. Which statements do you agree with and what do you disagree with? Argue why this is the case.

2 **Teepee videocase.** Watch the video case study on YouTube. The case is discussed in this chapter as an example of how social entrepreneurship is expressed; but do you agree? Is the story about social entrepreneurship? To what extent does the story meet the requirement of creating value for other people by creating or discovering a new opportunity and realising it through organising?

3 **Visit China.** In recent years,, the Chinese government has invested trillions of dollars in new infrastructure, education, health and new welfare systems. Investment is expected to rise by 20–30 per cent over the coming years. China's next growth wave could create massive opportunities for many companies that can deliver solutions in the field. Your task is as follows: in light of developments in China, find a social idea from which you could benefit. Next, figure out how you will translate the idea into an opportunity, so it can form the basis for a viable organisation.

 LITERATURE

Austin, J., Stevenson, H. & Wei-Skillern, J. (2006) 'Social and commercial entrepreneurship: Same, different, or both?', *Entrepreneurship, Theory and Practice*, 30(1), 1–22.

Dees, J. G., (1998). The meaning of social entrepreneurship, available at http://www.caseatduke.org/ (last accessed 23 May 2012).

Dees, J.G., Emerson, J. & Economy, P. (2002) *Strategic tools for social entrepreneurs: Enhancing the performance of your enterprising nonprofit*, New York: John Wiley & Sons Inc.

Harding, R. (2006) 'Social Entrepreneurship Monitor: United Kingdom 2006', Barclays, London Business School.

Harding, R. & Cowling, M. (2004) 'Social Entrepreneurship Monitor: United Kingdom 2004', Barclays, London Business School.

Harding, R., Hart, M., Jones-Evans, D. & Levie, J. (2007) 'Global Entrepreneurship Monitor: United Kingdom 2007 Monitoring Report', London Business School.

Hindle, K. (2010a) 'How community factors affect entrepreneurial process: a diagnostic framework', *Entrepreneurship and Regional Development*, December, 7–8, 1–49.

Hindle, K. (2010b) 'Skillful Dreaming: Testing a General Model of Entrepreneurial Process with a Specific Narrative of Venture Creation', *Entrepreneurial Narrative Theory Ethnomethodology and Reflexivity*, 1, 97–135.

Hindle, K. & Lansdowne, M. (2005) 'Brave spirits on new paths: toward a globally relevant paradigm of Indigenous entrepreneurship research', *Journal of Small Business and Entrepreneurship*, Special issue on Indigenous entrepreneurship, 18(2), 131–141.

Johnson, S. (2000) 'Literature Review on Social Entrepreneurship', White paper, Canadian Centre for Social Entrepreneurship, University of Alberta, Canada.

McKernan, S.-M. (2002) 'The Impact of Microcredit Programs on Self-employment Profits: Do Noncredit Program Aspects Matter?', *The Review of Economics and Statistics*, 84(1), 93–115.

Peredo, A.M. & McLean, M. (2006) 'Social Entrepreneurship: A critical review of the concept', *Journal of World Business*, 41(1), 56–65.

Terjesen, S., Lepoutre, J., Justo, R. and Bosma, N. (2011) 'Global Entrepreneurship Monitor Report on Social Entrepreneurship', Global Entrepreneurship Research Association.

Thompson, J., Alvy, G. & Lees, A. (2000) 'Social entrepreneurship – a new look at the people and the potential', *Management Decision*, 38(5), 328–338.

11

Synthesis and recap

As an entrepreneur you must be prepared to run the gauntlet between paradoxes. You must, for example, find a balance between planning and improvisation. One minute you are in a planning phase with its deskwork and calculation; then the next minute you set your inventiveness and improvisational behaviour free. Sometimes these processes occur synchronously, sometimes asynchronously. But whatever phase you are in, you as an entrepreneur must be able to walk a tightrope in a universe of paradoxes because that is what is required for the entrepreneurial process to succeed. At this point, we finally want to cast a unifying glance at the paradoxes that we have dealt with along the way and ask: is there a connection between them? The entrepreneur certainly experiences a connection in the practical world, but is there also a deeper theoretical context? Perhaps paradoxes can be added together in groups, and maybe we can find a meta-paradox hidden in the pattern of the many paradoxes that we have presented in the preceding chapters.

The book's paradoxes

Being an entrepreneur is about balancing in the universe of paradoxes. Paradoxes are not then a matter of choosing one over the other, but about finding the right balance in your specific situation. This choice varies according to who you are and what process you seek to develop. However, you may as an entrepreneur safely assume that you cannot settle for either extreme, however much it may appeal to you. One entrepreneur may love the start-up phase where ideas are bubbling, there is room for improvisation, and nothing is firmly established. Another entrepreneur may be more comfortable when the project's basic idea is established, and it is important to realise the idea through action, planning and organising.

However, regardless of preferences, there are no entrepreneurial processes where only one side of the paradox is present. Ideas are barely conceived before the first immediate evaluation is made, and throughout the organising phase there is a constant need for new ideas as to how the product

Table 11.1 The book's paradoxes

Born	or	Made
Discovered	or	Created
Instrumental	or	Legitimate
Planning	or	Improvising
Exploit	or	Explore
Rational	or	Embedded
Management tool	or	Creativity curb
Top-down	or	Bottom-up
Business	or	A better world

can be presented, how to cultivate customers, recruit staff, etc. So, irrespective of personal preferences and stages of the process, entrepreneurs operate in a universe of paradoxes, where there is a need for pragmatic 'both-and solutions' rather than 'either-or solutions'. One can therefore say that the entrepreneurs – or entrepreneurial teams – who master the paradoxes of the entrepreneurial process are the likely winners in the race between the many projects that are constantly being launched across all possible areas.

That's why we have chosen to build the chapters of this textbook around some key paradoxes. We believe that paradoxes are important, just as they are within the field of organisational and management theory in general (De Wit & Meyer 2010, Hatch & Carliffe 2006, Scott & Davis 2007). Moreover, we have, through the paradoxes, pointed out that whilst some paradoxes are central to the creation phase, others are important in a later phase or related to specific contexts. Finally, we have focused on the essence of entrepreneurship: the interplay between the discovery or creation of opportunities to be evaluated and exploited by the organisation, instead of more functional aspects such as finance and marketing.

Let us start by summarising the paradoxes, as they were presented in the book's introductory chapter. The summary is presented in Table 11.1.

The paradoxes should not be understood as incompatible extremes. In our interpretation of cases we emphasise that it's more a question of balance between seemingly contradictory perspectives on the same topic. It is not therefore a choice that has to be made between extremes, but rather a balancing act for the individual entrepreneur or team of entrepreneurs; a tightrope walk, between the extremes. Both perspectives of a paradox typically contribute to our understanding of what's happening in the entrepreneurial process.

A synthesis of the paradoxes

Is there a relationship between the paradoxes shown in the left and right hand sides of the table, i.e. between on the one hand born, discovered instrumental, planning, exploit, rational, management tool, top-down and business, and on the other, made, created, legitimate, improvising, explore, embedded, creativity curb, bottom-up and better world. Is there a kind of meta-paradox hidden in this puzzle?

One can actually argue for the existence of a meta-paradox. Where the left hand side of the table above can be summarised under an objectivist approach, the right side is likely to be summarised as a subjectivist approach (Burrell & Morgan 1979). The objectivist and subjectivist approaches reflect two different theoretical directions. The former suggests that there exists an objective world independent of man and his actions, where the outside world, in terms of human action, can be known, described and predicted. In the subjectivist approach reality is not externally given, but is internal and based on the individual's subjective understanding. Reality is created through human actions, experiences and understanding: social reality is thus created rather than discovered.

In the following we will further explain how the aforementioned meta-paradox is embodied in entrepreneurship.

An objectivist approach

The left hand side of Table 11.1 summarises the objectivist approach to entrepreneurship. Here, individuals and groups of people behave in as economically rational a manner as possible. The connection on the left hand side is that entrepreneurs find an opportunity, evaluate it through use of instrumental tools and start organising it: an almost linear process that can be plotted in advance. Among other things these activities include entrepreneurs adjusting their networks for the purpose and developing a business plan. This allows entrepreneurs to manage their way through the entrepreneurial process more efficiently and safely. The process is deliberate, systematic, and controlled through planning towards achieving a specific and predictable goal – a profitable organisation. It is therefore considered possible to manage the entrepreneurial process with only the right knowledge, which is why top-down management and control from upper management is the key to achieving entrepreneurial behaviour. This approach assumes that there are optimal recipes for how one or more entrepreneurs should approach the entrepreneurial process. All this can be termed an objectivist approach to entrepreneurship, as the entrepreneurial process is given and therefore independent of individuals. It exists 'out there in the real world'.

As actors, entrepreneurs are just a form of 'cog' in the wheels of a machine that attempts to reach goals as quickly and efficiently as possible. The project, not the person, is the key factor. The entrepreneur's function is to develop and manage the entrepreneurial machine, so as to reach the previously established goals. Through planning, control of machinery, coordination and analysis the entrepreneur is able to steer the machine in the desired direction. The born perspective emphasises how the entrepreneur is assumed to be born for the purpose.

The objectivist approach also promotes the existence of a 'best practice' for developing a new organisation. The business plan considered to be a management tool is an example of such 'best practice' for organisational formation. The plan's objective nature is reflected by the fact that from the beginning of the entrepreneurial process it is to a great extent possible to predict what destinations the entrepreneur must visit in the process of realising the goal. The plan's various dimensions (financing, marketing, strategy, etc.) show that the entrepreneurial process consists of a set of activities which need to be planned and coordinated. Accordingly, it is central to the objectivist approach to present some universally applicable tools and structural regularities that can support the entrepreneur in directing the entrepreneurial machine.

Sarasvathy (2008) has characterised the objectivist approach as 'causal' since it is based on both the goals that the entrepreneur constantly aims at, and also the selection of means to achieve the goals. The entrepreneur is assumed to have access to the required means, such as resources and networks (more or less), or to rationally determine them at the start of the entrepreneurial process. They are taken for granted.

A similar causal approach is seen in classical organisation theory and the mechanical and rational approach to the formation and operation of organisations propounded by Taylor in the early 20th century (Scott & Davis 2007). Likewise, we find the approach reflected in decision theory, where the rational theory tradition is central, both historically and in modern decision theory. For organisations, however, it is bounded rationality rather than absolute rationality (Simon 1946). Bounded rationality implies that we are not aware of all the alternatives and consequences of the choices we make, just as in practice we accept satisfactory solutions rather than optimal solutions. Such an understanding also makes sense in entrepreneurship.

A subjectivist approach

The right hand side of Table 11.1 expresses a subjectivist approach to entrepreneurship. Here, the entrepreneur is motivated by and acts from many different logics that do not always fit into a traditional rational economic logic. The human being is at the centre, both at the individual level and at the group level. The individual becomes an entrepreneur through personal development and he or she has a decisive influence on the design and shaping of the entrepreneurial process. Nevertheless, the person who creates opportunities and decides to pursue them is a holistic human being who also has other priorities in life. The entrepreneurial process is thus far from a fixed entity given by something 'out there'. Rather it is an entity created by the thoughts, feelings, desires and experiences of the entrepreneur.

The subjectivist approach stresses, however, that the entrepreneur does not create the entrepreneurial process alone. The process is created and recreated through constant interaction with other people, which illustrates how the entrepreneurial process is socially constructed. Therefore, other people and networks are the basis within which the entrepreneurial process is embedded and constantly influence how the process works. So, far from being a linear process that follows predetermined phases and objectives, the entrepreneurial process is shaped by jumping back and forth and parallel sequences.

Another foundation of the subjectivist approach is scepticism about the value of planning and closely defined objectives. The future cannot be predicted, and both actions and decisions should depend upon what situations arise. This is true not only for entrepreneurs who find themselves in an early phase of the entrepreneurial process in which ideas and projects emerge and new organisations are being formed. In more mature and existing organisations where routines and systems have already, to a great extent, been determined, planning and the definition of objectives can be an equally difficult activity to complete, especially if the goal is to create something new. It is not possible to predict everything, and therefore it is important to let the entrepreneurs who carry out everyday activities have room to move. It is also crucial, according to this approach, to let innovation occur bottom-up, because the creation of new things can sometimes be a chaotic process, where objectives and planning do not always make sense and add value. Actually one can argue that a highly rational and planned approach can destroy opportunities for the entrepreneur and weaken the development of new ideas. Therefore the business plan is often seen a curb on creativity.

Rather than planning at the desk, the subjective perspective is about moving into the world and being guided by the idea, but open to change or new directions. For example, an idea might be redirected to a completely different clientele. Instead of being predictable, universally valid and targeted, the subjectivist approach sees the entrepreneurial process as a unique process, the outcome of which is as yet unknown. As Steyaert writes: 'Every entrepreneurial endeavour follows and writes its own story.' (Steyaert 1997: 15)

Only by acting and interacting with others can the entrepreneur figure out whether and how the opportunity can be organised – whether it is legitimate, and more precisely, how it should be carved out. Weick captured this with the phrase: 'How do I know what I think, until I see, what I say.' (Weick 1969: 207) So, it is a case of first saying and doing something, and then interpreting and understanding it. This highlights how the starting point for the subjectivist approach, which has also been pointed out by Sarasvathy (2008), is not closely defined goals. On the contrary, the starting point is the actions performed by the entrepreneur and the means to which he or she has access. Sarasvathy calls this approach 'effectual' as opposed to 'causal' because the starting point is the means which the entrepreneur mobilises in order to achieve an overall effect.

The relevance and possible combination of the approaches

Let's emphasise once again that both of the two broad approaches to entrepreneurship outlined here are important and should not necessarily be seen as competing opposites. There is a sound theoretical basis for both of them, and for the individual entrepreneur the key is to achieve a balance in any specific situation. Sometimes the balance leans towards the objectivist approach and at other times towards the subjectivist approach. Something similar applies when selecting study programmes and projects at the university. Here again there are objectivist and subjectivist sides which students should be able to handle simultaneously.

Both sides are therefore relevant. However, you can benefit from working with each of them separately, i.e. by choosing one side of the paradox and thinking through the project or the process from this angle. But it can certainly be valuable to see the project or process from both of the paradox's perspectives. With this method you can get deeper into the material and more effectively avoid the normative 'blindness' we all carry with us in terms of those particular angles that we find especially appealing. For example, when starting up, some people will be 'fired up' by the rational perspective, whilst others will be discouraged by such a 'calculative' approach. Both have, so to speak, a need to wear 'reverse spectacles' and see things from the opposite point of view. By considering entrepreneurship from multiple angles one can obtain a better understanding of why processes evolve, as they do, and not least, why success or failure is sometimes the result of an entrepreneurial process.

Your journey is just beginning

We are now approaching the end of our journey through this textbook and the learning universe associated with it. We hope you have enjoyed the journey, have been inspired and now feel better equipped to embark on your own entrepreneurial journeys in the context you are in. Whether you become an independent entrepreneur or go on to develop entrepreneurial projects within existing organisations or in your leisure time, we are fairly confident that you are, at some point in time, going to engage with new ideas, possibilities and their realisation, simply because it is so universal and important in people's lives and careers.

In going forward, we suggest that you, one way or another, get to grips with one or several entrepreneurial projects in practice. Only then will you really understand much of what we've written about and only in this way will you discover – perhaps hidden – talent and strengths that you have. It is in practical projects that you will experience just how difficult and frustrating it can be, not being able to find your way through the jungle of ideas, but on the other hand, the feeling of success that comes when the entrepreneurial project succeeds. It's a bit like watching a roller coaster from the ground: it is only when you've actually ridden on it that you know just how it feels.

Practical projects can be found in many ways. You can start a student business whilst studying, rather than having a student job, or together with others you can embark on a project in social entrepreneurship, for example, targeting the world's climate or poverty problems, or you can seek an internship in a company or organisation where you will work with the development of new opportunities in multidisciplinary project teams.

You can also develop your knowledge of the book's themes by pursuing them within the education system. If the book and its subject area has caught your interest, you can further your education at many universities around the world that offer courses focusing on the issues we have mentioned e.g. innovation or creativity. A study in the US has shown that students who are trained to foster new ideas and find or create opportunities become better at it than students who have not undergone such training and education (DeTienne & Chandler 2004). Here then, the old adage, 'practice makes perfect' is appropriate. There are also advanced courses in specific subjects such as the financing conditions that apply to start-up companies, management of growth, or the special procedures and rules relating to intellectual property protection.

You can also choose to participate in the many extra-curricular activities offered by universities and further education establishments globally. These include innovation-camps that typically run for 48 hours with the participation of business leaders and other organisational representatives; business plan competitions and training courses and mentoring in your local business incubator environment for students.

Perhaps you're not yet convinced that entrepreneurship is important to you. So, let us finally summarise three key arguments:

- Whether you want to get a job when you graduate, or want to start a new organisation, it strengthens your chances of success if you have already as a university student learned to master the key aspects of entrepreneurship, i.e. creation, evaluation and organising opportunities. Remember that in the modern world, the vast majority of jobs for the highly educated involve interdisciplinary project-based work on new ideas, opportunities and their realisation. Everything indicates that this will become increasingly important in the future because of the increasing pace of change and innovation levels in society.
- Should you wish to start your own organisation, possibly together with others, it is naturally important to prepare for it in college where you have chance to 'play' the role before it becomes serious and costs you a lot of money.
- A final argument is simply that it is fun to participate in entrepreneurial projects. As a student most of your time has been spent absorbing existing knowledge. Entrepreneurship is fundamentally different, although here too there is an academic field with established knowledge. It is basically about developing the ability to seize something that doesn't yet exist. And mostly it appears to be fun. The fun thing is that you are working to develop something new and typically do it in cooperation with people who have completely different experiences and academic backgrounds than yourself. It is often only in such contexts that we really understand the field we have learned and how it can be used.

Let's conclude with Harvard professor C. Otto Scharmer's argument that entrepreneurship and a future orientation is important:

> We also pour considerable amounts of money into our educational systems, but haven't been able to create schools and institutions of higher education that develop people's innate capacity to sense and shape their future, which I view as the single most important core capability for this century's knowledge and co-creation economy. (Scharmer 2007: 3)

 LITERATURE

Burrell, G. & Morgan, G. (1979) *Sociological paradigms and organisational analysis*, London: Heinemann Educational.

DeTienne, D. & Chandler, G.N. (2004) 'Opportunity identification and its role in the classroom: A pedagogical approach and empirical test', *Academy of Management Learning and Education*, 3(3), 242–257.

De Wit, B. & Meyer, R.J.H. (2010) *Strategy synthesis, resolving strategy paradoxes to create competitive advantage*, London: Cengage Learning.

Hatch, M.J. & Cunliffe, A.L. (2006) *Organisation theory, modern symbolic and postmodern perspectives*, Oxford: Oxford University Press.

Sarasvathy, S. (2008) *Effectuation: Elements of entrepreneurial expertise*, Cheltenham, UK and Northampton, MA, USA: Edward Elgar Publishing.

Scharmer, C.O. (2007) *Theory U – leading from the future as it emerges*, Cambridge, MA: SoL Press.

Scott, W.R. & Davis, G.F. (2007) *Organisations and organising: Rational, natural and open system perspective*,. Englewood Cliffs: Prentice Hall.

Simon, H. (1997[1946]) *Administrative behaviour*, New York: Free Press.

Steyaert, C. (1997) 'A qualitative methodology for process studies of entrepreneurship – creating local knowledge through stories', *International Studies of Management and Organisation*, 27(3), 13–33.

Weick, K. (1969) *The Social Psychology of Organizing*, Reading: Addison-Wesley.

Index